THE FOUR GOSPELS

An Introduction

THE
FOUR
GOSPELS

An Introduction

Volume II

Bruce Vawter, C.M.

IMAGE BOOKS

A Division of Doubleday & Company, Inc.

Garden City, New York

Image Books edition 1969

by special arrangement with
Doubleday & Company, Inc.

Image Books edition published February 1969

Imprimatur: ✠ Joseph Cardinal Ritter
Archdiocese of St. Louis
September 20, 1966

CONTENTS

Volume II

ABBREVIATIONS OF BIBLICAL REFERENCES

Gen	Genesis	Wis	Wisdom of Solomon
Ex	Exodus	Sir	Sirach (Ecclesiasticus)
Lev	Leviticus	Is	Isaiah
Num	Numbers	Jer	Jeremiah
Deut	Deuteronomy	Lam	Lamentations
Jos	Joshua	Bar	Baruch
Jgs	Judges	Ezek	Ezekiel
1–2 Sam	1–2 Samuel	Dan	Daniel
1–2 Kgs	1–2 Kings	Hos	Hosea
1–2 Chron	1–2 Chronicles	Joel	Joel
Ezra	Ezra	Amos	Amos
Neh	Nehemiah	Mi	Micah
Tob	Tobit	Hab	Habakkuk
Job	Job	Zeph	Zephaniah
Ps(s)	Psalm(s)	Zech	Zechariah
Prov	Proverbs	Mal	Malachi
Eccl	Ecclesiastes	1–2 Macc	1–2 Maccabees
Cant	Song of Songs		

4 Ezra	The apocryphal book of 4 Ezra also called 2 Esdras
1 QS	The *Serek* ("Manual of Discipline") of the Qumran sectaries

Mt	Matthew	Col	Colossians
Mk	Mark	1–2 Thes	1–2 Thessalonians
Lk	Luke	1–2 Tim	1–2 Timothy
Jn	John	Tit	Titus
Acts	Acts of the Apostles	Phlm	Philemon
Rom	Romans	Heb	Hebrews
1–2 Cor	1–2 Corinthians	Jas	James
Gal	Galatians	1–2 Pt	1–2 Peter
Eph	Ephesians	1–2 Jn	1–2 John
Phil	Philippians	Apo	The Apocalypse or Revelation

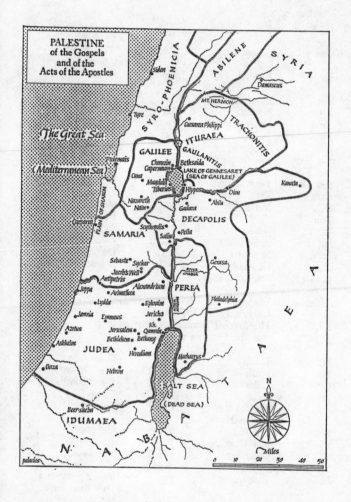

PALESTINE
of the Gospels
and of the
Acts of the Apostles

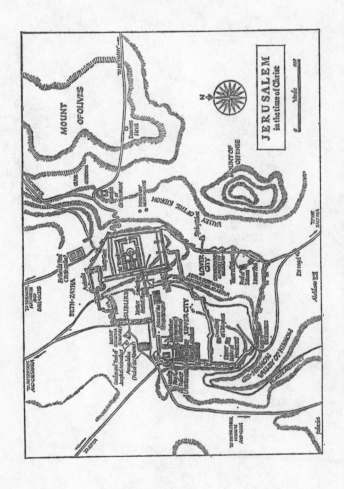

15. THAT THEY WHO DO NOT SEE MAY SEE

Jn 9:1–34   The story with which John continues his Gospel is certainly intentionally connected with the feast of Tabernacles of the preceding chapter, whatever may have been its original context. Above (see on Jn 8:12–20) Jesus proclaimed himself Light of the World. In this, the sixth of Jesus' "signs" of John's Gospel (see above on Jn 2:1–11), we see a dramatic demonstration of the triumph of light over darkness (cf. Jn 1:5). For this reason, it is doubtless of especial importance to John that this story tells of the giving of sight to a man *blind from birth*: the light which Jesus has come to give is the grace of divine life of which men are deprived from birth. The narrative is one of John's best, told with a respect for all of its simple dramatic qualities.

The disciples (who have not been mentioned by John in the preceding chapters) enquire, as people casually will, on seeing something that is of passing interest: *Who committed the sin, he or his parents?* It was commonly assumed that physical afflictions were personal retributions for sin. Either the sins of his parents had been visited upon him (cf. Ex 20:5; Deut 5:9), or God had made him blind at birth in view of the sins that he would commit in his lifetime. Jesus does not bother to affirm or deny the theory behind the disciples' question, but restricts himself to the case at hand. Neither the man nor his parents have made him blind; he has been blind in order to this time, *that the works of God might be made manifest in him,* that he might become a sign of *the light of the world.* In the best manuscripts, Jesus says, *We must do the works of him who sent me:* the Christian reader is invited to join in the continuing work of Christ performed in the Church, of which the healing of this blind man is a sign.

The sacramental gestures employed by Jesus are not without precedent in the Synoptic accounts of his cures (see above on Mk 7:31–37 and parallel and Mk 8:22–26). *Spittle* was commonly thought to have medicinal qualities. In this instance, however, it is used to mix a clay with which Jesus proceeds to *anoint* the blind man's eyes. "Anoint" is a strange word to use in this connection (it is certainly used in vs. 11, and the best manuscripts have it also in vs. 6), but John has probably deliberately chosen it in allusion to the rites of primitive Christian baptism. The earliest Christian exegesis of this passage correctly recognized that the evangelist intended his readers to find the realization of Jesus' "sign" in the baptism of the Church. For the same reason, the point is made that the man receives his sight only after he has fulfilled the command to *wash in the pool of Siloam.* Siloam was within the walls of the Jerusalem of Jesus' time, in the southeast corner of the city; its waters were used in the libations of the feast of Tabernacles. John assigns to it the popular etymology of "[someone] sent": it is the light-giving means employed by Jesus, the one who has been sent by the Father to be the Light of the World. In view of the controversy that follows, John may also be thinking of an earlier time when Jerusalemites rejected the divine grace symbolized by the waters of Siloam (cf. Is 8:6).

John undoubtedly sees irony in the bystanders' failure to recognize the man to whom Jesus gave sight and in their dispute over his identity (cf. Jn 7:40–43): the world which does not know Christ does not know those who are Christ's (cf. Jn 15:18–21); in verse 9 the man uses Christ's *I am* to identify himself. The man himself passes through the customary stages of affirmation of his faith as he is called upon, like every Christian graced by Christ, to give testimony before a hostile world. The person who in verse 11 is for him merely *the man called Jesus* is in verse 17 confessed to be *a prophet*, preparatory to his recognition as Son of Man in the dialogue with Jesus in verses 35–44. The issue for *the Pharisees* is, as before both in the Synoptics and in John, violation of the Sabbath. In this instance, however, the problem is further complicated for them since simultaneously they are trying to cast doubt on the reality of the event that has violated the Sabbath.

In verse 22 it is explained that *the Jews*, that is, obviously, the Jewish leadership, had adopted a policy of excommunication of all who would confess Christ. The kind of pressures which they would have been able to bring to bear in Jesus' lifetime doubtless did correspond to the formal excommunication inflicted on Jewish Christians in the time of the Gospel. This was a dire penalty in the tightly knit communities of that day, as it could affect a man's social and economic existence as well as his religious identity. In verse 27 the man who has now had his eyes opened in more than one sense through his dialogue with the Pharisees, is emboldened to ask, ironically, *Do you, too, wish to become his disciples?* The "too" manages to suggest the extent of Jesus' proselytizing in the face of all that they have been able to do. In their reply they unconsciously confess to the charge made by Jesus in Jn 8:14.

Jn 9:35–41   In the conclusion of the story which now follows Jesus the Light is shown confronting both faith and unbelief, and we see exemplified in what sense Jesus has *come into the world for judgment* (see above on Jn 3:14–21). The man born blind asks only to have Jesus offer himself as the object of his faith, and immediately responds with the Christian confession. The Pharisees, on the contrary, who have witnessed Jesus' sign unseeing, show themselves to be those who are really blind, with a willful

blindness that is inexcusable because the means of sight
have been present to them. Just as the loss of life for the
Christian is the paradoxical means by which he gains life,
and he who would try to preserve his life at all costs discovers that he has lost it forever (see above on Mk 8:34–9:1
and parallels), so has Jesus come *that they who do not see
may see, and they who see may become blind.*

Jn 10:1–21   Despite the abrupt change of pace as Jesus
now begins to speak of himself under quite
different figures, it seems to be certain that John intends the
present important passage to be set in close relation to the
preceding story and its sequel (cf. vs. 21). We can assume,
therefore, that at least for literary purposes the audience of
this discourse is the same as that of the preceding dialogue.

First of all, Jesus identifies himself as *the good shepherd,*
contrasting himself with the Pharisees who proved themselves
to be false leaders and teachers to the man born blind
(cf. Ezek 34:1–16). In Palestinian practice the sheep of a
given community are kept at night in a common sheepfold,
watched over by a *gatekeeper.* The sheep belonging to
individual owners are painted with distinguishing marks, and
also they are given distinctive names by their own shepherd
to which they respond. The shepherd to whom various sheep
belong enters the fold, therefore, by the ordinary gate
where he is recognized by the gatekeeper, calls his own
sheep by name, who recognize him and follow him out.
Only a thief would have occasion to climb over the wall
after the sheep. This is the first lesson, then, that Jesus intends by the use of this familiar figure, that they who are
the true sheep of the Shepherd of Israel will hear and heed
his voice (cf. Jn 8:43); it is predictable that his adversaries
did not understand what he was saying to them.

Jesus now shifts the figure somewhat: *I am the sheepgate.*
If the true shepherd is to be distinguished from the false by
his lawful entry through the gate, then *all who came before
me are thieves and robbers.* This is not to reject indiscrimi-
nately Israel's shepherds of the Old Testament and Jewish

times, but to define as interlopers all who do not belong to the true prophetic line of which he is the supreme exemplar. The figure of the gate, therefore, signifies both the guarantee of true shepherding and the way of the sheep into safekeeping: *whoever enters through me will be saved.*

Jesus contrasts himself, the good shepherd, with *the hireling*—in this context, the Pharisees of the preceding story—whose only interest in the sheep is selfish. The true shepherd to whom the sheep belong *lays down his life for the sheep:* the Palestinian shepherd was often called on to do just that (cf. 1 Sam 17:34 f.; Is 31:4). The application of the figure to Jesus in a most literal sense is obvious, as is the fact that *I know mine and mine know me:* Jesus has often rebuked his adversaries for knowing neither himself nor his Father, whereas in the Last Supper discourse (see below, page 197 ff.) he will dwell on the mutual knowledge of himself and his disciples as the extension of the shared knowledge of Father and Son.

Other sheep I have that do not belong to this fold: in context this doubtless refers to the Gentile mission of the Church of which John was a member. While Jesus in his earthly career had necessarily limited his ministry to Jews, the Church which had become mainly Gentile rightly recognized the universality of his Gospel and sought precedents for its catholicity in both his remembered words and actions (see above on Mk 7:24–30 and parallel). *There shall be one flock (poimmē) and one shepherd (poimēn):* though the Gospel of John, Jewish in its ultimate origins (see above in Chapter 1, page 38 ff.), continually recognizes the separation that had taken place between Church and Synagogue to the extent that it habitually speaks of "the Jews" in the third person, it nevertheless conceives of the Church as one, Jewish and Gentile, united under its one Shepherd (cf. Eph 2:11–22). What has made this possible is Jesus' atoning sacrifice: his free acceptance of the will of the Father means a resurrection to new life of himself and his sheep.

Lk 9:57–62   As Jesus' testimony leaves his hearers faced
Mt 8:19–22   with the decision of faith of which John so
                   often makes a point, we now return to the
Synoptic Gospels for various passages which Luke has connected with Jesus *on the way* to Jerusalem (see page 302 f.
Vol. I). Matthew, as we see here and in what follows,
has situated the same events during the Galilean ministry
in other parts of his Gospel. For various reasons that will
probably be evident of themselves it is much more convenient for us to follow Luke's orderly account for the time
being rather than Matthew's more complicated and artificial
disposition of the material. It is with these two evangelists
that we shall be mainly concerned for a while, with traditions
which they either possessed in common independently of
Mark or which were proper to themselves individually;
later, however, we shall rejoin the Marcan tradition as well.
These passages, as far as Luke's Gospel is involved, are
known as his "great insertion" into the Marcan outline.

We have before us three sayings of the Lord, only the first
two of which are reported by Matthew. It is Matthew, however, who identifies the first spokesman as *a scribe*, an avowal
which is particularly interesting coming from the First Gospel,
that Jesus found followers even from a group which generally
was bitterly opposed to him. We are not told what was his
eventual reaction to Jesus' reply, the sense of which is not to
point to his poverty precisely but rather to the extreme uncertainty and insecurity of his life lived in fulfillment of his
mission. Anyone who would be his disciple must be prepared
for a similar renunciation of worldly security, compared to
which even the vagrant animals enjoy an ordered and serene
existence. This is one of those deceptively idealistic statements of the Gospel which the casual reader is prone to take
in without reflection. It was surely not unimportant to
Matthew that the disciple in question was a person of status,
one of the privileged classes in Jewish society.

The second saying is another of the "hard" ones whose
very harshness is the best proof of its authenticity. *Leave
the dead to bury their own dead* is, taken in one way, an

absurdity. It is not that Jesus is suggesting, as some have thought, that all who are not at present his disciples are spiritually dead: this would imply a sweeping and uncharacteristically negative judgment that has no place in this context. It may be that in the Aramaic which Jesus used the same word did for "mortal" and "dead," thus: let those who are not yet concerned with the things of this world tend to its affairs. But most likely the sense is simply— or, perhaps, not so simply—that for the disciple of Jesus everything and everyone that could interfere with his call must be considered dead, his own parents included (see below on Lk 14:25–27). Inexorable as these words may sound to us, they could not have failed to sound even more so in the Oriental ears for which they were first uttered, conditioned as the people were to an intense, at times even exaggerated, veneration of the obligations of filial piety. By comparison the third saying reported by Luke, while it makes use of an expressive proverb to convey substantially the same message, comes as something of an anticlimax.

Lk 10:1–12
Mt 9:36–38, 10:5–16a
Only Luke has recorded the mission of another and larger group of disciples than the Twelve. Though there is no reason to question the reality of this group and its mission, it also seems to be evident that Luke had no really independent tradition that dealt with its activities. The saying of Jesus concerning *the harvest* which awaits its missionary zeal Matthew has brought into connection with the mission of the Twelve. Likewise, virtually every detail of the Lord's charge to this new group in the text that lies before us has either been copied from the common Synoptic account of the mission of the Twelve which we have already seen (above on Mk 6:6b–13 and parallels) or is additional material shared with Matthew who took that occasion to incorporate it into his missionary discourse of chapter 10.

It is not clear whether Luke speaks of this group of disciples as *seventy* or *seventy-two*: the evidence of the manuscripts is about evenly divided between the two readings and it is impossible to make a decision. Either number is intrinsically likely. Seventy had as venerable traditional associations as did twelve—the seventy elders of Israel (Num 11:16) come immediately to mind. Luke, however, may very well be thinking of the traditional number of the nations of the earth, which following Gen 10 was sometimes counted as seventy, sometimes as seventy-two. There is also the possibility that the tradition of the Septuagint lies behind the selection of the number. The Septuagint, whose name preserves the legend of its origin at the hands of seventy-(-two) translators, had once opened up to the Gentile world the Scriptures of the Old Testament, and now the disciples are being sent to bring the Gospel to the world. It is true, Luke respects his historical sources and does not suggest that Jesus actually missioned his disciples on this occasion to preach to Gentiles. But he carefully avoids repeating what Matthew has in his parallel, applied to the mission of the Twelve: *Go nowhere among the Gentiles and enter no town of the Samaritans, but go rather to the lost sheep of the house of Israel.* Also, of course, it is not without significance that this mission takes place after the conclusion of the Galilean ministry, in intimate association with Jesus' coming death for universal salvation.

If Luke wants us to think of the Church's universal mission in thus recalling this story, the discourse he has utilized is aptly suited to the purpose. It indulges in no romanticism, but combines prosaic advice with a realistic appraisal of the magnitude and dangers of the task ahead—*lambs among wolves*—and concludes with the perennial eschatological message of the Church: *the kingdom of God is at hand.* Nor is the gentle Luke reluctant on this occasion to cite the Lord's grim warning in time-honored Jewish language: *It shall be more tolerable for Sodom* (Matthew adds, and *Gomorrah*) *on that day—the day of judgment,* Matthew paraphrases—*than for that town* which rejects the apostolic preaching. It is interesting to note in these parallels how

often it is Luke rather than Matthew who has preserved the
Semitic structure of Jesus' words.

Lk 10:13–16   The theme of judgment causes Jesus to
Mt 11:20–24   advert to the cities of the Galilean ministry
and to marvel over the unbelief that he had
encountered there. The fact that *Chorazin* is named here for
the first time and nowhere else in the New Testament, yet
according to Matthew was one of *the cities in which his
greatest miracles were worked,* indicates to us again how
fragmentary is our Gospel account of Jesus' career. Matthew
has placed this passage within the Galilean ministry itself.

If *Tyre and Sidon,* the proverbially pagan cities of the
Phoenician coast, had received the graces showered on
Galilee, they would surely have repented, says Jesus. So
much the better will it be for Tyre and Sidon than for
Chorazin *and Bethsaida,* the city of Philip, Peter, and
Andrew, according to Jn 1:44. It is for *Capernaum,* however,
that his harshest judgment is reserved, in language recalling
the fate of other proud cities of the past (cf. Is 14:13, 15;
Ezek 26:20, 28:6, 8)—Capernaum which he had chosen as
his own city, where he had lived and was most familiarly
known to the people, so much so that it had been made a
reproach against him (cf. Lk 4:23). It is probably worth
noting that Tyre and Sidon still prosper to this day as cities
in Lebanon, while Chorazin (probably Khirbet Kerazeh,
about two miles northeast of Capernaum), Bethsaida, and
Capernaum have for centuries been nothing but uninhabited
rock piles.

Luke, who has included these apostrophes as part of
Jesus' instruction to the seventy(-two), in verse 16 concludes
with a saying of the Lord which appears often in the Gospels
and in various forms (cf. Mt 10:40; Jn 13:20).

Lk 10:17–20   Luke immediately describes the return of
the seventy(-two) disciples who were
elated over the success of their mission which had exceeded
their most optimistic hopes. Jesus' reply on this occasion has

often been misunderstood. *I saw Satan fall like lightning from the sky* is not said as a rebuke to their supposed pride in their accomplishment, but is, rather, a confirmation of their conquest of evil by the use of powers they had not known they possessed. At the same time, he does take the occasion to remind them of "the more excellent way" (cf. 1 Cor 13:1). Far more important than the charismatic graces they have received for their mission and the success they have achieved in it is that *your names are written in heaven*, that they, too, are to be counted among the elect who have accepted Christ's salvation (see on Lk 11:27 f. below).

Lk 10:21–22 Though the specific contexts differ—in
Mt 11:25–27 Matthew we are in the midst of a section in which the mystery of the kingdom is the theme following the missionary discourse to the Twelve— the following passage has essentially the same meaning in the two Gospels which have recorded it. It is, first of all, Jesus' paean of praise to the Father whose *good pleasure it has been to reveal these things,* the Gospel's message of salvation, *to little ones* (cf. above on Mk 9:33–37 and parallels) rather than to *the wise and learned* of this world: the scribes and Pharisees to whom Jesus was one of "the accursed people who know not the Law," the Judeans who despised him because he was a Galilean, the Galileans who would not credit him because he was lowborn and one of themselves. Of all the liberating effects of the Gospel message, which came almost unheralded into the religious world of New Testament times and still has its battle to fight for survival, undoubtedly the greatest and most revolutionary was its insistence on salvation as a matter of heart and soul rather than as an introduction into a system of esoteric "thinking," of a "wisdom" open only to elect "initiates" who have prepared themselves for it by study and mental discipline. The Christian principle has nothing to do with anti-intellectualism, but insists against every kind of Gnosticism or snobbish scribalism on the utter gratuity of God's grace (cf. 1 Cor 1:18 ff.).

Correlative with this principle is that of the source of what is Christian wisdom: *Everything has been handed over to me by my Father, and no one knows [who is] the Son except the Father, or [who is] the Father except the Son—and anyone to whom the Son chooses to reveal him.* The mystery which Christianity reveals, the knowledge with which it deals, does not concern things but persons. It is an introduction into a shared life and existence—such, on Semitic lips, is the meaning of "to know"—which is unique to a Father and Son; it is doubtless not without relevance that Luke also prefixed to Jesus' pronouncement the observation that *at that very moment he rejoiced in the Holy Spirit.* The participation in the life of the triune Godhead, this is grace and salvation; it is this that liberates us from purposeless existence and constitutes us new persons, children of God.

The Johannine flavor of this verse will not be missed by the attentive reader. "A meteorite from the Johannine heaven fallen upon the Synoptic earth," one commentator once called it. Others have remarked that it contains in essence all the christology of the Fourth Gospel. That this is not too great an exaggeration can be verified by comparing such passages as Jn 3:35, 6:46, 8:19, 10:15, 30, 14:9, 16:15, 17:6, 10. Above (see especially on Jn 8:48–59) and quite often in John's Gospel we hear Jesus claim an intimacy with the Father and a unique access to his being and will which can only be interpreted as John says it was interpreted, as the assertion of a divine Sonship transcending all human capabilities. Though we do not often hear the Synoptic Jesus speaking this language, we do hear him in this verse—and no verse is better authenticated in the Gospels of Matthew and Luke. Quite apart from its functional value in the Gospel context, therefore, this passage is a precious witness of historical tradition to the Christ of faith.

Lk 10:23–24   Most appropriately Luke follows the "Johannine" passage with a saying of Jesus which we have already seen Matthew use in a different context, in connection with the teaching in parables (see above on Mk 4:10–12 and parallels). The revelation of God which is to be found in Jesus' words and deeds, in the Christ-event, is the fullness for which the just of the Old Testament unconsciously yearned, walking in the light that was given to them. It is the same light that now shines in all its splendor (cf. Jn 1:17; Heb 1:1 f.).

Mt 11:28–30   Even more appropriate, however, is Matthew's continuation, drawn from a tradition proper to himself. Here again we hear an echo of the Christ of John's Gospel. *Come to me, all you who labor and are burdened, and I will give you rest:* Jesus addresses the *anawim* of the Beatitudes (see above on Mt 5:3–12 and parallel). He does not say, as any teacher could say, that he will endeavor to put his followers in touch with the God who alone can give spiritual peace and rest, who alone can satisfy the longings of our souls created to know and love him and to be happy with nothing else. He himself is the immediate source of peace and rest, for he embodies in his person all that was the ideal of the *anawim*: he is *meek and humble of heart* (cf. Zech 9:9). The *rest for your souls* which he promises (cf. Jer 6:16) is not, obviously, a passivity. It is a new way of life, a road to walk, even a *yoke*: Jesus throughout has been speaking as the Wisdom of God (cf. Prov 8:32; Sir 6:24–30, 24:18). But because of where the road leads, the *yoke is sweet and the burden is light.*

Lk 10:25–28   The story that next follows in Luke's outline is similar in many ways to one told later on by Matthew and Mark (see below on Mk 12:28–34 and parallel), and either we have separate versions of what was originally a single event or details of basically similar stories have been exchanged in the process of oral transmission (as we saw in the case of Lk 7:36–50 above). In view of the separate use made of the stories in the Gospels, for our purposes it is better to opt for the latter explanation. As Luke tells the story, *a certain lawyer* decided to *put*

him to the test as a teacher, asking what he should *do to
inherit eternal life.* Though the question may have been put
in good faith, it was somewhat inept. In the first place, Luke's
context has put the accent on salvation not by "doing" in any
legal or activist sense but by opening oneself in all simplicity
to the God of salvation revealed in his Son. Secondly, the
tenor of the question is the somewhat naïve assumption that
salvation may be obtained once for all by the doing of some
single thing. It is, therefore, very important that we understand correctly Jesus' reply. *In the Law what is written? How
do you read?* elicits from the scribe what the Gospels
would certainly endorse as an epitome of the spirit of the
Law (see above on Mt 5:17–20), expressed in the *Shema,*
the ancient prayer recited by devout Jews to this day,
combining the precepts of Deut 6:4 f. and Lev 19:18. *Keep
doing this,* then, says Jesus, *and you will live.* It is not by
performing any work, great or small, that a man can make
himself worthy of eternal life; but when he lives according to
the law of love he has the assurance of having passed
from death into life through God's power (cf. 1 Jn 3:14,
4:10–12).

Lk 10:29–37   Of what does the lawyer now seek *to
justify himself?* Probably, of the intimation
that his question could be answered so simply. He therefore,
and doubtless still in a legalistic vein, counters with the
classic problem of Jewish casuistry: *And who is my neighbor?*
(see above on Mt 5:43–45). It is this question that introduces perhaps the most famous of all the Lord's parables.

The Jerusalem-Jericho road descends from Jerusalem, some
2600 feet high in the hills of Judea, down to the area of the
Dead Sea basin in which Jericho is situated, about 700 feet
below sea level, passing through gorges and hills which in
spring have a thin layer of grass but the rest of the year
are barren. Almost every foot of the road provides a likely
hiding place for robbers, and as a result it has been a
favorite with them for centuries. Even in modern times it
has not been unknown for travelers to be waylaid on the

pavements that have replaced the old Roman road. The none-too-gentle way in which the man in the parable was handled by the bandits was very typical; he was fortunate to escape with his life.

It has been thought by some that the story of the parable was taken by Jesus from an actual event. It is, indeed, possible. Though *the priest* and *the Levite* add bite to the lesson, we could easily imagine a priest passing by, having left the Holy City after his period of duty in the temple, making his way to Jericho which was traditionally inhabited by priestly families. The point is, of course, that while these two eminently qualified under the Law, by anybody's interpretation of it, as "neighbors" to the man who is obviously supposed to be a Jew, it remained for the despised heretic *Samaritan* to show him the mercy and kindness that were their duty. It was he who applied the soothing balm of *oil and wine*, recognized as a disinfectant long before anyone knew about germs. It was he who took him to the *inn:* the "inn of the Good Samaritan" pointed out to the traveler in Palestine today, actually a police station inhabiting the ruin of a Turkish building constructed for the same purpose, probably does occupy a site that would have had a *khan* in ancient times, half way between Jerusalem and Jericho.

As the parable concludes, the lawyer's question has been answered; or rather, he has been taught that it was the wrong question to ask. "Love your neighbor" has not been commanded in order to put a limitation on love to indicate its direction. Rather than "Who is my neighbor?," it asks: "To whom am I neighbor?": *Which of these three, asks Jesus, proved himself to be a neighbor to the one who fell among thieves?* Whoever truly lives by the law of love will never ask who his neighbor is, for he will recognize him in every man. He will ask only what he must do here and now in order that he, too, may deserve the name of neighbor. Neighbor is a relative word: God has made every man a neighbor to us, and it remains for us to make ourselves a neighbor to every man according to his need.

Lk 10:38—42   Though the connection is not immediately evident, it is most likely that Luke intends the story that follows to be a further elucidation of "What must I do to inherit eternal life?" This charming little episode from the Lord's life introduces us to characters whose personality traits are strikingly confirmed by the independent testimony of Jn 11. Luke speaks of *Martha and Mary* here for the first time and never again, but from the familiar way in which Martha and Jesus exchange remarks, each not hesitating to chide the other, though in perfect good humor, we can deduce that he had been a visitor in the sisters' house before and that they all knew one another very well. Luke sets the scene in *a certain village* not, probably, because he did not know it was Bethany (Jn 11:1), but because in his perspective Jesus is still on his journey to Jerusalem (see above on Mt 19:1 f. and parallels), and it would be anticlimactic to indicate his presence in the Holy City before the appointed time: Bethany, where Jesus habitually lodged when in Jerusalem (cf. Mt 21:17; Mk 11:11 f.), was actually one of its suburbs. We may suppose that what is described here took place during one of Jesus' multiple visits to Jerusalem about which the Synoptic Gospels are silent but which are recognized in John's Gospel.

While Mary adopts the posture of a disciple, *seated at the Lord's feet listening to his word* (cf. Acts 22:3), *Martha was distracted with much serving*. The situation is a familiar one. Probably Martha had already sent some meaningful glances in Mary's direction that had gone unheeded before she took her complaint to Jesus. His reply that she is *anxious and troubled about many things*, his reiterated *Martha, Martha*, tell us that he was smiling at a friend whose little failings and excesses were well known to him. It is not that Mary had simply shirked her duty and left her sister to do all the work. It is plain that Martha had imagined that a great deal more was to be done than was really needful. She is the eternal elder sister who has a household to run, the hustler and bustler determined to kill her guests with kindness.

All this being understood, we will not misinterpret Jesus' meaning, as though he were making light of the practical necessities of life in favor of a kind of selfish and parasitical contemplative state. *There is need of but one thing*, he says to Martha. The "one thing" is not what Mary is doing in contrast to what Martha is doing, but the essential of what Martha is doing in contrast to the "many things" over which she is troubled. *There is need of but few things, or even only one* is the reading of some good manuscripts and by many this is believed to be the original reading. Whatever was required by hospitality for himself and his disciples had already been taken care of. Martha's many little duties in which she now wanted Mary to share were quite superfluous. Then, with a slight play on words: *Mary has chosen the good portion, which shall not be taken from her.* Without condemning Martha he praises Mary who has recognized that the most important of all things is to hear the word of life.

Lk 11:1–4   It is not inappropriate that while Luke is
Mt 6:9–15   concerned with the Lord's teaching on the
                           way to eternal life he should now bring in
the story of the introduction of what we know traditionally as the Our Father or Lord's Prayer. Matthew, as we know, has the same prayer in his Sermon on the Mount, where it appears as a kind of appendix to various teachings of Jesus on prayer, interrupting a well-balanced series of examples in which Christian simplicity is being contrasted with contemporary religiosity. Luke's story, while no point is to be made of its chronology—he says, again, that it occurred *in a certain place*, holding to his journey-to-Jerusalem outline— is perfectly credible in itself. It is only to be supposed that Jesus, like every religious teacher, and *as John* the Baptist *taught his disciples*, should have instructed his followers in prayer. There is an ancient adage, *lex orandi lex credendi*, which is to say that every belief manifests itself in its own proper way of praying. In the ancient Church the Our Father was learnt by catechumens but could be recited only by the

baptized, so much was it identified with the profession of the Christian creed. We retain something of this tradition in our rite of Baptism and in our recitation of the Our Father at the conclusion of the Canon of the Mass before Holy Communion.

The liturgical use of the Our Father is indeed ancient. It appears in the Didache substantially in its Matthaean form, with the instruction that it is to be prayed thrice daily. In the Didache a liturgical doxology has been appended, "for yours is the power and the glory forever," which in one form or another has made its way into many of the manuscripts of Matthew's Gospel and thus into many of the older vernacular versions of the Bible. It is doubtless liturgical use in the various local churches rather than an individual evangelist's tendency to shorten or lengthen the Prayer that accounts for the "longer" and "shorter" forms in which we find it in Matthew's and Luke's Gospels respectively. Neither form, we may be sure, corresponds precisely to the Aramaic original uttered by Jesus. While Luke's shorter version probably represents a form of the Prayer which had undergone less material expansion, in various instances it is evidently farther removed from a Semitic original than is Matthew's. It is well to note that the liturgical adaptation of the Prayer is by no means restricted to its development prior to the canonical Gospels. As used in public prayer today by people of whatever language, the Our Father hardly if ever corresponds exactly to the text of either Luke or Matthew. The standard English version that is recited with incidental variations by most Protestants and Catholics seems to have been standardized in the time of King Henry VIII. A history of this kind is by no means isolated. Prayers such as the Jewish *Shema* mentioned above and the *Shemoneh Esreh* (the "Eighteen Benedictions") have the same record of development and adaptation as does our distinctive Christian prayer.

We think of it as a distinctively Christian prayer, though as a matter of fact it was first offered to devout Jews who in reciting it were not conscious of departing from any tradition of their past. It is not so much in content as in context that it is Christian, as becomes evident when we begin to study its very first line. Matthew has *Our Father who are in heaven*. In Aramaic "who are in heaven" would be a single word, the equivalent of our adjective "heavenly." This is a fairly standard Jewish designation of God, the purpose of which is not to suggest his remoteness from the world but rather his omnipotent transcendence of it: the "kingdom of heaven," after all, as Matthew understands it, is the coming of God's power down upon earth. Luke has, simply, *Father*, and it is most likely that it was in this form that Jesus first uttered the prayer. The New Testament, the Gospel of John especially but by no means exclusively, retains a vivid memory of the intimate way in which Jesus addressed God as "Father" or "my Father" (see above on Lk 10:21 f. and parallel), a distinctive address that was a departure from normal Jewish usage. So much did this impress itself on tradition that *Abba*, the Aramaic word which he used, has also been remembered and recognized as peculiarly Christian (cf. Mk 14:36; Rom 8:15; Gal 4:6). It is to acknowledge the extraordinary intimacy into which we enter with God through Christ that, "taught by our Savior's command, . . . we *dare* to say, Our Father . . ."

May your name be sanctified. This is a typically Jewish *Qaddish* prayer which is paraphrased by the second petition (in Matthew and Luke) and the third (in Matthew only). To ask that God's *kingdom may come* upon earth and that his *will be done on earth as it is in heaven* is to ask much the same thing, and this same thing is the sanctification of God's name, that is to say, the public and universal acknowledgment of his holy and saving power (cf. Zech 14:9). In Jewish ears, and in the ears of the earliest Christian Church, there was doubtless a once-for-allness connected with these petitions that we miss today. Without losing sight of this original perspective, however, the Church has continued to pray in these terms as each age has revealed more of her destiny to herself, recognizing that the eschatological kingdom is also realized in each existential moment. God's name is made holy to the extent that his holiness enters more and more into the lives of men; in this sense his kingdom continually "comes."

In the next petition, common to both Matthew and Luke, the Prayer turns from the kingdom itself to its members. The two Gospel verses are sometimes translated as though they said precisely the same thing, but actually there is considerable difference between them. While Matthew has *Give us* (once for all) *today our _____ bread,* in Luke we read *Give us* (continually) *day by day our _____ bread.* It is easier to take Luke's version first, because it is probably an adaptation. In both verses I have substituted a dash for the adjective which we customarily translate "daily," simply because we do not know the exact meaning of the Greek word (*epiousion*). "Daily" was the translation which St. Jerome found in the Old Latin version of the Gospels of Matthew and Luke when he began the life's work of revision and translation that eventuated in the Vulgate Bible. (The Old Latin Gospels, which may have appeared as early as the end of the second century, are among our earliest interpretations of the New Testament.) Jerome left "daily" as it stood in Luke, and probably rightly. Luke, as we know, displays a more than usual concern for the poor and their needs, and it is therefore most likely that he understood the petition in terms of their day-by-day concern for subsistence (cf. Lk 6:21). Following a suggestion by Jerome himself, some modern scholars have theorized that the Aramaic word underlying *epiousion* would have been *delimhar.* If so, the request would be, literally, for "tomorrow's bread": this is the prayer of the poor. Obviously, this direction of attention toward physical needs does not exclude but rather presupposes the dependence of the poor on God for every good thing, spiritual as well as material (see above on Mt. 5:3–12 and parallel).

It is not so evident, however, that this is the way Matthew understood the petition. Here Jerome changed the Old Latin translation of *epiousion* to *supersubstantialem,* relying on the supposed etymology of the Greek word. Whatever he may have wanted "supersubstantial" to mean for his readers, it is clear enough that he did not believe "daily" was right.

What would *delimḥar* signify in this context, a "tomorrow's bread" that is asked for today and once for all? Very likely, it is the bread of the kingdom (cf. Mt 15:26; Lk 14:15, and see above on Jn 6:26–51a). If this is the correct interpretation, this fourth petition of the Our Father agrees strikingly with the first three. It is likewise easier to see why Christian tradition, as reflected in our liturgical usage, has always put the Our Father into such close relationship with the Eucharistic bread.

Forgive us our debts, the Prayer continues in Matthew's Gospel. This petition embodies a Semitism that is doubtless original, which is paraphrased by Luke as *forgive us our sins.* Luke, however, shows his awareness of the underlying figure in his next clause: *for we also forgive everyone who is in debt to us.* This clause, too, is something of a paraphrase, smoothing out the ruggedness of Matthew's *as we have also forgiven our debtors* and, probably, stating as a continuing principle of forgiveness what was first envisaged in Matthew's version as a once-for-all remission of sin in view of the coming final judgment. No one would be so foolhardy as to ask God's forgiveness only in proportion as he has forgiven others, for by that very fact he would be asking for something less than complete forgiveness, and furthermore there can be no real proportion between what we forgive and what we hope to be forgiven us by God. The point is, however, that God's forgiveness is for those who are disposed for it, who know the need of forgiveness and its value. Only the man who has himself forgiven knows what it means to ask for forgiveness and is prepared to receive it. This is why it is so important to forgive. That is the meaning of the little commentary that Matthew has attached to the Prayer at the end (vss. 14 f.), and that was the sense of the parable of the unforgiving servant that we saw in Chapter 14 (see above on Mt 18:23–35).

Do not lead us into temptation we find in both Matthew and Luke. Though there is a sense in which God tempts man, that is, puts him to the test (cf. Gen 22:1), it is equally obvious that he is not a tempter in the conventional sense, an inciter to evil (cf. Jas 1:13). The expression is a Semitism, the intention of which is "Let us not succumb to temptation." But what is the temptation in question? As the prayer has developed in Christian usage, doubtless any temptation of any kind is meant. The first Christians, however, probably thought first and foremost of the final great trial coming upon the earth, the last onslaught of Satan and his minions which must be overcome by the elect before the end of all (cf. Apo 3:10). In keeping with this is Matthew's parallel, *but deliver us from [the] evil,* which may also be translated *from the evil one.*

Lk 11:5–8   Luke also adds his own commentary on the Prayer by way of the parable of the importunate friend, the meaning of which is fairly pellucid. A knowledge of the Palestinian scene only draws its picture more sharply. The house besieged by the friend would have consisted of a single room: kitchen, larder, and parlor by day, bedroom by night. When the mats had been spread over the floor and everyone was in bed, it would indeed be an inconvenience to disrupt the entire household literally to dig out what was needed. Still, if only to ransom a part of his night's rest, the householder will eventually give in if his friend plagues him long enough. So persevering must be prayer, says the Gospel. Not, of course, that God will not hear us the first time; that is not the point of the parable. The point is that we must not lose heart when, for reasons of his own, God delays, or seems to delay, the answer to our prayers. The point is driven home by further sayings of the Lord which we have already seen in the context of the Sermon on the Mount (see above on Mt 7:7–11 and parallel).

16. FIRE ON THE EARTH

Lk 11:14–23
Mt 12:22–30
Mt 9:32–34
Mk 3:22–27

We continue with Luke's order of events: "chronology" would obviously be the wrong term to use in this connection. Both Luke and Matthew give us the occasion of the charge of diabolism made against Jesus in the exorcism of a man who was *dumb* (in Mt 12, *blind and dumb*), while Mark simply notes the charge as made by *scribes from Jerusalem*. Mark and Matthew, however, situate the controversy within the period of the Galilean ministry, where it doubtless belongs; for Matthew this is only one of a whole series of controversies between Jesus and his adversaries. For good measure, Matthew has a doublet of the same story which he has placed earlier in his Gospel, in a context which shows the manifestation of Jesus' power in the face of the growing animosity of *the Pharisees*.

Jesus is accused—in Luke's timeless sequence Mark's scribes and Matthew's Pharisees become *certain people in the crowds*—of being diabolically possessed (the same charge in Jn 7:20, 8:48, 52, 10:20 imputes insanity to him), in the sense that his power derived from *Beelzebul the prince of demons*. Beelzebul, originally *ba'al zebul* (Baal the Prince), had once been the name of a Philistine god; the Jews tended to identify the gods of the Gentiles with demons (cf. 1 Cor 10:20 f.). In the Hebrew Bible the name was deliberately

corrupted out of contempt to *ba'al zebub* (Baal [lord] of
the flies), which explains the "Beelzebub" of many of the
Gospel manuscripts. Luke also adds that *others were demanding from him a sign from heaven* (cf. Mt 12:38, 16:1;
Mk 8:11; Jn 6:30).

Jesus first mocks the absurdity of their claim, born of
desperation. Satan overthrowing the power of Satan would
be like civil war in a kingdom or commonwealth. Satan is not
so foolish as to destroy himself. Moreover, he asks, according
to Matthew and Luke, if exorcism can so readily be
ascribed to diabolical influence, what does this make of the
exorcisms performed by the Pharisees' own *children,* that is,
their disciples? *They will be your judges:* Jesus' adversaries
will stand condemned by the very doctrine they have taught.
It is, in fact, this widespread conviction of the power of
exorcism through *the spirit of God* (=the power of God=
Luke's *the finger of God,* cf. Ex 8:15; Deut 9:10; Ps 8:4)
that must prove to Jesus' hearers that *the kingdom of God
has come upon you.* The little parable common to the three
Gospels concludes the illustration. The only way to enter a
strong man's house and rob it at will is first to have the
strong man tied securely. If Jesus is, in fact, now plundering
Satan's stronghold, then Satan's power must have been
definitively broken. We have seen all along that this is the
essential message of Jesus' healing miracles and exorcisms.

Matthew and Luke conclude with a saying that is verbally
the reverse of another uttered on an entirely different
occasion and to an entirely different purpose (see above on
Mk 9:38-41 and parallels). Jesus speaks here as the gatherer
of the eschatological community (cf. Ezek 34:13), and the
times permit only the option that is possible between Christ
and Satan: *He who is not with me is against me, and he who
does not gather with me scatters.*

Mt 12:31-32   Matthew and Mark quite properly con-
Mk 3:28-30   tinue this scene with the Lord's words on
Lk 12:10   blasphemy against the Spirit of God, the
so-called "unforgivable sin." Jesus does not,
of course, say that any sin is really unpardonable, for such

a statement would put limits both on God's mercy and his power. He does assert that there is sin that will not be forgiven. If God's mercy is without limit, neither is it mindless: to represent God as an overindulgent father who automatically condones every offense is not to hear the teaching of Christ. Blasphemy against the Spirit—deliberately and in cold blood to ascribe the manifest workings of God to the power of evil—is a perversion of spirit, a reprobate sense which deprives itself of the divine mercy simply by denying its existence.

The meaning of Jesus' pronouncement becomes clearer in Matthew's Gospel, where the distinction is drawn between speaking *against the Son of Man* and speaking *against the Holy Spirit*. St. Jerome's commentary is apposite: "He who speaks a word against the Son of Man is scandalized by my flesh . . . that I am the son of a carpenter, and have brethren, James, and Joseph, and Jude, and that as a man I eat and am a drinker of wine; such an opinion and blasphemy, though it lacks not the guilt of its error, will however be forgiven because of the weakness of the flesh. But he however who plainly perceives the works of God, who is unable to deny the power but is impelled by envy of the same to calumniate and ascribe the works of the Holy Spirit to Beelzebub—for him there is no forgiveness."

Neither in this age nor the one to come is an emphatic paraphrase of Mark's *never*. "The age to come" as distinguished from "this age" or "this world" is Jewish language for the messianic era, which in the New Testament has been used to refer to the age of the Church (cf. Heb 2:5).

Luke has put his version of this saying in the quite different context of Jesus' warnings to his disciples against the temptation to deny him in times of persecution. Following verse 9 the sense is: Whoever disowns Christ simply as another man, that is, who denies being a follower of Jesus of Nazareth as Peter did, commits sin; but only he who repudiates Christ's divine mission as God's emissary and Son blasphemes against the Holy Spirit whom Christ has manifested.

Mt 12:33–37 Matthew concludes this episode with the use of a parable which both he and Luke have already employed in other contexts (see above on Mt 7:15–20 and Lk 6:43–45). Here the purpose is to drive home the point that the evil and malicious speech of Jesus' adversaries is a true index to their character as men.

Jn 10:22–39 We may find it convenient to turn now to the last of Jesus' discourses to the Jerusalemites recorded in John's Gospel. The evangelist connects it with the mid-December feast of *the Dedication* (Hanukkah), the Jewish celebration which commemorates the reconsecration of the Jerusalem temple in 165 B.C. by Judah the Maccabee after its profanation by Antiochus Epiphanes (cf. 1 Macc 4:36–59; 2 Macc 1:18). Judaism did and does observe Hanukkah as a festival of freedom, "the feast of Lights." Lamps were lighted to symbolize the light of liberty, and in various other ways it was regarded as a kind of continuation of the feast of Tabernacles and was sometimes even called by this name (cf. 2 Macc 1:9, 10:6). These resemblances partially explain the similarity of this discourse to the lengthy ones centered about the feast of Tabernacles which we saw in our preceding two chapters. As before, Jesus is *in the temple* area, *in Solomon's porch,* an area protected against the winter cold on the east side of the outer temple court.

The Jews ask Jesus to *tell us in plain speech whether you are the Messiah.* Although John habitually makes Jesus' messianic affirmations more explicit than those in the Synoptics, that such a question could be asked by the Jerusalem crowds this late in the ministry is doubtless an indication of the same historical "messianic secret" that underlies both traditions (see above on Mk 1:22–28 and parallel). As in the Synoptics, Jesus avoids here any direct affirmation or denial of the messianic title. As before, he points to the witness of his works to his identity, a witness, however, which can only be seen by the eyes of faith (cf. Jn 8:12–20, etc.). He returns to the theme of the good shepherd (see on Jn

10:1–21 above), this time to speak of the "pasturage" of *eternal life* into which he leads his sheep, a result which is guaranteed by the omnipotence of the Father and his oneness with him.

I and the Father are one is more than an assertion of the harmony of will and action between Jesus and the Father (see on Jn 5:16–30 above); it presupposes the radical unity asserted in Jn 1:1. The Jews correctly perceive this: *You, who are a man, make yourself God* (cf. Jn 5:18, 8:58 f.). For the evangelist, of course, this is a superbly ironic conclusion, since in reality Jesus is a God who has made himself man (cf. Jn 1:14).

Jesus' continuing argument has often been misunderstood. *It is written in your Law* (cf. Jn 8:17), he reminds them, "*I have said, 'You are gods.'*" The citation is of Ps 82:6; the Jews sometimes spoke of the entire Old Testament as "the Law": cf. Jn 12:34, 15:25. The Jews are not asked for an exegesis of the Psalm, but simply to reflect that in the Scripture, the word of God itself, they can hear God the Father declaring others than himself to be "gods." The title itself, therefore, is not *ipso facto* the *blasphemy* which they are making it out to be. Rather, they must ask with what right and in what sense the title may be used. If it was used in Ps 82:6 in one legitimate way, may it not be used now in another? How it is now being used—*that the Father is in me and I am in the Father*—is, as always, being demonstrated in *the works and words* of a Son of God *whom the Father consecrated and sent into the world.*

Jn 10:40–42   With the conclusion of this discourse John marks a provisional termination of the period of Jesus' public ministry by taking him to the same Perean district presupposed in the Synoptic outline at this stage (see above on Mt 19:1 f. and parallels). To where the witness to the Word had first begun (see above on Jn 1:19–24) Jesus now returns; and the Baptist's witness continues in the *many* who *believed in him there.*

Lk 11:24-26   Resuming the Synoptic passage with which
Mt 12:43-45   we began this chapter (above on Lk 11:
                      14-23 and parallels), we find an eschato-
logical warning of Jesus which has been topically associated
with the discussion of the implications of his exorcisms. The
point of the parable is clearly set forth in its concluding
words: *the final condition (ta eschata) of that man becomes
worse than the first;* Matthew only underlines what is implied
in Luke when he adds, *thus will it be with this evil generation.* The very perversity of those who confront Jesus with
the charge that his works are Satanic rather than divine is
the proof that, in their case, his proclamation of the kingdom in deeds of power will be only a temporary relaxation of
the grip of evil. They will be the worse for their rejection of
grace and of the prophetic word. The power of evil over
them will increase rather than diminish because they have
shown themselves incapable of distinguishing the kingdom of
God from the rule of Satan. The expelled demon with
his reinforcements will, therefore, find it quite easy to gain
admittance with them, and so it will be.

The parable presupposes the popular Jewish demonology
of the times. The demons are pictured as wandering through
the *dry* and desert *places,* thought of as their natural habitat
(cf. Lev 16:10; Tob 8:3; Is 13:21; Bar 4:35; Apo 18:2),
seeking *rest,* that is, a human person in whom they can take
up abode. The proprietary *my house* of the demon (cf. 2 Cor
5:1) strikes an intentionally ominous note. It is doubtless not
to the point of the parable to enquire who has *swept* the
house and put it *in order* as the demon finds it on his return.
The point is that the "house" is always an attractive lodging
to Satan, who will take possession when he can.

Lk 11:27-28   The connection in context of the following
                      two verses proper to Luke does not appear
immediately, but in reality it is quite close; the association of
ideas is quite like that of a previous passage we have already
seen, which, as a matter of fact, Matthew places in this

very context (see above on Mk 3:31–35 and parallels).
Struck with admiration for Jesus' teaching, thinking to please
him and, at the same time, expressing her own holy envy,
a woman in the crowd cries out: *Blessed the womb that bore
you and the breasts you sucked!* How fortunate to be the
mother of such a son! The praise of Mary is in reality the
praise of Jesus.

Jesus does not deny the validity of the woman's honest
words. He can turn them, however, to an even more important consideration, and he does so. *Rather, blessed they
who hear the word of God and keep it!* The way out of the
evil and perverse generation whose last lot will be worse
than its first lies not through blood relationship with Jesus—
an evident impossibility for many—but through a spiritual
relationship available to all. This relationship consists in becoming Christ's disciple, which means to take in his word
wholly, with one's whole being, thus becoming a new person:
this is to do so as well as to hear the word of God (cf. Jas
1:22–25). This was as true for Mary as for anyone else.
"More blessed is Mary for believing the faith of Christ," said
St. Augustine, "than for conceiving the flesh of Christ."

Lk 11:33–36 It is at this point (Lk 11:29–32) that
Luke introduces the passage on the sign of
Jonah which we have already seen (above on Mk 8:11 f.
and parallels). The following verses are also paralleled elsewhere (see above on Mk 4:21–25 and parallel, and on Mt
6:22 f.). In their present context, Luke uses them to contrast
with the evil generation on whom all signs are wasted those
who have an eye of sincere faith to perceive the brilliant light
of his word which can illumine their whole being.

Lk 11:37–54 For topical reasons also, but possibly in
virtue of an original historical context as
well, Luke now brings in this fairly lengthy rebuke of
Pharisaical piety. Much of the material is reproduced by
Matthew in his chapter 23, a passage which is likewise
paralleled by Luke. It would appear that Matthew has made

use of the same source employed by Luke, but has assimilated the material to that of the later context, where it
will be more convenient for us to consider his parallel and
variant application of the verses that we now have before
us. The situation described by Luke, not without precedent
in his Gospel (see above on Lk 7:36–50), presupposes the
Pharisaical doctrine of the "tradition of the ancients" which
we have already had explained to us by Matthew and
Mark (see above on Mk 7:1–13 and parallel). It does not
seem likely that *the Pharisee* who *asked him to dine with
him* (literally, "to breakfast"—but the Greek word was commonly used for any meal) was only pretending the hospitality
he offered, attempting to trap Jesus in some way. That *he
was astonished that* Jesus *did not first wash* sounds like
genuine and honest surprise at the unexpected. On the other
hand, this fact alone indicates that he could have known little
about Jesus that did not go beyond polite curiosity. Of
course, we have no way of knowing when and where this
event occurred.

Now you Pharisees. The reaction of the Pharisee, probably
expressed externally in some fashion, becomes the signal for
quite plain words on Jesus' part. Coming from a guest to a
host, they were not altogether diplomatic. Apart from their
service to the truth, however, it is possible that they had a
salutary effect on this particular Pharisee. Jesus' first attack
centers on the underlying error that has occasioned the
present instance of Pharisaical scandal. You people, he says,
carefully *clean the outside of the cup and the dish,* but you
are little concerned when your own souls are filled with
corruption. This is the peril to which legalism exposes the
religion of even honest men: a preoccupation with trifling
externals can easily pre-empt all their attention and lead to
forgetfulness of the realities they were once supposed to
externalize (see above on Mt 6:1–4). Jesus' next words are
obscure, but their sense seems to be: *Give as alms what is
within* the vessels you wash so carefully, *then everything
will be really clean for you.* What is needful is that they
themselves be inwardly clean; if this were the case, the rest

would take care of itself. The best way for them to "clean" their cups and dishes is by emptying them for the sake of the poor, as a work of mercy.

However, the three "woes" that follow (cf. above on Lk 6:24–26) entertain little hope for any such performance on the part of the Pharisees. They *tithe mint and rue and every herb*—insignificant garden produce of which neither the Law nor firm custom demanded the tithe—so eager are they to show their devotion to religion, but they have no time for *justice and the love of God.* In such pronouncements we hear the ancient voice of Israel's prophets (cf. Is 1:10–17; Hos 6:4–7; Amos 5:21–24, etc.). *These you ought to have done without neglecting the others:* Jesus' condemnation of a distorted interpretation of the Law is not a condemnation of the Law itself, whose claims he recognizes (see above on Mt 5:17–20).

The Pharisees *love the first seat in the synagogues and the salutations* which accompany men of conspicuous religion. But in reality they *are like hidden graves over which men walk unawares.* The Law, dating from an age that had no sterile gauze or hermetical sealing to prevent the spreading of disease and corruption, wisely designated legally "unclean" anyone who came in contact with a corpse or a grave, which is to say that it segregated him from his neighbors for a week (cf. Num 19:16). Graves were, as a consequence, usually well marked, lest anyone should come in contact with them without knowing it. Thus the point of the comparison. The Pharisees' semblance of piety and the good esteem which they enjoyed concealed their corrupting influence from those who were inclined to put confidence in their example and counsel.

At this juncture one of the scribes (called *lawyers* here by Luke; cf. vs. 53) rightly remonstrates with Jesus, pointing out that his strictures are in reality addressed to his professional class. Rightly, that is, since the Pharisees were mainly dependent for their religious attitudes on the scribal students and teachers who belonged to their party (see the remarks on the Pharisees in Chapter 1). The association of scribes and Pharisees is, as we have seen, habitual in the Gospels and certainly to be expected at the meal which serves as the setting for this passage.

The scribe's intervention earns three "woes" for his class paralleling those addressed to the Pharisees. First, says Jesus, they *load men with intolerable burdens* (cf. Acts 15:10); we have seen ample evidence of this in considering, for example, the scribal rigor concerning the Sabbath, which could make its observance dehumanizing (see above on Mk 2:23-28 and parallels), or the elaborate rules of ritual purity which they derived from the Law and which were an impossibility for the generality of men. Yet at the same time, by clever dodges and tortuous subterfuges, they could excuse themselves from the Law's fundamental prescriptions: here we can remember the "korban" oath by which duties even to parents could be avoided (see above on Mk 7:1-13 and parallel).

The second "woe" is not as easy to understand as the first. The scribes, Jesus goes on, *build the tombs of the prophets.* Is this meant ironically, of the entombment of the dynamic prophecy of Israel in the frozen system of scribal legalism, the reduction of the prophetic word to the role of a source book for casuistic commentary? It is possible. More likely, however, is it that Jesus has in mind the actual building and rebuilding of physical tombs which were intended to honor the traditional grave sites of the prophets of old. By this means men professed reparation for the sins of their *fathers who killed* the prophets (cf. Mt 23:30). All in vain, however; their conduct otherwise shows how much they were of the same mind as their fathers, and however much they protest other dispositions, they approve their deeds in fact (cf. Acts 7:51-53). Therefore in reality they form, together with their ancestors, a consistent tradition of conduct: they complete the work of their fathers, as it were, by providing tombs for those whom the former slew.

The Gospel finds the history of the past being repeated in the Christian present, when once again prophets are being killed and entombed. *The divine wisdom* knew from the beginning that the *prophets and apostles* whom it sent into the world would be killed and persecuted. It will demand account of this innocent blood, just as of this present generation account will be demanded of all the innocent blood shed *from the blood of Abel to the blood of Zechariah*. This last is a reference to the salvation history of the Old Testament; Abel (Gen 4:8) was the first and Zechariah (2 Chron 24:20 f.) the last man whose murder is described in this history, since in the Jewish canon of Scripture the Book of Genesis stands at the beginning and the Second Book of Chronicles at the end.

Finally, Jesus returns to his earlier charge. The scribes, he says, are like men who have stolen the key to a door; they do not use the key to enter themselves, nor will they allow those to enter who want to. Here it is question of *the key of knowledge*, the knowledge of God to be found in his Law. They themselves strive neither to know nor to do God's will, and they have made access to it impossible for those who have trusted in their teaching. It is not surprising, in view of the uncompromising tone of Jesus' strictures, that Luke closes this passage on a scene of violence or near-violence. The text suggests that *the scribes and Pharisees* were prepared to assail him physically as well as to trap him in his speech.

Lk 12:2-9 Neither is it surprising that Luke brings
Mt 10:26-33 in at this point the saying of Jesus on the "leaven" of the Pharisees which we have seen above (on Mk 8:13-21 and parallels). As we noted, in verse 49 above the evangelist moved quite naturally from the purview of Jesus' Palestinian audience to the situation of the Church for which he was writing his Gospel. The same association of ideas now prompts him to include Jesus' words to his disciples on their conduct in the face of persecution, a passage to which Matthew has given a similar context as part of the Lord's missionary discourse to the Twelve.

In both Gospels the discourse embodies a saying which we have seen before, in a different context and with a

different meaning (above on Mk 4:21–25 and parallel). Here
the hidden thing that is to be revealed refers to the apostolic
preaching. This is certainly the case in Matthew's version,
and probably in Luke's as well: that is, *whatever you have
said in the dark* among yourselves and with me . . . *shall
be proclaimed upon the housetops.* The verb "proclaim"
(*kēryssō*) corresponds to the term used for the apostolic
preaching, the *kerygma.* Jesus does not minimize the dangers
that will await his disciples in their mission: they will face
discrimination, torture, and death. Yet however fearful such
things may be, they must *fear them not* but rather reserve
their fear for God. Their enemies have power, indeed, to
kill the body, but only God can *destroy body and soul*
together and forever. This may sound like a harsh and
ignoble kind of motivation, but it is not intended so. To die,
after all, under whatever circumstances, is the common lot
of man. No earthly power can do more to him than unas-
sisted nature will eventually do. But what no earthly power
can do, man can do to himself. He can destroy his own
identity forever, taking occasion from the trials of life to
reject the Author of his being who thus becomes his inexorable judge. The fearsome God who destroys and buries
in hell appears only to him who has refused him as a loving
Father and at the same time denied his own sonship.

Jesus has not spoken of God to frighten his disciples,
though the thought of his power must frighten the weak
and fearful. God loves them, wants them, watches over
them. He uses a homely example reminiscent of the Sermon
on the Mount (see above on Mt 6:25–34 and parallel).
One of the commonest, most valueless creatures he could
name was the Palestinian *sparrow: two for a farthing* (the
Roman *as*)—about one cent—says Matthew; *five for two
farthings,* says Luke. Yet God watches over each one of
these, and *not even one of them* dies without his knowledge
and permission. Christ's friends must realize, then, how
precious is each one of them individually in God's eyes
and how much the object of his solicitude which extends
to the numbering of the hairs of their heads. When their

trials come, therefore, let them stand fast, confident and fearless. Those who acknowledge him in the face of all their common enemies will be sustained before men and, above all, in the final judgment of God; those who reject him will be rejected (see above on Mk 8:34–9:1 and parallels). Here Luke has brought in Jesus' saying on blasphemy against the Spirit which we saw earlier in this chapter (above on Mt 12:31 f. and parallels).

Mt 10:16b–25 Earlier in the discourse Matthew has
Lk 12:11–12   cited other teachings of the Lord on the
                  same subject which are here partly paralleled by Luke in his conclusion (cf. also Jn 14:26). To *be prudent as serpents and simple as doves,* to combine sagacity with ingenuous honesty in dealing with a hostile world—the Gospels, quite evidently, look beyond the immediate Palestinian scene with which Jesus dealt into the continuing history of the Church—this is surely not easy. It means to know when to be bold, when reserved; when to speak, when to remain silent, yet never to be silent when it is necessary to speak; when to act and when to let events take their natural course. Hard though it be, however, the disciples must remember that they are not alone. They will have the assistance of *the Holy Spirit* to guide them, *the Spirit of your Father,* as Matthew puts it. On this promise the Church has lived ever since.

Brother will deliver up brother to death . . . It is not an attractive picture that Jesus paints. The saving message of Christ will divide families, or rather belief and unbelief will divide them, and the ties of blood will be forgotten in the ensuing strife. The rule still holds, that the disciple must expect to receive the treatment of his Master, if he is disciple indeed (cf. Lk 6:40; Jn 13:16). If they have dared *call* even *the master of the house Beelzebul* (see Lk 11:14–23 and parallels at the beginning of this chapter), *how much more* will they do so with *those of his household!*

Jesus instances an example of the prudence to be exercised by his disciples. *When they persecute you in one village, flee to another.* The call to Christian witness is not a summons to fanaticism: removing oneself from the attentions of a persecutor can be an act of charity toward him and qualify as the simplicity of the dove. *You will not have gone through all the villages of Israel,* Jesus adds, *before the Son of Man comes.* This is another of those puzzling statements of Jesus like that of Mt 16:28 which we saw on page 287 f., Vol. I (on Mk 8:34–9:1 and parallels; cf. also Mk 13:28–32 and parallels below). The early Church most certainly understood it and other words of Jesus of its kind as pointing to an imminent termination of "these last days" (Heb 1:2) in the glorious consummation of God's kingdom; indeed, the continued "delay" of this eagerly awaited end became a source of scandal to many as the Church continued on (cf. 2 Pt 3:3–10). What did Jesus himself mean by such a saying? We shall be in a better position to answer this question when we come to consider his *ex professo* teaching on the last days in our Chapter 21 below. For the moment, let us understand what Matthew has taken it to mean. The evangelist's context supposes no speedy conclusion of the Church's mission limited to the towns of Palestine, but a continuing witness before the governors and kings of the Gentile world (vs. 18), a mission which extends to all the nations of the earth (cf. Mt 28:19 f.). For Matthew, then, "Israel" here means nothing less than the new people of God which the Church is sent to form (cf. Mt 2:6, 19:28). Until the Lord comes, he says, there will always be another place for the Church to go, retreating before violence, and in going there to bear yet further its testimony to the Gospel of Christ.

Mt 10:34–36   Violence has been the theme of Jesus'
Lk 12:49–53   warnings to his disciples, and it is on this
                    theme that he continues to dwell. It is one
of the paradoxes of all time that this Man of peace, whom the New Testament can call peace itself (Eph 2:14), should be the source of strife and dissension, that he should have occasioned some of the vilest as well as the noblest of the

conduct possible to man. For this reason he can say that
he has come not *to bring peace on earth . . . but a sword,*
not *to give peace on earth . . . but division.* Both Matthew
and Luke cite Mi 7:6 in illustration of his meaning, words
by which the prophet intended to signify all that was ab-
normal and enormous in human relations.

The sense of the Gospel, however, is not merely to reiterate
warnings of things to come. *I came to cast fire on the earth,*
cries Jesus—the figure has changed, but the meaning remains
the same—*and how I wish that it were already kindled!*
He not only anticipates the violence, he also welcomes it!
The word of Christ is not all milk and water, sweetness and
light. If the kingdom is to come only through violence—a
violence which is not of its making—then, violence or no,
let the kingdom come! If the violent of this world are to
have their way forever, then nothing of good will ever be
accomplished. If good men are to be dissuaded from good
because doing good provokes violence, then evil has tri-
umphed for all time. We have it from the lips of Christ that,
when the cause is right, it is the man of peace in whose
wake and at the tips of whose nerveless hands injustice and
inhumanity pursue their untrammeled paths, while the man
who is attended by violence does the works of God. We
have it from his lips and we have it from his life: *I have a
baptism with which to be baptized, and how I am hemmed
in till it is done!* This is an "imitation of Christ" to which all
too few Christians have been equal.

Mt 10:37–39, 11:1   Matthew proceeds toward the end
Lk 14:25–27, 17:33   of his missionary discourse by joining together three sayings of Jesus ap-
propriate to this context, two of which he has already used
elsewhere taken from the common Synoptic tradition (see
above on Mk 8:34–9:1 and parallels). One of these two,
as we also noted before, is likewise proper to the Johannine
tradition (cf. Jn 12:25). The three sayings have been repeated by Luke as well, at two intervals in his "timeless"
sequence of the Perean ministry.

The difference in meaning caused by the changed contexts is not appreciable; it is mainly a question of specific applications. It will pay us to examine, however, the third of the sayings which we have not seen up to this point. Here again it is interesting to note that it is Luke, rather than Matthew, who has preserved the Semitic rigor of Jesus' words. *If anyone would come after me and not hate his father . . .* is softened to *Whoever loves his father or mother more than me.* We are not invited by pronouncements of this kind to weigh our separate loves in a balance and compare them in the abstract. The sense is, rather, that no earthly love or bond must ever be allowed to interfere with our prime allegiance to Christ. This is made quite evident when in Luke's version the Lord says that we must even hate ourselves. The Christian finds his true fulfillment in complete surrender to his Savior, renouncing in the process when called upon to do so all that men would consider to be the claims of self-interest. It is perhaps worthy of comment that while Matthew has put these lines in a discourse of Jesus to the Twelve, Luke has them in an address to the *great multitudes* which were following him, among whom, presumably, were those who were on the verge of committing themselves to discipleship. Neither Gospel can be accused of proposing the calling of a Christian as an easy one.

Lk 12:13–21   Matthew closes his discourse with his customary formula (see above on Mt 7:28 f.). In Luke, Jesus' teaching at first directed to his disciples (vs. 1) is now interrupted by the request of *someone in the crowd,* an intervention which focuses his attention on the whole assembly and leads to a discussion closely related to the foregoing.

We do not know the circumstances involved in regard to *the inheritance* about which the man hoped that Jesus would arbitrate between him and his brother. He had seized this opportunity of calling out to Jesus as a respected rabbi whose authority would be worth something if used in his behalf. Jesus, however, as we know, habitually refused to intervene in such matters, leaving them to be handled in the conventional way, as he does now. He did take the occasion to warn against covetousness, which is not to say either that the man's desire for his property was inordinate or that he was dishonest. Jesus' teaching on the Christian attitude to wealth is more far-reaching than that.

Covetousness—the word *pleonexia*, which is used in the New Testament mainly by Paul, means "the desire for more" —is an evil for man not because it necessarily makes him defraud others or otherwise do them an injury, but because it can lead him to miss the meaning of life and thus to destroy himself. It can make him forget that *a man's life does not consist in the abundance of his possessions*. It is for this reason that Col 3:5 calls covetousness "idolatry": it worships a false god by setting up another goal of life than that for which man was created.

What Jesus understands by covetousness we learn from his parable. We see a certain rich farmer—today he might be growing wheat in Kansas or corn in Iowa—who brings in a bumper crop, so great that he is forced to tear down his available barns and build greater ones. This he does, and with all his possessions snugly laid in, it seem that he can quite justly congratulate himself on a good job well done. He has security; he can now take things easy and live off his accumulated capital. The picture Jesus drew would have appealed to his hearers, and was so intended, as that of a respectable, solid citizen, one of the bedrocks on which a stable society rested. Nor should we imagine that the average Christian reaction today would be much different. We, too, are inclined to see in this man the prudent organizer, the good planner whom we would trust with our own goods, the man of substance who has done well for himself and his family.

God, however, calls him *fool*, and in doing so indicates how far apart our judgments can be from those of Christ. As far as Jesus is concerned, the man was neither wise nor prudent nor sensible, but a fool. The very night he found himself at last prepared to lead the good life without fear of want, that night God decreed his life forfeit. He was *not rich toward God*. This does not mean necessarily that he was an irreligious man who had consciously cut God out of his life: the parable does not suggest this. He was a fool, rather, because he felt that his future was in his own hands, that whatever he was to become, he would be "self-made"; he was a fool because he thought to reckon with every eventuality of life, only to find out too late that no single one of them had really been under his control. Not only a crude love of riches corrupts, but also a preoccupation with them—and this holds, of course, for the poor as well as the rich man. It can lead to a practical forgetfulness of God that is perfectly compatible with public protestations of thanksgiving to a God of bounty who smiles on success and industry and who frowns, as all responsible men frown, on the shiftlessness and lack of forethought that alone account for poverty and want. It is not difficult to see why Luke continues in this context with certain words of the Lord which Matthew has put in his Sermon on the Mount (see above on Mt 6:25–34 and parallel).

Lk 12:32–34 Luke goes on in the same vein, including material that has been paralleled in part in Mt 6:19–21 above. Concern for worldly goods is not the only hindrance to a wholehearted and purposeful seeking of the kingdom, but it is a major one. Jesus speaks as the Good Shepherd (see above on Jn 10:1–21), affectionately addressing his *little flock*, that is, his disciples (vs. 22) as distinct from the multitude present (vs. 1). *Do not be afraid*, he tells them. He had begun by warning them of what they had to fear, but he had also told them why they should discount their fears. They are a little flock, small in the eyes of the world and defenseless, but they have what the world cannot see. They have God and they possess his kingdom if they will receive it from him. What need have they of anything else? *Sell what you have*, he directs, *and give alms*.

This command of the Lord was taken precisely at the letter by the primitive Christian Church that emerged in Jerusalem following Jesus' resurrection and ascension (cf. Acts 2:44 f.). This same mother church, we must add, itself speedily became impoverished and economically dependent on the more vigorous Christian communities which soon began to proliferate throughout the vast Gentile world (cf. Rom 15:25-28; 1 Cor 16:1-4; 2 Cor 8:1-4). In the fifties and sixties of the Pauline churches the charitable communism of the Jerusalem church of the thirties must already have seemed a quixotic anachronism from a never-to-be-repeated age of Christian innocence. This is not to say simply that Christians discovered Christ's law to be impossible and therefore settled for something less. Rather, as we said above in this chapter (on Mt 10:16b-25 and parallel), the Church had to rethink, and to rethink continually, the enduring meaning of a revealed word which, as the Holy Spirit had now made quite clear, was to guide it not for five or ten or twenty years but for an indeterminate future that was beyond calculation. Some would always be able to take this word at the letter and thus fulfill in their lives a vocation to anticipate the eschatological fulfillment of the Church, just as others would be able to do through a life of celibacy or some other charismatic calling; but the Church could not then and cannot now ignore its duty to perpetuate itself in a world that is not yet eschatological and in which an eschatological vocation will always be the exception rather than the rule. Again, therefore, we must ask: How did Luke construe this pronouncement for the Church he knew and for which he wrote?

The answer to this question is fairly obvious. Not every Christian can literally sell all that he has and distribute what he gets in alms, for if everyone did so there would be none left to carry on the ordinary life of society; and it is this ordinary life of society that Luke presupposes as he shows the Church fulfilling its destiny in Paul's hands throughout the Acts of the Apostles. Everyone can, however, take as his own the spirit in which Jesus uttered these words, and in doing so he can accomplish the end toward which they indicated a means. He can acquire the detachment from wealth of which the Lord has been speaking in the preceding passages. He can recognize that his duty to his neighbor is not defined by the extent of his surplus goods but must be fulfilled at cost to himself. He can learn, then, the function of Christian almsgiving, which is not only to relieve the need of the poor but also to benefit the giver by destroying in him the spirit of covetousness.

Lk 12:35-40   An exhortation to vigilance now follows in Luke's compilation. That part of what Luke reproduces here turns up again in the major eschatological discourse of the Synoptic tradition (see below on Mk 13:33-37 and parallels) reflects the eschatological heritage of Jesus' preaching of the kingdom and of the primitive Christian Church. Luke obviously does not exclude this perspective but neither does he consider the Lord's words to be confined to it. The eschatological moment in which the Christian encounters his Judge likewise overtakes him pre-eminently in death, whose precise instant no man can ever possibly know, but also in every wakeful minute of his life, when he forms the judgments and does the deeds on which his eternal destiny depends. Every moment of decision is, in this sense, eschatological.

The parable told by Jesus pictures a master who is to return from *a wedding feast* and who has charged his servants to be waiting for him: a wedding feast has been deliberately chosen because it was an event whose duration was entirely unpredictable, thus making the rest of the story plausible. The point of comparison is, of course, that the Lord is coming at no known or determined time. The servants, then, are to have their *waists girt and* their *lamps burning* at all times so that they will be in instant readiness to receive their master. The flowing garments of the time were worn loose when one was at leisure, but had to be girt close about the body when any active work had to be done. Doubtless no earthly master would actually have treated his faithful slaves as does the man in the parable, reversing the roles of master and man (cf. Jn 13:3–20). The very exaggeration of the story, however, points up its message: a reward far beyond our deserts is in store for those of us whom Christ our Judge finds ready at his summons. In verse 38 the uncertainty of the time of visitation is stressed—for a Church that had reconciled itself to a "delay" of the Lord's coming—*even if he comes in the second or the third watch* of the night. The Romans divided the night into four watches of roughly three hours each, depending on the season of the year, and the Jews in Palestine followed this system. Probably, however, the reference here is to the more ancient Jewish practice which knew only three night-watches (cf. Jgs 7:19).

The other little parable used by Jesus likewise dwells on the idea of uncertainty. No thief in his right mind, of course, announces his coming, so that his victim will be alert and on his guard. Just so, the Lord does not announce his coming, but appears unawares as *the thief* who *breaks into the house*. This "breaking into" the house, incidentally, is not precisely what is meant nowadays by the "breaking and entry" of a police blotter, implying the picking or the forcing of a Yale lock. Palestinian houses were, and sometimes still are, walled of mud and wattles, and a thief might easily find it more convenient to remove a wall than to get through a stout door.

Lk 12:41–48   In Luke's context *Peter* now asks whether
Mt 24:45–51   *this parable* of Jesus applies *to us*, the
               Twelve, *or to everyone*. The question might seem natural enough in view of what has gone before, since the Lord's attention has been often divided between the disciples and the accompanying multitude. Actually, however, it is pointless. Peter had no doubt at all that what Jesus had said, especially in verse 37 regarding the reward for faithful service, was meant for the Twelve. What he was asking was whether others were to be included as well. This is the kind of question that he asked according to

Jn 21:21, and equivalently he receives the same answer here. His duty is to take in the word as he receives it without concerning himself about what others do or are intended to do. Actually, it is difficult to decide whether the evangelists understand the parable above and the one that now unfolds as designating pre-eminently the Twelve and therefore said with reference to apostolic functions in the Church (cf. the apparent echo in 1 Cor 4:1–3), or expressive of the common eschatological lot of all Christians. Some of the details of context favor the former, most of the content favors the latter interpretation. For practical purposes we need not attach too much importance to the distinction.

The parable presupposes the situation of a trusted slave appointed as overseer of his master's estate, a not uncommon occurrence. It is much to the point to observe that the reward for faithful service is even greater responsibility in the same order. Whether uttered in specific reference to service in the Church or extending to the Christian's total activity in the world, the lesson is much the same and is quite an important one. Authentic Christian eschatology is not "pie in the sky" unrelated to this present world; when the Christian enters into the reward of his Master he begins a life for which he has been preparing all along and which he has even been leading already in all of his actions and involvements. Christian service, which has as its model the life of the Servant of all, is ordered toward the world which God has created and which he has loved to the extent of sending his own Son for its salvation.

Conversely, what of the servant who takes advantage of his master's absence, abuses his trust, plays havoc with his goods and abuses his fellow servants, doubtless planning to put things to rights again at some final moment that never comes? The day of reckoning arrives with the unexpected return of the master. He will, the Gospels say, *cut apart* the faithless servant. This is a strange expression, but perhaps some light is thrown on this word (*dichotomeō*) which occurs only here in the New Testament by a Hebrew expression (*yabdîl*) which etymologically is the same, and which was used by the Qumran sectaries to mean *separation* from the elect community. This idea, which has Old Testament precedents (cf. Is 56:3, 59:2), seems to be what is intended here: such a person will have *his lot with the faithless*, as Luke puts it; *with the hypocrites*, says Matthew, who also adds the expressive words found often in the Gospels to describe the hopelessness and desolation of eternal perdition: *where they weep and gnash their teeth* (cf. Mt 8:12, 13:42, 50, 22:13, 25:30; Lk 13:28).

Luke at the end has included some allegorical details which contribute a further lesson related to the foregoing and clarified by his conclusion. What he is saying is that there are degrees of punishment meted out in accord with the various degrees of guilt that are incurred.

Lk 12:57–59   Luke now introduces the Lord's words on the effect of his coming which we have seen earlier in this chapter (on Mt 10:34–36 above), and also the saying on "the signs of the times" which is as appropriate in this context as in the one where we saw it previously (above on Mk 8:11 f. and parallels). The final lines with which he closes this chapter we have also had in a Matthaean parallel (on Mt 5:21–26 above). It may be very well that in Luke's context we have this saying in its original emphasis, whereas Matthew has somewhat adapted it in applying it to fraternal charity. The time of decision is now, says Jesus; now *right judgment* must be made; after now will be too late. Now come to terms, now seek salvation in repentance. The judgment of God is ever near, and it is inexorable.

17. WAITING IN PEREA

Lk 13:1–9   The Lucan passages with which we begin have a general connection with the context of the last chapter. Jesus takes occasion from two recent disasters to issue a further eschatological warning and summons. Concerning the circumstances of the incidents themselves we have no further source of information beyond Luke's Gospel. *The Galileans whose blood Pilate had mixed with their sacrifices* evidently were Galilean pilgrims to Jerusalem who had committed what either was in fact or what Pilate imagined to be an insurrection and were therefore slaughtered by the Roman governor. Either possibility is likely: the Galileans were always restless under Roman domination, and Pilate was extremely suspicious of rebellion and merciless in dealing with it. The Roman garrison was situated on the very edge of the temple area (cf. Acts 21:30–32); obviously what happened was that the troops simply poured down upon the Galileans who were thronged together in the courtyard while their sacrifices were being carried out by the priests within.

An unexpected death, especially a violent death, was popularly regarded as God's punishment for personal sins. Perhaps in the case at hand the question of the lawfulness of rebellion was in the air. Jesus does not concern himself with these issues. All men, he reminds his listeners, are under judgment and subject to death *unless you repent.* The Galileans have died, for whatever cause, not because they were more egregious sinners than others, but their deaths can at least serve as object lessons for others. So also *the eighteen on whom the tower in Siloam fell:* the reference is to another misfortune about which we are not otherwise informed. Without repentance *all will perish in the same way,* not necessarily by Roman swords or falling stones, but violently and unexpectedly.

It is in this context that the parable of the barren *fig tree* follows. As respects God's judgment all men are in a sense living on borrowed time. At any time they could be cut down, and if they have not yet been, it is only because in his mercy they are always being given one final chance to show themselves worthy of his concern.

Lk 13:10–17   Luke intends the story of the healing of the crippled woman to have a topical connection with the foregoing, though it resembles even more some of the controversy stories involving the Sabbath that we have seen before (see above on Mk 3:1–5 and parallels). The connection here is the demonstration of the proximity of the kingdom of God in the loosing of Satan's power which had *bound this daughter of Abraham for eighteen years.* Though this healing miracle was not precisely an exorcism it was produced much to the same effect, since afflictions of the woman's kind were popularly ascribed, as we see, to a personal *spirit of infirmity.* When the event actually occurred we of course do not know, though it probably belongs to the early part of Jesus' ministry when *he was teaching in one of the synagogues.* The story is told with the attention to detail that speaks for its having been taken from life. This is particularly evident, perhaps, in the words of *the ruler of the synagogue* who, rather than attack Jesus directly, tries to lecture the crowds who would not presume to answer him back, placing the blame on them as though they had come to the synagogue expressly to be healed, which was not the case. His pompous *come on those* six other *days to be healed and not on the Sabbath* even manages to suggest that miracles of healing were going on everywhere on a twenty-four-hour schedule and could be regulated at will. It was probably these devious courses as well as his Pharisaical scandal that earned the Master's retort, *Hypocrites!*

Lk 13:22–30   In this appropriate context of controversy over the coming of the kingdom Luke has included the parables of the kingdom which we have already seen (above on Mt 13:31 f. and parallels; Mt 13:33 and parallel). Then, after reminding us that Jesus is *journeying toward Jerusalem* (see above on Mt 19:1 f. and parallels), he has him *teaching through towns and villages* till he reaches the scene of this present passage.

Will only a few be saved? was a natural question which inevitably Jesus must have been asked countless times in his preaching of the kingdom. The rabbis generally thought that the number of the saved would be rather small—as, for that matter, many earnest souls have thought throughout history, not always without a certain complacency concerning their own status among the saved. Small or great, however, the number was usually related exclusively to the Jews; the Gentiles, by and large, were left out of consideration as a matter of course. Descent from Abraham and Moses was what counted (cf. Jn 8:31 ff., 9:28 f.), that and the faithful observance of the Law and the traditions of the ancients. Since ignorance of the Law and the traditions, from the standpoint of the professional scribe, was more the rule than the exception, it was not felt that the number of the elect would be large (cf. Jn 7:49). It was a certain smugness, therefore, that lay behind the posing of the question, Will many be saved?

It is this kind of irrelevant question that Jesus never answers. Neither does he respond to it here. His saying about *the narrow door* (here the door of a house rather than the gate of a city) has the same meaning as its parallel

in Matthew (see above on Mt 7:13 f.). *Keep trying to get in,*
he teaches them, for the time is late and the kingdom of
God is like a room into which everyone must crowd at once:
in such a press of people it is normal that *many will strive
yet not be able to get in.* His accent is on the urgency of
the situation and the need for effort; he does not speculate
on the relative numbers within and without the door. And
the door is soon to be shut! In verses 25–27 Luke applies
to the present figure words of the Lord very like those
which Matthew reproduced in another context but to the
same purpose (see above on Mt 7:21–23 and parallel). In
turn, this leads to the sternest warning of all, which strikes
at the complacency in which the original question had been
asked. Luke's verses 28 f. parallel Mt 8:11 f. and have the
same function (see above on Lk 7:1–10 and parallel). Blood
descent from Israel's ancestry is no guarantee of membership
in the kingdom, which can be given instead to the Gentiles.
The last shall be first and the first shall be last is a saying
of Jesus which appears in several Gospel passages. Here it
probably refers less to the possible substitution of Gentiles
for the Jews—though in Luke's perspective the substitution
now had in fact taken place, in the Church—than to the
general theme of the entire passage, which is now summed
up: in the pell-mell struggle that is involved in the entry
to the kingdom, see that you are not among the last, the
too late!

Lk 13:31–33 The next episode, which is told us only
by Luke, is entirely at home in this story
of the Perean ministry. Perea, like Galilee, was the domain
of *Herod* Antipas, and it was here in Perea that Herod had
had John the Baptist put to death (see above on Mk 6:14–29
and parallels). It is not entirely clear what role the *certain
Pharisees* played in the little drama that unfolds before us.
Jesus' telling them to bear his message back to the tyrant
may have been merely rhetorical, but at the same time it
seems to indicate that he put them in the same class with
Herod. On the other hand, had they really been privy to

Herod's plans and in sympathy with them, they would hardly have brought a warning to Jesus of any kind. Probably we are dealing with a case of a coincidence of interests rather than a plot. Herod, we know, had heard of Jesus and was curious about him, and whatever he had heard was doubtless not to his liking. To say that Herod had decreed his death is certainly to say too much: *He wishes to kill you,* the Pharisees related. But it is most likely that he had said something to the effect that the land would be well enough off without Jesus—"Will not someone rid me of this troublesome priest?" It was probably intelligence of this kind that the Pharisees brought. It was to their interest to be rid of Jesus' presence, and news like this could easily send a person hurrying across the nearest frontier, since in those days it was extremely unhealthy to come to the unwelcome attention of a king.

Jesus, however, will not be intimidated. *That fox,* he calls Herod: in the Bible a fox is a predator rather than an animal of guile. *Today and tomorrow and the third day* is the time that remains to him: the expression means a determined period, but a period determined by God, not by Herod (cf. Hos 6:2). Furthermore, he adds ironically, it can hardly be destined that his life should end in Perea, for it is Jerusalem that has the monopoly in the slaying of prophets!

Lk 13:34-35 It is the mention of Jerusalem that causes
Mt 23:37-39 Luke to introduce at this point Jesus' lament over the Holy City, a passage which Matthew has reserved for the peroration of a lengthy discourse delivered in Jerusalem itself against the Pharisaical leadership of Judaism. The city is symptomatic of all rebellious Israel in this apostrophe, of course, as it is so often in the Old Testament, *rejecting the prophets and stoning those sent to it.* But symptomatic or not, it is of the city that Jesus speaks when he touchingly compares the mercy shown through him to the tender solicitude of a mother hen who spreads her wings to protect her young from harm. His *how*

often confirms the Johannine tradition complementing the Synoptic, that Jesus' acquaintance with and ministry in Jerusalem was not confined to the one week of his passion, death, and resurrection toward which Luke is looking in his Gospel.

Your house is left forsaken, pronounces Jesus, echoing the words that an earlier prophet spoke of an earlier Jerusalem and its king (cf. Jer 22:5). Jerusalem, having rejected its destiny, is desolate, whatever be its present proud pretensions. *I say to you, you shall not see me* (cf. Jn 7:34, 8:21) *until you say, "Blessed is he who comes in the name of the Lord!"* (Ps 118:26). Do the evangelists think that this will eventually happen (an "until" does not necessarily imply a change of state, cf. Mt 1:25), or do they look on this as the Lord's irrevocable judgment on Jerusalem? We cannot be sure. Luke, however, by placing this passage where he has, has evidently seen a partial fulfillment of Jesus' condition in his triumphal entry into Jerusalem on Palm Sunday (cf. Lk 19:38), and therefore, in all likelihood, an earnest of the salvation of Israel in God's own time (cf. Rom 11:26 f.).

Lk 14:1-6   Luke now offers something of a change of pace in his "great addition" as he begins to tell a story that we have the initial impression of having heard before because of its resemblance to a common type (see above in this chapter on Lk 13:10-17); actually, however, this seems to be a story apart. The scene is set *in the house of one of the leaders of the Pharisees* where Jesus has been invited *to eat a meal on the Sabbath.* The setting is natural enough—of course we do not know when or where it is to be placed in the life of Jesus—and there is no reason to suspect that the invitation was anything less than a gesture of honest hospitality or that Jesus was seated among people who were antecedently hostile to him. *The lawyers and Pharisees* who were present *were watching him,* it is true, but seemingly more out of curiosity and of interest than of evil intent. The *man with dropsy* who suddenly appeared *before him* would have had no problem in intruding upon an Oriental banquet, and there is no indication at all that he had been introduced to provide a provocation. His swollen condition as he stood there spoke eloquently of his need; he had no cause to put it in words.

It is Jesus who forces the issue: *Is it lawful to heal on the Sabbath, or not?* (cf. Lk 6:9). The doctors of the Law recognize that this is no theoretical question, for here stands the man who, they realize, is to be healed. They evidently accept his argument that since a man can retrieve *an ass or an ox from a well* on the Sabbath, it should be permitted to heal a man (see above on Mt 12:9–13). (Some of the better manuscripts have "a son" in place of "an ass"; but this would appear to be an attempt to make things a little too easy for the legal mind.) *They could not reply to this:* they were not necessarily seeking an answer at all costs which they could not find; it is possible that they were genuinely puzzled. This older generation of jurists had been conditioned to certain automatic responses according to ingrained custom, and it did not come easy to them to devise new answers to new questions. The Gospel leaves them in a quandary rather than in a state of obduracy.

Lk 14:7–11 Jesus now seizes the opportunity from the present occasion to inculcate another of his teachings. The background for what Luke calls his *parable* may strike us as a somewhat stilted and stuffy social atmosphere, if not downright childish. However, protocol of a different kind probably plays as pervasive a role in our lives as the seating arrangements at table did in the lives of Jesus' contemporaries. What we tend to reserve for extraordinary affairs and state occasions was for these Orientals part of the daily routine. There were dozens of converging titles by which one man could claim precedence over another and which by comparison might make the arrangements of a Washington hostess seem like informality itself. Age, public position, learning, attainments, wealth, all had their claims, conferring on one the right, and a jealously guarded right, to be seated at one of the first places, that is, nearer the host. It was seeing this familiar ceremonial being enacted before his eyes that prompted Jesus to speak.

Jesus speaks of *a marriage feast* possibly out of a concern not to point his finger too directly at those present on this occasion, also because an event of that kind was more formally and solemnly observed than an ordinary meal. He neither condemns nor approves the social customs in question, but simply takes them for granted. Everyone present could appreciate, perhaps from sad or happy experience, the situation that he describes. It would indeed be a humiliation for one who had confidently taken one of the first places to find himself obliged publicly to relinquish it to a later arrival of greater dignity and thus have to make his way to one of the places below. On the contrary, what a joy to be able to walk, at the host's invitation, from a lower to a higher place reserved for him! The wisdom of seeking *the lowest place*, therefore, could hardly have been better brought out. And that, of course, is the point of the parable: *everyone who exalts himself will be humbled, and he who humbles himself will be exalted* (cf. Mt 23:12). Jesus has been teaching neither social etiquette nor the methods of face-saving. Humility, pursued for the glory of God and not of man, is the only way into God's kingdom, while pride bars the way completely.

Lk 14:12-14   Jesus also has a word for his host that reiterates teaching we have seen above in the Sermon on the Mount (on Mt 5:46-48 and parallel). The duties of hospitality were precise and taken very seriously in the East, as they still are. We can probably presume that at this banquet there was a sprinkling of the four classes of people noted by Jesus: *friends, brothers* (close relatives), *kinsmen* of less degree, and *rich neighbors*. Friend was hospitable to friend, brother to brother, kinsman to kinsman, and a rich neighbor of course could always count on a hearty reception. All this was reciprocal, a comfortable charity that worked hardship on no one. All well and good, Jesus tells the Pharisee, but he must also allow that this kind of cautious generosity simply follows the dictates of self-interest and carries with it its own present recompense. If he would have the reward of God and not of man, let him do good to those who cannot repay him. True charity is disinterested; it *will be repaid at the resurrection of the just*.

Lk 14:15–24   Mention of "the resurrection of the just" calls forth an exclamation from *one of those at table*, the kind of mutual congratulation and blessing to which Orientals are prone in moments of joy and satisfaction. Throughout this encounter Jesus' comments, though pointed, have been given in a pleasant way, and there is no indication that any of his teaching had been taken amiss. *Blessed he who shall eat bread in the kingdom of God!* was, of course, uttered with some of that complacency we have already remarked. The man who said it obviously had no doubts that the kingdom of God would be a prolongation of the good-fellowship of this present table, a perpetual banquet prepared by the Lord on Mount Zion (cf. Is 25:6) for such good fellows as these.

Hence the point of Jesus' parable which now follows. It is in all likelihood the same in origin as that told in Mt 22:1–14 below. The two evangelists or the sources on which they depended have so altered and adapted it, however, and applied it to different contexts, that it is necessary to consider the two passages as independent of each other. Here the purpose is to apply another correction to Jewish complacency about the kingdom and to insinuate once more the consequence of Jewish rejection that is dear to Luke's heart, the mission of the Church to the Gentiles. Both of these emphases are historically authentic in the teaching of Jesus, and for this reason Luke's version of the parable may be closer to the primitive form than Matthew's which is heavily allegorized.

The parable tells of *a man* who *gave a great banquet* to which *he invited many*. Following this preliminary invitation, which the parable supposes to have been accepted, he then *sent his servant,* as was the custom, when the lavish preparations had been completed and the presence of the guests was now expected. Had the servant not been sent, the invitation would have been deemed cancelled, which would have been an insult to the guests. By the same token, the refusal of the invited guests to honor the summons is a grave violation of the laws of politeness. Their excuses are paltry. *They all as one began to make excuses* is probably calculated language in view of the parable's application: it suggests a concerted conspiracy of refusal. No one, naturally, would have bought a foot of land without first having inspected it thoroughly, nor would he have acquired a single ox without knowing all about it in advance. Furthermore, no newly wedded wife would have had the slightest say about the goings and comings of her husband. The man in question may have been citing Deut 24:5 in his own favor; if so, he was guilty of what Jesus has previously stigmatized, using the letter of the Law to violate its spirit in respect to his humane duties.

His banquet spurned, the man now turns first to the byways of the town, bringing in *the poor and maimed and blind and lame* to replace his able and affluent, but absent, guests. Here we are to think of the ones called "sinners" by those seated comfortably about the Pharisee's table, who were entering the kingdom in place of the doctors and students of the Law (cf. Lk 15:1; Mt 21:31). *And still there is room!* Thereupon the master of the house gives the order for his servant to leave the town itself and to fill up the empty places with people who are outsiders (cf. Rom 11:17–25; Eph 1:11–13). The parable ends abruptly. Nothing is said of what the Gentiles will make of the kingdom, for that is not to the Lord's purpose. The warning to Israel, however, hangs heavy in the air as he concludes.

Lk 14:28–33 Luke now abandons the banquet scene and takes Jesus on his journey surrounded by a huge crowd. These are people evidently of good disposition, but equally with the Pharisees in need of instruction on the conditions of the kingdom. This instruction Jesus proceeds to give, beginning with words which we have already seen in the preceding chapter (above on Mt 10:37–39 and parallels). No one must assume that it is easy to follow Christ. It means the renunciation of all that could stand in his way, whether this be father or mother or even his own life itself. Let no one venture on this path without first counting the cost. This warning he illustrates with two little parables. He first pictures a person of substance *about to build a tower*, that is, probably, a large farm building, who if he is wise will begin by calculating his resources, lest the end result be nothing more than an unfinished local "folly" decorating the landscape and he become a laughing-stock. Possibly the parable originally referred to some notorious instance of such improvidence. Or a *king going to encounter another king in war:* it is unpardonable to begin a war that one cannot win. For those who cannot win wars, negotiated peace is a necessity. The point of the parables, of course, is not that one has the option of entering or declining to enter the kingdom of God, but that one must be forewarned of the terms of his commitment and be prepared to meet them. Otherwise he may begin well and end miserably: here Luke introduces the figure of salt that has lost its taste (see above on Mk 9:49 f. and parallel).

Lk 15:1–2 The kingdom of God continues to be the subject of these Lucan passages as the evangelist joins together three parables which both respond to a well-known situation in Jesus' life and have served ever after as a precious source of reassurance to the repentant sinner of the Church for which Luke wrote and of which we are the heirs. The situation is, again, the Pharisaical scandal taken at the low company for which Jesus had become famous and for which he seemed to have an attraction rather than for the respectable elements of the population. The text says, with something of an exaggeration no doubt, that *all the publicans and sinners were drawing near* *to hear him;* at least they were coming in such numbers that as a class they could be listed as his followers, whereas the Pharisees and scribes as a class would doubtless have to be numbered among his enemies (see also above on Mk 2:13–17 and parallels). Not all those whom the pillars of Jewish society regarded as sinners were necessarily more reprobate morally than their fellows, it is true, but it is also true that Jesus was undoubtedly being pursued by a motley assembly that included sinners by anyone's accounting as well as by Pharisaical election. As the parables go on to show, this was not to Jesus' discredit, but rather testified to the bankruptcy of the religious establishment that had lost its sense of mission and now had no higher ambition than to devote itself to the serious purpose of saving the saved.

Lk 15:8–10   The first parable is that of the lost sheep, which we have seen above in a different context (on Mt 18:10–14 and parallel). Luke has it that *there will be more joy in heaven over one sinner that repents than over ninety-nine righteous who need no repentance.* The righteous often find this a hard saying, but it will be explained in better detail in the third parable.

The second parable is like the first, except that it figures something that was lost through carelessness rather than through its own willfulness. The *drachma* was a Greek coin of the same value as the Roman denarius, worth comparatively little in itself, but representing much to the *woman* of the story whose total wealth consisted in ten of them. Possibly they were her dowry money. At any rate she goes to extraordinary measures to find it, illuminating the dark house and sweeping the dirt floor, sifting until she has found it. As the shepherd with his lost sheep, therefore, she lets everything else go in her all-out effort to find what was lost. And again her joy in finding it is intense—greater than had she never lost the coin.

There is joy before the angels of God over one sinner who repents. The implications of this pronouncement should not

be overlooked. He who says "sinners" thinks in categories
rather than of persons. It is easy to hate, to despise, or
merely to dismiss categories, because they are abstractions
independent of experience. He who says "one sinner" thinks
of a person who has sinned. The lesson of all these parables
is the value that God attaches to each human person, in
whatever category he has placed himself.

Lk 15:11–32   The third parable, certainly the best
known of this triad, has only one or two
other rivals among the many passages of the Gospels for first
place in the affections of most readers. We think of it
traditionally as the parable of the Prodigal Son, though Lost
Son would be the more apt title; the son's prodigality is
only a detail of the story, not its point. Because of its
multiple values and message, we sometimes forget that it,
too, was told originally to justify Jesus' association with
sinners. That purpose quickly becomes obscured, however,
as our interest is focused on the personalities of its protago-
nists. The parables of the lost sheep and the drachma were
concerned with objects whose recovery was a precious joy
to their owners, but in this story we have to do with a living, human person who is as much affected by the process
of loss and gain as is the father who loses and regains him.
This parable, then, which is in part allegorical, we think of
first and foremost as a word of love and reassurance to the
repentant sinner himself.

According to the Law the younger of two sons was
entitled to one third of his father's estate as his *share of
property* (cf. Deut 21:17). The father was under no obliga-
tion to make a distribution of his goods during his lifetime;
the father in this story does agree to do so, contrary to the
advice of one of Israel's sages (cf. Sir 33:19–24). Apparently the elder son does not take possession of his share,
but leaves it under his father's administration while he continues to live in the family home. The foolish younger son
quickly *squandered his property,* and it was not long before
he was reduced to the occupation of a swineherd—the lowest

level of degradation for a Jew. In speaking of the youth's subjection to the *citizen* of *a far country* who is obviously a pagan, is Luke thinking of the publicans—pre-eminent "sinners" in Jewish eyes—who had sold themselves to the Roman state?

The *pods* eaten by the swine are the fruit of the carob tree. They are insipid and hardly fit for human consumption; however, on these the youth *would glady have fed* (some manuscripts have *fill his belly*), simply to stop the pangs of hunger rather than to gain real food and nourishment. It is in these straits that he at length comes to his senses and recognizes the enormity of what he has done. His resolution to return to his father is not, by his own accounting, based on any motive other than his miserable condition contrasted with the lot of the poorest in his father's house. The speech that he rehearses to recite to his father is, however, an expression of true repentance, and it is by this means that the parable makes its point. Similarly, we could hardly uphold the father of the story as a model of sobriety in his treatment of the boy either before or after his wild oats had been sown. He runs out to meet him, does not even permit him to complete his carefully prepared confession, and proceeds to lavish on him every honor, not stopping at necessities but indulging every exaggerated mark of affection that the Oriental reserves for a favorite son who can do no wrong. The parable is not telling fathers how to deal with wayward sons, however, but trying to convey how great is God's happiness at the return of a sinner and how incredible is his mercy that extends far beyond anyone's just deserts.

And it is this, of course, that others of God's children often find it hard to understand. The elder son in the story speaks like one of the Pharisees (cf. also Lk 18:1–14 below), as one who has *served many years*, who *never disobeyed a command*. Indignant at his father's treatment of the ne'er-do-well, he himself becomes prodigal in his comparisons. His brother, whom he designates obliquely as *this your son*, had not merely been good-for-nothing, but *devoured your living with harlots*. He accuses his father of meanness in his regard. We begin to see a not unfamiliar phenomenon in the life of religion. It is a fact that we can easily set a greater price on virtue than does God himself, because we forget that we are all equally the objects of God's mercy, some in one way, others in another. If we have led a righteous life, or at least middling righteous, which is doubtless what most of us would lay claim to, it is all too easy to give ourselves full credit for what we have done. It is all too easy to compare ourselves favorably with the wastrel who has made his peace with God at the last moment, a comparison that is usually compounded with envy of a man who has somehow had the best of both worlds. But *you are always with me, and all that is mine is yours:* the righteous man has been the recipient of God's mercy all along. How many times has he not been shielded from temptations that he never knew, strengthened when others were weak? Because God rejoices more over the repentant sinner than over the righteous who need no repentance does not mean that he values lightly either the righteous or righteousness. He alone values it rightly, for it was of his doing. He has rejoiced over the righteous all along, and now is the time for another rejoicing.

Lk 16:1–13 Righteousness continues to be the theme of Luke's Gospel in the passages that follow, with the Pharisees always standing somewhere in the background. Perhaps, too, there is a connection of thought centering on the dangers and responsibilities of wealth, one of Luke's characteristic concerns, as the parable of the prodigal is succeeded by the others of this chapter. This next parable is also popularly misnamed. We think of it as about a Dishonest Steward, which of course it is; but again, it is not the steward's dishonesty but his sagacity that is the point of the parable, as is shown at the end of the story.

The parable tells of an overseer, apparently a freeman in this case, who held the position of trust ascribed to the slave of the story we saw above in Lk 12:41–48 and parallel. Having been found out in some embezzlement, probably, he

faces the prospect of losing his position and of being forced
to find another in order to live. He has no talent for common
labor and he is ashamed, or afraid, to have to beg. So he
hits on another plan. *Calling his master's debtors one by one,*
he systematically reduced their debts by about half. Some
commentators have suggested that this did not constitute
another act of dishonesty, by which he continued to defraud
his master, but rather that he forewent his own commission
on these debts as overseer. Even today promissory notes are
sometimes written not in the amount of the principal but
with advance interest and other extras already totaled in.
This may be true, since otherwise his master displayed an
admirable detachment with regard to his own property when
he proceeded to commend the steward's resourcefulness. But
in any event, *the master commended the dishonest steward
because he acted prudently.* There is the lesson of the
parable. Finding his security threatened, the steward made
quick and efficient use of the means that were at hand to
buy friends for himself against the lean years ahead. His
dishonesty, whether before or after his discovery by his
master, is not commended, merely his shrewdness. By his
principles, whether crooked or not, he acted wisely.

Whether verse 8b is also part of the parable depends on
the main thrust one is disposed to find in the story as it
appears in Luke's context. If the Lord's lesson includes
teaching on the prudent use of wealth—and this interpretation would seem to suppose that what the steward did
with his master's bills of debt was not dishonest—then the
parable doubtless ends with verse 8a. What follows would
then be an application of the parable. But if, on the other
hand, the main intention all along has been to illustrate to
Christians the need of expeditious and prudent action on
their part, the parable certainly includes these words: *for
the children of this world are wiser in dealing with their
own generation than are the children of light.* The alacrity
and skill with which the steward dealt with the crisis facing
him serve as a model to Christians facing their crises of

decision, which must be dealt with on principles of divine rather than worldly wisdom.

By any accounting, the following verses represent applications of the parable, all of them concerned with wealth and its uses. *Make friends for yourselves with the mammon of wickedness,* Jesus says, which means: make wise use of your wealth that will be to your true good. Mammon, money, is qualified as wicked perhaps because the mammon of the parable was such, but certainly because in Luke's mind its tendency is to make men wicked. Similar expressions were used by the rabbis and at Qumran, just as we speak jocosely —and sometimes affectionately—of "filthy lucre." Jesus' teaching regards the Christians' eschatological future: their use of worldly goods is to be such that *when it* [wealth] *fails, they may receive you* (=you will be received; the "they" is impersonal) *into everlasting dwellings.* Again, the proportion by which we are faithful in our trust with worldly goods (*a little thing*) will be the measure of our chance at heavenly things (*a great thing*). If we do not know how to handle *the wicked mammon,* how shall we know what to do with *the true wealth?* Wealth, after all, always really *belongs to another:* it is ours only fleetingly and does not go with us. All the more reason, if we have proved ourselves faithless in this extraneous thing, not to be entrusted with what is our very own forever. Luke now brings this series to a close with the saying on God and mammon which can be seen at Mt 6:24 above.

Lk 16:14-18   Jesus has been talking to his disciples (vs. 1), but now his attention is diverted by *the Pharisees who had heard all this.* Luke says that they *were lovers of money* in the sense that their notion of wealth as a token of divine favor tended to an attitude toward it which was diametrically opposed to that of Jesus ("the mammon of [=which leads to] wickedness"); in their theoretical teaching and belief, the Pharisees were not materialists, but rather opposed the materialism of the Sadducees. The verses that follow are intended as the introduc-

(see above on Mt 5:3–12 and parallel). Despite his abject poverty, his physical sufferings, his degradation when even dogs, unclean animals, lick his sores, he shows no resentment, no despair or hatred, asking only the bare pittance of food necessary to keep him alive. In this alone of Jesus' parables does one of the characters receive a name, which has doubtless been carefully chosen for the occasion (Hebrew *el'azar*= "God helps"); however, some have suggested that even here the name may have been picked up in oral tradition from the story of Lazarus of Bethany who returned from the dead and was not believed (vs. 31; cf. Jn 11:1–44, 12:9 f.).

Abraham's bosom does not appear to have been a conventional term for a place of repose for the dead, but rather expresses the idea of the messianic age as a banquet in the company of Abraham and the patriarchs of old (cf. Mt 8:11; Jn 13:23). It is hard to tell to what extent some of the details of the parable represent contemporary popular ideas about the afterlife and to what extent they have been made to order for the sake of the story. At all events, the parable has not been told to suggest that Hades is divided by a chasm over which conversation takes place between the wicked and the just, or that a lost soul can feel compassion for those who are to share his fate. The point is made in Abraham's response to the rich man's petition and in the latter's reaction to the response (vss. 29 f.): the way of salvation has been indicated by *Moses and the prophets*, but the Pharisees will not heed it (cf. vss. 15–17 above). For this selfsame reason, the parable concludes, the "signs" for which Jesus was continually being asked (cf. Lk 11:16, etc.) would equally have been of no avail.

18. THE LAST JOURNEY

Lk 17:3–6   In this chapter we shall see the end of Luke's "great addition" to the Marcan outline and at last rejoin the other Synoptic Gospels to resume their common tradition. Luke's verses with which we begin seem to have no close connection with his preceding context nor, for that matter, among themselves, except in the sense that they respond to various catechetical purposes in this highly catechetical Gospel. As before, Jesus is speaking *to his disciples*. We first read three isolated sayings of Jesus, all of which appear elsewhere in the other Gospels. The first we have already seen above almost verbatim (on Mk 9:42–48 and parallels). The second, on forgiving one's brother, seems to synthesize two Matthaean passages (see above on Mt 18:15–18 and 18:21 f.) where the context was much more obviously ecclesial than it is here. The third, uttered in response to the disciples' request to *increase our faith,* we saw Matthew incorporate into a previous story told by the Synoptic Gospels (see on Mk 9:14–29 and parallels above), and both Matthew and Mark will use it again in a later context. The other instances of this saying speak of the power of faith to move "this mountain" (the mount of the transfiguration and the Mount of Olives, respectively); here it is *this mulberry tree* (the saying had doubtless got

associated with a tree from the context of Mk 11:22 f.;
Mt 21:21). The disciples seem to have been asking for a
special charism of faith in view of the demands of their
apostolate: Luke refers to them here as *apostles*. But Jesus
assures them that faith itself, when it is true faith, is more
than sufficient for the greatest works they will be called on
to do, of whatever order.

Lk 17:7–10   The fourth saying brought in by Luke is a
little parable proper to his Gospel. Neither
does it appear to be closely connected with its surrounding
context. Taking the contemporary institution of slavery as its
point of departure, it teaches the eminently Pauline doctrine
of justification through God's mercy and not through works.
The *servants* in the parable are simply slaves who belonged
to their master body and soul according to the laws of the
time. They did not look for consideration from their master,
nor for his thanks, and no matter what service they faithfully
performed, the master regarded it as due him by right, with
no credit to his slaves. As it happens, this was an intolerable
social order which evolving man quite properly abolished.
Neither does the Gospel intend to suggest, of course, that
God has made this imperfect human institution the model
of his way of acting with us, his servants. The point of the
parable is, rather, that he would most rightly do so if he
chose. For we do belong to God body and soul, in a way
that no human being can really belong to another.

We can give nothing to God, for we can add nothing
to his existence by our own efforts, and no matter how much
we do it is only what he has the right to expect of us.
We owe him our being and everything that we are and have.
If the Gospel also frequently speaks of a heavenly reward
(literally *misthos,* wages) that God will bestow on us in
return for our service (cf. Mt 5:12; Mk 9:41; Lk 6:23,
etc.), it is only because of the divine promise that our good
works thereby possess a value. Without it, they would have
none. The good works of the Christian, along with Christian

justification and salvation itself, are alike the manifestation
of God's grace and mercy.

Lk 17:11–19   Reminding us yet once more (cf. Lk 9:51 f.,
13:22) that Jesus is *journeying toward
Jerusalem*, Luke tells us that *he was passing between
Samaria and Galilee*. This sounds very much as though
Jesus had recently left Galilee and was traveling down the
western side of the Jordan Valley toward Jericho (cf.
Lk 18:35). If geography and chronology were really an
issue for Luke at this point, we should have to suppose that
at some undetermined time Jesus left Perea for a final visit
to his Galilean homeland. However, we may be sure that
the evangelist is merely preparing us for a story in which
we find Jews and Samaritans associating together. In the
case at hand, this fact is not remarkable. The life of the
leper was usually one of utter hopelessness, in which he was
little disposed to bother about social distinctions. Though
this story has various resemblances to others in the Synoptic
tradition, it seems to have its own proper identity as a
narrative proper to Luke. Again the evangelist is permitted
to record something favorable to a Samaritan in contrast
to his Jewish brethren (cf. Lk 10:29–37), a presage of the
success of the Church's later mission to the Samaritans
(cf. Acts 8:4–25).

The lepers were careful to observe the sad rules under
which they had to live, standing *at a distance* to beseech
Jesus' aid. Jesus likewise instructs them to *go to the priests*
(cf. Mk 1:44 and parallels) who were empowered to judge
when a man no longer had leprosy and could be readmitted
to society. As we have already noted, many different kinds
of skin disorders were called "leprosy" along with the actual
dread disease itself, and to be on the safe side all were
treated the same. Since the Samaritan and the others, who
presumably were all Jews, would have gone to separate
priests for scrutiny, it is not surprising that the former returned by himself. The point that is made is not that he
alone possessed faith: all ten lepers were doubtless healed,

and for the same reason. Only he, however, displayed that gratitude for grace that is so much the heart of genuine religion and the cause of its vitality.

Lk 17:20–21 Jesus' answer to the Pharisees in this next section begins a short treatment on *the coming of the kingdom of God* which at first glance seems to be somewhat contradictory. Actually it is not; it does, however, reflect the same tension that exists throughout the entire New Testament between what is sometimes called "realized" eschatology and "final" or standard eschatology. Jewish eschatology itself was comparatively straightforward. Those Jews who possessed eschatological views (not all did, by any means) were looking for an end-time, "the age to come," when the Messiah would inaugurate God's kingdom or reign, putting an end to evil once for all and establishing good for all time. The kingdom would come through judgment, fire, and tribulation, but come it would surely and definitively, and when it came "this age" would be gone forever and there would be a new heaven and new earth for God's elect. Within this framework there was, of course, room for an infinite variety of theories about details—the fate of the dead, the role of the Gentiles, the number of the elect, the character of the Messiah, and so forth, and so forth; still, the basic essentials were simple enough. This age and the age to come. The now and the kingdom of the future. When was it to be? Every rabbi was doubtless asked the same question.

By contrast, Christian eschatology became far more complex. The earliest Jewish Christians did not at first realize that this was so: they thought of the kingdom as did their fellow Jews, and looked for Jesus, as the Messiah, to inaugurate it. When instead he died on the cross, they were puzzled and disillusioned; had they believed in vain? (cf. Lk 24:21). The resurrection reassured them. Jesus their Messiah still lived. Now, then, he would surely establish the kingdom? (cf. Acts 1:6). But the risen Lord departed from their sight, though he remained present with them through his Spirit. Obviously, then, his glorious coming, his *parousia*, was reserved for the future: then at last would come the resurrection of the dead, the judgment, the end of all, the kingdom (cf. Acts 3:19–21). Would this be quite soon? The early Christians thought so—why should the Messiah have come but to bring in the kingdom? But later, as time went on, they began to have doubts, and from these doubts and the abiding presence of the Spirit of Christ came far deeper insights into the purposes of God. Had Jesus' teaching on the kingdom been quite as routine as they had imagined? If he had spoken of it in conventional apocalyptic language as any rabbi would, had he not also spoken of it at times in quite prosaic terms, as a reality that one might easily overlook if he did not see aright? What did all those parables of the kingdom mean— parables about growing seeds, of wheat awaiting a harvest, of leaven mixed in dough, and all the rest? Was it not possible that Jesus, the Messiah, had indeed already brought in his kingdom, even though the kingdom was yet to come? Was this really a contradiction? What of his teaching on life and law, on oaths and promises, on love and filial respect, on divorce, and marriage, and humility—was this intended merely to help them mark time over a few weeks or months till a final cataclysm would send it all to oblivion? Or was it the laying down of an ethic designed to enable them to witness to a world which God loves (cf. Jn 3:16), a world of whose vastness no one at that time could have had the faintest idea? And what of this Christian community, this *qāhāl*, this *ekklēsia* (see above on Mk 8:27–30 and parallels), of which they were members and whose quickening Spirit they knew; did they not find in it, in its life and love and liturgy and sacraments, at least a beginning of the blessings which God had prepared for the people of his kingdom? (See below on Mk 10:23–31 and parallels.)

Hence we have in the New Testament "final" and "realized" eschatology. The Christian knew that a kingdom that was yet to come had, somehow, already begun. He knew

that this realization diminished neither the one nor the other.
He could look for the resurrection of the dead while believing himself already to be one of the resurrected: such is
the conviction of John's Gospel. Like Paul, he could say in
one epistle—even in one chapter of the same epistle—that he
was looking forward to becoming one of God's sons and that
he was already one of God's sons (cf. Rom 8:15, 23). The
final times are now (cf. Heb 1:2), and they will continue to
be now as long as God has intended that the Church shall
endure.

What does all this make of Jesus' reply to the Pharisees?
*The kingdom of God does not come so that it can be
observed,* he says. We can imagine a saying like this in the
lifetime of Christ even though we can imagine it much more
readily in the life of the early Christian Church. Apocalyptic
language (cf. 1 Thes 4:16) was recognized as being, at least
in some part, figurative. Furthermore, not everyone shared
the apocalyptic viewpoint. Therefore, it might well be that
the kingdom of God is within you, that is to say, *among you,*
already begun, in your midst. Jesus was certainly well aware
that his preaching and teaching, his miracles and exorcisms,
had already inaugurated the kingdom of God. And obviously,
not all recognized this.

Lk 17:22–37   With hardly a change of voice, though
now his words are addressed *to the dis-
ciples,* Jesus begins to speak of the coming of the kingdom in
somewhat different terms. What he says is for the most part
expressed in fairly conventional apocalyptic language, and
this together with the fact that a great deal of the speech is
paralleled in the later eschatological discourse common to all
three Synoptic Gospels makes it easy for us to see that Luke
has composed it from various statements of Jesus made on
different occasions.

From what has gone immediately before, we should be
surprised to hear Jesus speaking of the kingdom's coming
either as a remote or proximate future event, and indeed he
does not. His emphasis is entirely on the suddenness and un-

expectedness of the *parousia* and the culmination of the last
days: in this way, the kingdom is always imminent and the
eschatological moment is always now. *One of the days of the
Son of Man* probably is a Semitism for "the first of the days
of the Son of Man," that is to say, the beginning of the last
times. They will come with the suddenness of a *lightning
flash,* he points out, and only in view of the Son of Man first
having achieved his destiny of service, which is by far the
present consideration of greatest importance: *first he must
suffer many things and be rejected by this generation.*

The practical conclusion from all this is perpetual vigilance.
As in the days of Noah (gen 6:9–9:17), as in the days of
Lot (Gen 18:16–19:27), judgment comes when men are
least prepared. And when it comes, no concern for worldly
affairs will any longer be relevant; those who look back will
do so only to share the fate of Lot's wife (Gen 19:26). Two
people going about their ordinary affairs, to all appearances
entirely alike, yet one is marked for judgment and the other
is not; and when it comes, no one knows. It is quite evident
that, despite the language of future eschatology, Jesus' emphasis is on here-and-now readiness for God's summons,
however it comes.

It is this emphasis that renders somewhat fatuous the
disciples' question. *Where, Lord?* they ask—where will all
these people *be taken* to have judgment executed on them?
Jesus replies with a characteristic no-answer, doubtless having
in mind biblical figures like those of Is 18:6 and Ezek
39:4, 17. The "eagles" of the text are undoubtedly *vultures:*
neither Hebrew nor, curiously, Greek distinguished between
the two birds.

Lk 18:1–8   Two passages remain of Luke's special material, both of them fairly well-known para-
bles. The connection with the preceding context is not hard
to find. Persevering and persistent prayer, which is the lesson
of the first parable, is the obvious corollary of the vigilance
of which Jesus has been speaking. The comparison of God
with the *judge who neither feared God nor regarded man* is,

of course, rather to contrast the two. If even an unjust judge will finally do justice in spite of himself for one who is sufficiently persistent, then all the more will the God of justice who loves his children hear their persistent prayers. Perhaps Jesus' question at the end is not as gloomy as it sounds. He has just spoken of God's vindication of his elect, therefore he does expect to find faith. Nevertheless, the question is a warning and drives home the point of the parable, for without prayer there certainly will be no faith.

Lk 18:9–14   There is more to prayer than persistence, of course. The main thing is that it should be genuine prayer. This second parable takes its place among numerous Gospel passages which inculcate the spirit of true religion at the expense of contemporary forms of externalism. For Luke it is the culmination of an extended treatise on Christian righteousness which he has systematically contrasted with the formalism associated by him—somewhat uncritically, as we know—with the Pharisees.

The two participants in the parable provide a contrast almost like that in the parable of the Good Samaritan. The Pharisee, by his own standards, was all that was respectable and proper. The publican, by the same standards, was quintessentially a sinner. But in the eyes of God the roles are completely reversed. The Pharisee's words are more a proclamation than a prayer: Luke says, indeed, that he *prayed to himself,* and perhaps he intended this to be taken ironically. The Pharisee says all that we would expect him to say, and more. He is a model of sobriety and external decorum. Not only does he keep the Law faithfully, he performs works of supererogation which he feels should place God firmly in his debt; he *fasts twice a week,* on Mondays and Thursdays following Pharisaical tradition, and *gives tithes of everything* and not merely of those things specified in the Law. He asks God for nothing, for he feels the need of nothing. And, of course, he receives nothing. He is left with the righteousness that he has designed for himself, which is as nothing in the eyes of God.

It is the prayer of the despised publican that is received by God. *Be merciful to me the sinner* are his words, which match his humble mien. This is the prayer of a man who truly knows himself as he stands before God. He cannot know other men as the Pharisee thought he could; as far as he is concerned and can testify, he is the only sinner in the world standing in the presence of him who hates sin. The publican has brought all that any man can bring and the only thing that any man should bring if he would be *justified* in the sight of God. Conscious that man's righteousness is like worthless rags (Is 64:5), he is disposed for the grace of God which alone can give him righteousness. On this Pauline note Luke brings his treatment of Christian justice to a temporary close.

Mt 19:3–9   And once again it is necessary to pick up
Mk 10:2–12   the threads of the Synoptic continuity where
             Luke left it toward the beginning of his lengthy journey-section. Matthew and Mark also, as it happens, attach great significance to this final division of their Gospels preparatory to the passion and resurrection narratives. For Matthew, in particular, the Church as it were journeys along with Jesus and passes from Judaism into the liberty of the Gospel. It is for this reason that there are in this section so many conflict stories representing Jesus' controversies with the rabbis. This first episode is a case in point. Luke, doubtless because of its Jewish coloration, has omitted it, though he has already given above (16:18) the Lord's *logion* embedded in the story; essentially the same *logion* is recorded by Paul as the Lord's command in 1 Cor 7:10 f.

Here by exception it appears that the Matthaean version of this parallel account is the more original and that Mark's is a story that has been considerably adapted. This becomes evident from the very beginning in the question that is put to Jesus. The *Pharisees* must have asked Jesus *whether it is lawful to divorce one's wife for any cause,* as Matthew has it: the tenor of this question is, "What are the lawful grounds for divorce?" The question was one much debated by the rabbis. The legitimacy of divorce itself, sanctioned by the Law of Moses, was not a point at issue. Thus there is something unreal about the question as phrased by Mark (in a few manuscripts of Mark "Pharisees" is omitted and the question is anonymous), *whether it is lawful for a man to divorce a wife.* Mark is interested merely in giving the Lord's teaching on marriage and divorce and not in the circumstances of the Jewish legal discussion that originally prompted it.

The law of Deuteronomy (24:1) envisioned divorce as taking place when a husband found "something indecent" in his wife and thus decided to repudiate her. As we have already explained (above on Mt 5:31 f.), this law was mainly concerned with protecting woman's rights in some small way and was not a pronouncement on the grounds for divorce. Nowhere in the Law, as a matter of fact, is any such thing spelt out. Not unnaturally, however, the subject came up frequently in moral discussions, and the rabbis generally fixed on the "something indecent" of Deut 24:1 as offering some index of the divine will in the matter. But what was "something indecent"? In the time of Jesus there were two radically opposed interpretations current in the rabbinical schools. Those who followed the tradition of the liberal Rabbi Hillel— one of the formulators of the Golden Rule (see above on Mt 7:12)—did not restrict the "indecent" to the immoral. This school, which in practice was followed by most Jews (cf. Mt 1:19), held that a man was free to divorce a woman for anything that he found displeasing about her, even, say, if this should be only that she had spoilt his dinner or railed at him in public. Common sense and the Semitic love of family undoubtedly kept the application of the principle well within reasonable bounds, while the law of Deut 24:4 effectively discouraged the temptation to hasty divorce. Nevertheless, at least in theory it could fairly be said that the school of Hillel taught that it was lawful for a man to divorce his wife for any cause whatever. Opposed was the school of Rabbi Shammai (Shammai was a contemporary of Hillel), which taught that "something indecent" meant unchastity and that alone. It was into this dispute that Jesus was invited to enter.

Jesus does not, now or ever, permit himself to be entangled in fruitless casuistry. The casuistry in this case, the determination of legitimate causes, was fruitless because divorce itself is no law of God; at the very best, the legislation on divorce in Deuteronomy represented a divine concession to human weakness and *stubbornness*, making the best possible of a very bad bargain. *At the beginning* God had no divorce in mind. Marriage, Jesus reminds his hearers, was first intended for one man and one woman, not for a man and a succession of wives (cf. Gen 1:27, 2:24). Marriage so constitutes *one flesh*—one body, one person—that to destroy it is as unnatural as dividing a man's body into parts (cf. Eph 5:31). Furthermore, God himself is the author of the marriage bond and, therefore, the third party to every marriage contract. Not even mutual consent between husband and wife, as a result, is of any avail to dissolve a marriage. *What God has joined together, let not man separate.*

This teaching was not altogether new in Jewish ears. Other prophetic voices had troubled Israel's conscience in the matter in the past, and the Old Testament is a reflection of it. The texts which Jesus quoted are typical of a prevailing Old Testament view which regarded marriage as in principle monogamous and indissoluble. (It is doubtless relevant at this point to observe that the Jews, without having any laws to forbid divorce among themselves, nevertheless have established and maintain an enviable history of marital stability.) No Jewish teacher had, however, as far as we know, ever dared formulate as the divine will what Jesus now does in all confidence: *Whoever divorces his wife and marries another, commits adultery.* When Mark goes on to apply the same pronouncement to the situation of a woman divorcing her husband, he is without doubt adapting the Lord's teaching to a Gentile Church. The situation did not exist under Jewish law and would hardly have come up in a discussion with Pharisees. A Jewish wife could not divorce her husband, though under certain conditions she could sue to force him

to divorce her. Undoubtedly some Jewish women took advantage of Roman law which permitted women to institute
divorce proceedings; however, they would have been regarded as nothing less than apostates.

In Matthew's quotation of the Lord's words occurs the
well-known exceptive clause, *except for immorality;* an equivalent expression is found also in Matthew's use of the saying in the Sermon on the Mount (Mt 5:32). When we
compare the Lucan, the Pauline, and the Marcan forms
of Jesus' *logion* on divorce and remarriage with the Matthaean, we are left in no doubt that Matthew's version, as
regards these clauses, is an adaptation. But an adaptation to
what? Certainly not, as some have thought, to a positive
exception to the absolute principle expressed in verse 6, per-
mitting divorce and remarriage on the grounds of marital
infidelity (essentially, the doctrine of the school of Shammai).
In addition to the fact that "immorality" (*porneia*) is hardly
the word that Matthew would have used to express this
idea—rather he would have said "adultery" (*moicheia*)—such
an interpretation would make him contradict himself. What,
then, does *porneia* mean? Most likely it has the same meaning
that it has in Acts 15:20, 29, where it refers to sexual
unions within certain close degrees of kinship or legal relationship as listed in Lev 18:6–18. Such unions the rabbis
called by the Hebrew word *zenuth,* "fornication," which is
translated by the Greek *porneia.* Marriages of people so
related were abhorrent to the Jews, but were often common
enough among the Gentiles. So common, in fact, that the
rabbis would sometimes permit them in the case of proselytes
who had entered Judaism from a Gentile background. What
Matthew seems to be saying, then, is that Gentile converts to
Christianity could and should break off these illegal sexual
unions, which in his eyes were no-marriages, without fear of
thereby offending against Jesus' prohibition of divorce. This
was not to weaken but rather to strengthen the force of this
prohibition. The "exceptive" clauses inserted into Jesus'
teaching by Matthew or his source are the kind of adaptation
of the word which would have been expected in the Jewish-

Gentile church of Antioch for which the First Gospel was
in all likelihood written, the same church for which the
apostolic decree of Acts 15:28 f. was formulated.

Mt 19:10–12   In Matthew's Gospel *the disciples* who
have heard Jesus' reply to the Pharisees
and his stern interdiction of divorce come to the conclusion
that perhaps *it is better not to marry.* The same thought has
doubtless occurred to many a Christian on the threshold of
the altar: it is not necessarily a counsel of despair, but rather
a recognition of all that marriage means, not as a selfish and
casual liaison but as a commitment for life. Who is to presume himself equal to such a commitment? Thus we have the
full force of our Lord's reply: *Not everyone can accept this
teaching, but only those to whom it is given.* This is not to
say, obviously, that marriage is for only a limited few, or
that one is free to take or leave alone his teaching on the
indissolubility of marriage. He is saying simply that Christian
marriage is a grace—a sacrament, it would later be called—
and not merely a natural contract arranged through the
inevitability of the sexes. Marriage is one thing, Christian
marriage is something else. The fate of marriage taken as a
human arrangement and nothing more—its history has been
written mildly in the divorce regulations of the Law of Moses,
and a far more dismal history can be read in the laws of the
Gentiles long before and long after Moses. Christian marriage
is a grace: it is God who calls people to this life and who
gives them the power to live it.

There is here a rather important Gospel teaching that
Christians have not always properly understood. Graces
cannot be legislated. Understandable though it may be that
Christian nations will desire their laws to reflect the religious
convictions of their peoples, it is a very questionable wisdom
that has prompted a country or a state to translate into civil
and actionable law a divine word that has been sent into the
soul and conscience of Christian man. For Christian man
such a thing is unnecessary in the first place and a usurpa-
tion of the liberty with which God has made him free; for

non-Christian man—who is at least as frequent in a Christian country as in any other—it is an intolerable burden, the imposition (in the name of God) of a duty which God has not revealed to him and which, therefore, he has not given him the means to fulfill. A sad, sad record of hypocrisy and collusion has dogged the footsteps of good, earnest people who have made the mistake of confusing the Gospel with a *corpus iuris*.

As Jesus goes on to say, not everyone, then or now, has been called to the state of Christian marriage. *There are men incapable of marriage from birth:* such persons, by the Jews considered the most unfortunate of all men, were of course well known. Well known, too, were those who had been made such by the violence of other men. Less well known were those who *for the sake of the kingdom of heaven* rendered themselves incapable of marriage. Jesus is not thinking now of the castrated priests of the mother goddess Cybele: as he saw it, they were hardly tending toward "the kingdom of heaven." It is impossible to believe that he was not thinking of himself, of John the Baptist, of the Qumran people, of those who, like Paul (cf. 1 Cor 7), would later form a great Christian host who could find their fulfillment in renouncing marriage rather than in embracing it. If marriage is a grace, it is not necessarily given to all, for God has other graces as well. *Let him who can, accept* the grace he is given.

Celibacy in itself is merely a negation, but a celibacy in which God's will is seen and pursued is one of the graces of the kingdom. This can be a source of great consolation to many, to enrich lives that would otherwise have been empty. There are other ways than by physical mutilation by which men or women may be made incapable of marriage by other men. Celibacy for such people is the result of no conscious choice but is the conclusion of circumstance. Yet the grace of God can also be offered through circumstance, and if accepted can transform sterility and futility into meaningful existence.

Mk 10:13–16   It is somewhat fitting that a pronounce-
Mt 19:13–15   ment on marriage should be followed by
Lk 18:15–17   this rather appealing story of Jesus and
the children. Probably no association is intended with *the house* which Mark mentioned in verse 10
simply to distinguish, as he usually does, between Jesus'
public preaching and his private instruction of his disciples.
The scene is perfectly natural and could have been enacted
anywhere at any time. Mothers in the admiring crowds about
Jesus bring their children to a respected teacher that he may
touch them in prayer and blessing. Natural, too, is the
reaction of the disciples, who thought they were serving
Jesus' best interests by discouraging such flattering but also
time-consuming attentions.

The vehemence of Jesus' reprimand of the disciples, on
the other hand, shows that in his eyes they were missing
something very important concerning his ministry. *To such
as these belongs the kingdom of God,* he reminds them.
Mark and Luke also include here a saying which Matthew
used in an earlier, similar episode (see above on Mk 9:33–37
and parallels). Consultation of the earlier passage should also
put us on our guard against attaching to this pronouncement
an unintended sentimentalist judgment on the supposed
virtues of children that make them worthy of the kingdom of
God. The kingdom belongs to such as these, and every
Christian must be such as these, precisely because these
receive it as a free gift, bringing to it nothing but themselves,
their openness and receptivity to the workings of God, incapable as they are of helping themselves in any way. What
these children are by nature, all must become by free choice
who will enter the kingdom of God. This is what it is to be
childlike; it has nothing to do with childishness.

Some commentators think that this passage served a
further catechetical purpose in the Church that transmitted
it to the evangelists. In all three Gospels when Jesus says of
the children, *Do not hinder them,* a Greek verb is used
(*kōlyō*) which elsewhere in the New Testament (Acts
8:36, 10:47, 11:17) appears in contexts involving baptism;

another form of the verb is likewise used in Mt 3:14. There
are in addition a few hints in other early Christian literature,
all of which support the theory that this word was a
technical term employed in the ritual of Christian baptism to
render the *nihil obstat,* the "nothing hinders" verdict on a
catechumen presenting himself for the administration of the
sacrament. If this is the correct understanding of the
background of this expression, it is possible that the Church
which used it to translate whatever Aramaic term Jesus may
have employed did so with the intention of finding in Jesus'
acceptance of the children a precedent for the baptism of
infants. The passage was often invoked in the early Church
as providing such a precedent, we know. The question of
the baptism of infants was much fretted during the first ages
of the Church, and it is conceivable that the form-critical
analysis of this Gospel pericope reveals one of the earliest
answers to the question.

Mk 10:17–22 The *rich young ruler* of the next passage
Mt 19:16–22 is something of a composite figure. All
Lk 18:18–23 three Gospels agree that he was rich, it is
             true, but only Matthew says that he was
young, and only Luke identifies him as a ruler of some un-
specified kind. The story explores the by now well-worn
Gospel theme of the danger of riches to the Christian life, but
also contains certain teachings proper to itself which make it
unique in the Synoptic tradition.

First of all, there is the man's greeting, *good master,* and
Jesus' reply, as found in Mark and repeated almost verbatim
by Luke, *Why do you call me good? No one is good except
the one God.* Matthew was apparently sufficiently impressed
by the difficulties involved in this answer, by which Jesus
seemingly repudiated any claim to the divine attribute of
goodness, that he paraphrased both question and answer so
as to put the discussion on an abstract level, leaving Jesus'
person out of it. However, Jesus' words here doubtless represent the Synoptic equivalent of various pronouncements with
which we are already familiar from John's Gospel (for

example, see above on Jn 5:16–30). Always he refers to his
Father the attributes which he has been sent to reveal in his
life and teaching. "Good master" was an unusual title, fulsome even though well meant. The young man's "good"
rolled from his tongue far too readily. Since he is being
asked about *eternal life* (another Johannine phrase), Jesus
feels obliged to focus attention immediately on its only
source. God alone is truly good, and everything good that
man is or does can only reflect this goodness. The Son of
Man is no exception to this rule.

As we have already seen brought out in a previous story
recorded by Luke (above on Lk 10:25–28), it is most typical
that the young man should ask what he must *do* in order
that, once for all, he may have eternal life. Though expressed
differently, Jesus' reply is not much different from that of the
former occasion. There is no esoteric way to salvation that is
not already known to all. The man *knows the commandments*. Keeping God's commandments is a mark of one's love
for him (cf. Jn 14:15). And since a man is what he loves,
whoever has embarked on this route is on the way to eternal
life with God.

The young man of the story felt that he was on this way,
as perhaps he was: Mark says that *Jesus looked on him with
love*. Mark's and Luke's record of his reply as *all these things
I have kept since childhood* might just possibly be an indication that he was a very young man indeed. It is for
nothing up to this point in his life, however, that the young
man is censurable. He himself, nevertheless, recognizes that
something is lacking in his life, something of which he is
capable and of which he senses the need. The explicit *What
more must I do?* of Matthew's Gospel is implicit in all that
he has said according to Mark and Luke. Here we have a
bold spirit who will not abide what is not final and total.
Unfortunately, like so many good men before and after
him, he discovers that it is easier to have high ideals than
to live by them. His is the tragedy that a man of low ideals
will never experience, when he finds that his reach has
exceeded his grasp.

If you would be perfect, Jesus replies, there is indeed a course available to him, the *one thing remaining* by which he can realize the potentialities that God has given him: *follow after me.* Jesus invites him to do no less than share his own life as an immediate disciple, an invitation that was not given to all. For this young man the acceptance of this invitation necessitated his dispossessing himself of all he owned and sharing the poverty of Christ, a necessity that was not imposed upon all. And so, a face which a moment before was radiant with enthusiasm now becomes clouded over. The challenge has been offered, and is reluctantly refused. The young man went away *sad at heart,* but he did go away, *for he had great possessions.*

This passage has justifiably been used to provide an evangelical basis for the tradition of the "religious" life which is venerable in Christianity and which is represented in various ways in Protestantism as well as in Catholicism. "Religion," in this restricted (and doubtless unfortunately chosen) sense of the term, means a vocation not to a higher form of Christianity, which does not exist, but to a distinct form of Christian life that seeks to realize in some fashion—anticipate is one way of saying it, but perpetuate is perhaps even more accurate—the eschatological figure of the Church. Just as celibacy is obviously for the few rather than for the many, but in those few can show forth an aspect of the kingdom of God that marriage does not (cf. Mk 12:25 and parallels), so it is with the life of evangelical poverty (see above on Lk 12:32–34). What the Church as a whole cannot and should not do can be the vocation of some to do for the Church. Such is the distribution of graces in the Church (cf. 1 Cor 12:4–31).

Mk 10:23–27   Jesus takes the occasion of the departure
Mt 19:23–26   of the rich young man to warn once more
Lk 18:24–27   about the dangers of wealth in respect to
               the kingdom of God. Mark, whose account
is summarized by Matthew and Luke, records that *the disciples were astonished at his words.* Then as now, the rich

man was regarded as the one who had the easiest time of it, in salvation as in everything else. If the poor were in some special way under God's care, this was, after all, simply because there was no one else to watch out for them; the rich man could take care of himself. He had the leisure and the opportunity to know the Law and the means to fulfill it by almsgiving and other good works. If he nevertheless is in danger, *then who can be saved?*

Predictably the Lord tells them that in their sense of the question no one can be saved, rich or poor. *But what is impossible with men is possible with God.* No man saves himself, but he is saved wholly by the grace of God. What is needful is that he remove the obstacles to grace, and a rich man has tremendous obstacles to remove. For this reason *it is easier for a camel to pass through the eye of a needle than for a rich man to enter the kingdom of God.* There is no point in attempting to mitigate the extreme hyperbole of this expressive figure by imagining that there was a well-known passageway called "the needle's eye" or by supposing *kamēlos,* "camel," to have been misread for *kamilos,* "hawser." The figure says what it has to say with complete Semitic extravagance.

Mk 10:28–31   In context, Peter's intervention is now quite
Mt 19:27–30   understandable. Unlike the rich young
Lk 18:28–30   man, he and the other disciples *have given
               up all things and followed* Jesus. The warn-
ing against the dangers of riches therefore holds no terrors for them. What, then, will be their reward? In his comments on this passage St. Jerome rather dryly reminds Peter that he was not a rich man but a fisherman: what he had left was a boat and a few nets. All the same, he had made the sacrifice that the rich man had refused, for he had left all that he had, and no man can do more than this. What is more important, as Jerome went on to say, he and the rest had really followed Jesus. We know with what generosity they had done so, without haggling over conditions or terms. They had gone where they knew not, simply out of faith

and good will, and they had served him well, if imper-
fectly.

Matthew inserts at this juncture a saying of Jesus of
which there is a variant parallel in Lk 22:28-30, a saying so
"primitive" in the Jewishness of its formulations that it must
be very nearly precisely as Jesus uttered it. *In the new
creation* (cf. 2 Pt 3:10; Apo 21:1-5), promises Jesus, *when
the Son of Man sits upon the throne of his glory,* these faithful Twelve *will themselves sit upon twelve thrones judging,*
that is to say, ruling, *the twelve tribes of Israel.* Nowhere
else in the New Testament is the kingdom of God described
in more material and earthly terms. However the saying may
have been initially understood (see above on Lk 17:20 f.),
it is certain that Matthew interprets it of the apostolic government of the Church.

All three Gospels go on to record the Lord's promise not
only to the Twelve but to *everyone* who has imitated their
example in renouncing family, friends, and possessions for his
sake. Each version has modifications of its own: it is interesting to find that according to Mark, for example, Jesus included *persecutions* among the favors reserved for his
friends (cf. 1 Thes 3:3; 2 Thes 1:5). Even more interesting,
however, is what is made quite explicit in Mark and Luke,
that besides *eternal life in the age to come* Jesus promises a
here-and-now reward, and a reward that is of the same order
of the things that have been renounced. Mark is most
emphatic about it: *a hundredfold now, at this very time.*
This does not mean, obviously, a hundred houses or a hundred wives for one. It does mean a more than compensating
sense of possession, of social existence, of family relationship
to be found within the kingdom (cf. Mk 3:35; Rom 16:13;
Phlm 10, etc.). When we reflect that this exchange is often
the material and social wealth of one who by this world's
standards is both poor and alone—a man who has embraced
monastic poverty for the sake of the kingdom has very
literally "left house and wife and children"—we can again see
the relevance of this entire sequence to those charismatic
callings which prefigure the eschatological Church.

Matthew and Mark conclude with Jesus' saying about the first being last and the last first (cf. Mk 9:35; Lk 13:30, etc.). Here the purpose is probably to underline the divergence between the value judgments of God and of man. Many who in this life are held to be of little or no consequence, "last" by man's accounting, shall prove to be "first" in the eternal kingdom; and they who are the mighty of this earth, on whom the world's destiny has turned, may have no part at all in the world to come.

Mt 20:1–16   It is this saying and this theme that Matthew takes up in the parable of the Laborers in the Vineyard. If this parable continues to perplex a great number of readers who feel that the mode of conduct it depicts as God's is, from any human standpoint, eccentric and not altogether fair and square, it must be concluded that it deserves to rank among the most successful of Jesus' parables, for that is exactly the effect that it set out to produce. It shows how the last become first through a divine mercy that men find incomprehensible, yet with the preservation of justice for all. Jesus very likely intended it to be a cautionary story for the Pharisees, but its message is perennial, applicable equally well to any earnest soul who knows that he has deserved well of the Lord, who nevertheless finds his faithful service made of no more account than the momentary performance of him who answered the roll call at the last possible minute. It reminds us again that salvation is in any case God's free gift, and also warns against the assumption that membership in the eschatological kingdom and the pilgrim Church is one and the same thing. The Church, it is true, is ordained for the kingdom: it is a sign, a sacrament, of eternal election (cf. Rom 8, etc.); but the converse is not necessarily true, that where there is no perceptible sign there is also no election.

The parable, as parables so often do, combines a basically plausible story with some details that are too good to be true, which have been deliberately constructed to bring out the intended lesson. Thus, on the one hand, hiring workmen *in the early morning* for a day's work is natural enough. It is still common in the Near East for day laborers to assemble early in the public places of the town or village to bargain for their services with an employer or his agent. Settling for *a denarius,* the ordinary daily wage, was also to be expected. But it would have been unlikely that any vineyard would require the services of so many men, nor would they have been hired at different times during the day, much less at the very end. Here, to add climax to the story, laborers are engaged *at the third, the sixth,* and *the ninth hour,* that is, around nine o'clock in the morning, at noon, and three o'clock in the afternoon, and finally *at the eleventh hour,* only an hour before sunset, when work ceased for the day. We may be sure, too, that no real-life workers would have undertaken their job just on faith that the owner of the estate would pay them *whatever is fair.* Finally, the men would hardly have been paid in reverse order; Jesus tells the story this way to explain how the original group of workers can see what the others have received, since otherwise as soon as they had received their wages they would have gathered their tools together and gone home.

We see *the foreman,* then, passing out the coins of payment in the sight of all. Those who have worked only an hour, and that in the cool of the evening, receive a denarius, a truly generous wage far beyond their deserts. We are not told what the intervening groups received—they are not really important to the story except to contribute to the suspense—but presumably they also received a denarius from their rather single-minded employer. Those who have toiled since dawn now expect to receive more, since it seems to them that generosity should be extended to them in like proportion. But when it comes their turn to be paid, they too get each a denarius. Then begin the objections!

And, of course, those who object have not a leg to stand on. The man had agreed with them on a definite wage, and they had made a contract together. The contract had now been fulfilled on both sides, to the letter. There is no question of anyone having a claim in justice to anything further, not even if the owner of the vineyard had given the rest of his workers ten denarii each. The alternating liberality and strict application of justice that he has displayed may appear quite baffling to all, but there is precisely the point of the story. So does God's way of acting often seem baffling to us.

When the parable is applied, we begin to see the enormity that is involved in the workers' complaint: *Could it be that you are showing envy because of my generosity?* No objection whatever can be made against God's justice. What it amounts to, then, is that we can only feel chagrin that he has seen fit to deal more kindly with men than our mean natures deem proper. The reaction of the workers is a natural one, so natural that we must be constantly on guard against it, lest we find that with many high-sounding words and much righteous indignation we are really doing nothing more noble than to rail against the incomprehensible goodness of God.

19. BETHANY AND JERICHO

Jn 11:1–16 Somewhere paralleling the vague chronological sequence of the Synoptic events that have preceded and that will immediately follow, John intends us to read the story of the raising of Lazarus. This miracle is the last and greatest of the "signs" of Jesus which John has distributed over the first half of his Gospel (see above on Jn 2:1–11), quite literally fulfilling the words which Jesus uttered in Jn 5:28. All the "signs" reveal in some fashion the life-giving, saving power and presence of the Word of God, his "glory," but none other quite as definitely and directly as this one. Furthermore, in John's eyes it is this work of Jesus above all that sets in motion the chain of events that culminate in Jesus' ultimate work of salvation, his sacrificial death (cf. Jn 11:45–53, 12:9 f.), which for John is his "glorification" (see above on Jn 3:14–21). In view of its extreme importance for John, it is perhaps surprising that there is no parallel to the story in the Synoptic tradition. However, all the Synoptic Gospels make mention of similar miracles (cf. Mk 5:35–43; Mt 11:5; Lk 7:11–17), and we know by now how variously the Synoptic and the Johannine traditions have gathered and utilized their material (cf. also the remarks on Lk 16:19–31 above, on the name "Lazarus").

Bethany, today called by the Arabs *El-azariyeh* (an

obvious corruption of the name "Lazarus"), is a village on
the southeast of Jerusalem, separated from the Holy City by
the Mount of Olives. John identified it as *the village of Mary
and her sister Martha* who are known to us from the Gospel
of Luke (see above on Lk 10:38–42). It was with this
family, in all likelihood, that Jesus resided when he came to
Jerusalem (cf. Mt 21:17; Mk 11:11 f.). John's reference to
Mary as she *who anointed the Lord with ointment and wiped
his feet with her hair* presupposes that the reader is already
familiar with a story he himself has not yet related (Jn
12:1–8); the evangelist has no thought of connecting Mary
with the incident described in Lk 7:37 f. Though Lazarus
is not mentioned elsewhere in the Gospels, the text before us
bears out what Luke tells us of Jesus' intimacy with his
family in Bethany. The names of Lazarus, Martha, and Mary
were quite common in Palestine: a single Jewish tomb in the
vicinity of Bethany discovered last century yielded all three
names, together with those of Judas, Simon, and Jesus!

There are certain intentional resemblances between this
story and that of Jesus' first sign in Jn 2:1–11. The message
of the sisters to Jesus, *he whom you love is ill,* is a discreet
and implied request, like Mary's statement at Cana (Jn 2:3).
In the same way, Jesus at first appears to be on the point of
disregarding their petition, though all the time he has in
mind an action that will show forth his glory (cf. Jn 1:14,
2:11). There are also, as in so many of the Johannine
dialogues, deeper levels of meaning—the Johannine irony—in
various of Jesus' and the disciples' statements. When Jesus
says that *Lazarus has fallen asleep,* for example, using the
Christian euphemism for "has died" (cf. 1 Cor 15:6, 20,
51; 1 Thes 4:13, 15, etc.), the disciples take his meaning
literally for the healthful sleep of convalescence, but also
utter a truth that expresses the Christian belief in the resurrection: *Lord, if he has fallen asleep, he will be saved.*
Lazarus appears in this story not merely as the brother of
Martha and Mary and as the friend of Jesus, but as typical of
every Christian to whom the Lord also gives life; hence the
reiteration that he is one whom Jesus loved.

A subsidiary theme of the story is Jesus' impending death and the danger that he faces in returning to Judea (cf. Jn 10:31, 39). *Are there not twelve hours in the day?*: the daytime is the period of Jesus' ministry, before the coming of night and darkness (cf. Jn 1:5, 9:4); the time for this is determined by God, not by man (cf. also Lk 13:32). When Jesus shows himself resolute in going up to Judea, *Thomas*, a disciple merely named as one of the Twelve by the Synoptic Gospels, expresses a loyal willingness to share his Master's fate, which again echoes the formula of Christian faith in Jesus' salvific death and resurrection (cf. Rom 6:3 f.).

Jn 11:17–32 John correctly observes that *Bethany was about fifteen stadia from Jerusalem*, that is, something under two miles. That Lazarus had been in the tomb *four days already* is stressed doubltess in order to emphasize the reality of his death: some of the rabbis taught that for three days after death the soul continued to hover over the body and only on the fourth day did it depart. As was true of Jesus' first manifestation of his glory at the end of the first week of the new creation (Jn 1:19–2:11), again it is on the seventh day that Jesus achieves this ultimate manifestation (cf. vss. 4 and 6).

This time it is Mary who *remained quietly at home* while Martha went out to greet Jesus as he entered the village. The Lucan portrayal of the sisters, however, is basically the same as that of this story. The large number of *the Jews* who were present is explained by the mourning rites of the time, which usually lasted seven days after death. Burial always took place as soon as possible, since there was no way of preventing the rapid decomposition of the body. On the other hand, travel was slow, and thus it would require a number of days for all the friends and relatives of the deceased to put in an appearance and console the bereaved family. It is noteworthy that in this passage "the Jews" simply means these concerned people and has no pejorative connotations as it so often does in John's Gospel.

Martha's conversation with Jesus is a singular combination

of faith and lack of undertanding. She greets him with the
Lord of Christian faith, and her initial statement expresses
her confidence in his power and half-request that he will
make use of it in respect to her brother. But when Jesus
assures her that Lazarus will rise again she thinks only of the
Jewish belief in the final resurrection of the dead. It is this
belief, accepted by Christ and Christianity, which Jesus
proceeds to reformulate in Christian terms: *I am the resurrection and the life; whoever believes in me, though he has
died, shall live; and whoever lives and believes in me shall
never die at all*. The source of the resurrection stands before
Martha. It is he who will raise the dead on the last day
because he is the very life of God come into the world (cf.
Jn 5:26); and for the believer this selfsame eternal life is
already a present reality (cf. Jn 6:40). Martha makes this
formulation her own, and in doing so says more than she
understands, since Jesus is about to signify what he has
uttered by the raising of Lazarus from the dead. She now
summons Mary with the call that will greet every Christian
at the resurrection: *The Master is present* (the verb is
parestin, from which comes *parousia*) *and calls for you.*

Jn 11:33–44   The magisterial Christ of John's Gospel is
                   fully human for all that he is a divine
person come into the world. He weeps in the presence of the
grief of Mary and the other mourners. *He trembled,* says the
text, and twice over an expression is used which denotes
intense emotional involvement, of indignation or of anger.
This seems to represent the Johannine equivalent of something we have already found in the Synoptic tradition (see
above on Mk 1:40–45 and parallels) concerning Jesus' reaction to the reign of sin and its consequences and his
recognition of the life-and-death struggle to which he is
committed.

The more practical of the two sisters remonstrates with
Jesus in what she takes to be his ill-advised desire to look for
a last time on the features of his friend. Far from being a
comfort, such a sight can be a repulsive shock. Thereupon

Jesus tells her that the faith to which she had previously given utterance will now find an immediate realization: *you will see the glory of God.* His prayer to the Father is an accompanying sign *for the crowd:* his will is always one with the Father's and needs no leave to be exercised, but it is necessary that this work be seen as the carrying out of a life-giving mission (cf. Jn 5:19–24). Thus the men nearest the vault roll back the stone that covers its entrance, and at the summons of Jesus (cf. Jn 5:28 f.) Lazarus comes forth with the burial cloths still loosely wrapped about his face and body. Jesus' further command to *loose him and let him go* was probably not only a practical direction but also intended to demonstrate the reality of the miracle. However, this Gospel story is no exception to the rule that such events are briefly described with an economy of detail that wastes no time on incidentals. Once the fact has been stated, the story is at an end.

Jn 11:45–57 As usual in John where the words and deeds of Jesus are shown in their living character of revelation inviting response, there is a mixed reaction to the raising of Lazarus. *Some of the Jews . . . began to believe in him, but some of them also went off to the Pharisees and told them what Jesus had done.* The latter did not necessarily have a hostile intent, but neither is it indicated that they were much affected by what they had seen. Their report leads to a summoning of *the Sanhedrin* by *the chief priests and the Pharisees* ("scribes" would be more accurate here, as designating the second major component of the supreme Jewish tribunal). It is not necessary to suppose that this was a formal session of the Sanhedrin; it suffices that a cabal of Jesus' enemies drawn from its members should have gathered together to discuss his case and the threat which he offered.

The chief element of concern expressed on this occasion was the popular belief in Jesus as Messiah. For all of those present, Messiah could only mean the leader of a Jewish liberation movement. To the Sadducean priesthood the idea of such a thing was abhorrent in principle; to the scribes Jesus was unacceptable on other grounds. *Everyone will believe in him, and the Romans will come and destroy our holy place and our nation.* This is Johannine irony: this precise thing did happen, though through a somewhat different causal connection than was then imagined. The same irony reaches its height in the words of *Caiaphas, who was high priest that year* of Jesus' death, whose part in the story of Jesus' passion and death we shall see later on. Caiaphas' "prophecy" is a study in cynical expediency, doubtless called forth to synthesize an opposition and policy on the part of men whose motives were disparate and partly conflicting. He is willing to dismiss as irrelevant the question of whether Jesus is guilty of any crime. Guilty or not, sincere or not, good teacher or bad, miracle-worker or fraud, sent from God or from the devil—the practical fact is that he is a danger to the established order. *It is better for you that one man die for the people rather than that the whole people should perish;* on such unlikely lips and unconsciously, we find the Christian doctrine of the atonement!

Caiaphas was evidently able to evoke a responsive chord in the minds and wills of those who were plotting against Jesus. John may very well have anticipated this conspiracy in order to connect it more closely with the story of the raising of Lazarus (cf. Mk 14:1). At all events, we now see Jesus withdraw once more from the danger zone *to a town called Ephraim,* doubtless to the great relief of the Twelve who had followed him to Bethany with such quaking hearts. Ephraim is usually identified with a little village on the borders of the Judean desert, about fifteen miles northeast of Jerusalem.

It is on this note of a temporary stay in impending violence that John makes his first mention of the last and decisive *Passover* of Jesus' public ministry. In his chronology, as we shall see (cf. Jn 12:1), the Passover is only a week away, and already throngs of people are gathering *in Jerusalem to purify themselves* of various ritual irregularities that would prevent their celebrating the feast. Again it is a

matter of speculation whether Jesus will present himself in
Jerusalem for a great feast (cf. Jn 7:11). Actually, of course,
he was to celebrate this Passover in a way that none of them
had imagined, but at the time it seemed scarcely likely that
he would dare to make an appearance.

Mk 10:32–34   The Synoptic Gospels, too, are bringing us
Mt 20:17–19   closer to this last Passover, in their own
Lk 18:31–34   more leisurely fashion. Here we find them
all together again "on the way to Jeru-
salem," on a journey that is fast drawing to a close. This
"third" prediction of the passion, it scarcely needs to be said,
like the first two (see above on Mk 8:31–33 and parallels;
Mk 9:30–32 and parallels) had put Jesus' intimations about
his future into the explicit descriptions of the known Gospel
fulfillments and has made no effort to preserve the precise
language in which he spoke at that time. This is acknowl-
edged plainly in Luke's account (vs. 34), though he also
intends to say that the disciples were dull of understanding
because of their preconceived ideas about the Messiah and
the kingdom of God, as we see illustrated in the next episode
told by Mark and Matthew. At all events, that Jesus'
disciples were expecting his triumphal resurrection following
his death is contrary to all of the later Gospel evidence.

Mark's account, considerably shortened by Matthew and
Luke, pictures Jesus striding ahead of the somewhat reluctant
disciples, who are puzzled and fearful. On the steep and
narrow paths of Palestine most of the walking had to be done
single file, and it was customary for disciples to let their
master precede them. In this case, however, the evangelist
seems to be suggesting the same kind of dispositions on the
part of Jesus and the disciples that were recorded in Jn
11:8–16 above.

Mk 10:35–45   How little ready the Twelve were to ac-
Mt 20:20–28   cept Jesus' conception of his mission as that
of a Servant of the Lord and of the king-
dom of God as one of service in his image and likeness, can

be seen from this story about the two disciples who, after Peter, have the greatest prominence in the Synoptic tradition. That the story was something of an embarrassment to the same tradition that recorded it, seems to be evident from the various ways in which it has been treated in the Gospels. While Mark, as usual, records what he had to record without undue sensitivity to its implications, Matthew has taken advantage of a variant form of the tradition which ascribed ambition less directly to *James and John* and rather to *the mother of the sons of Zebedee*. The proverbial and often overpowering aspirations which mothers entertain for their favorite sons lend sufficient credibility to Matthew's version of the story; further, we know that among Jesus' intimate disciples, a category which extends beyond the Twelve, there were also many women (cf. Lk 8:1–3). Luke, for his part, finds it convenient to omit this story entirely, though in a later context (see below on Lk 22:24–30), doubtless under Johannine influence, he incorporates its lesson for the disciples into his story of the Last Supper.

To *sit at the right hand and the left hand* of the Lord *in* his *kingdom* or his *glory* obviously means to possess the best and second-best preferential places after Christ himself. It is not necessary to suppose that their ideas about the kingdom were completely and crassly materialistic: the Gospel has represented Jesus speaking in similar terms not long before this (see above on Mk 10:28–31 and parallels). Nevertheless they were, to say the least, extremely naïve, as the question itself shows best of all. Hence there is genuine and compassionate irony in Jesus' exclamation: *You don't know what you are asking!*

To drink the cup was a recognized figure for embracing one's destiny or undergoing it, as was, seemingly, *to be baptized* (cf. Lk 12:50), though this latter Marcan expression may be a Christian paraphrase (Old Testament precedents might be Pss 42:8, 69:2; Is 43:2; Cant 8:7). At any rate, Jesus demands of James and John whether they are prepared to share his fate, in terms that make it clear that it will be no easy one, and they reply confidently that they are ready.

Thus the irony of their initial request is completed. Though
Jesus says that only the Father, whose Servant he is, may
assign places in his kingdom (see above on Jn 5:16–30),
that they will indeed drink his cup and share in his baptism
means that they will also have assured positions in his glory.
The triumph and victory of the Christian is to be con-
figured to Christ, and suffering and persecution thereby become a sign of divine predilection (cf. 1 Thes 3:3; Col
1:24). James, as a matter of fact, the elder of the two
brothers, was beheaded by Herod Agrippa about A.D. 44
(Acts 12:2), the first of the Twelve to suffer martyrdom.
John does not appear to have been martyred, but he was
tortured, exiled to the island of Patmos, and died long after,
among the last of the "first generation" Christians upon the
earth.

The *indignation* felt against James and John by the rest of
the Twelve may very well have been motivated by something less than a contrasting humility in the spirit of Christ's
teaching (see above on Mk 9:33–37 and parallels). What
Jesus says, therefore, he says to all. Previously he had
spoken of the dispositions which must characterize every
member of his kingdom. What he had taught then applies
eminently to the present question of the leadership of the
kingdom. Christ's Church must be governed, like any other
organization of men. But in its government it cannot imitate
the power structures of the kingdoms of the earth, for it is
the kingdom of God whose head became the Servant of
all. If the lot of every Christian is to be the servant of God,
the lot of Church leadership is to be the servants of servants.
In this passage the key words *servant* (*diakonos,* from which
comes "deacon") and *slave* (*doulos,* used of Christ in
Phil 2:7) were significant in the early Christian vocabulary.

The example, always, is Christ himself. *The Son of Man
did not come to be served but to serve:* this epitome of
Jesus' mission as he himself saw it is, in turn, the explanation
of the second part of the statement that follows. *To give his
life as a ransom for many* describes the extent and the end of
Jesus' ministry of service: it is to perform the role of the

suffering Servant of the Lord (Is 53:10 f., paraphrased here;
cf. also Phil 2:6–11), whose sacrificial obedience is redemptive for the multitude of the people of God. (The
"many" of the Gospel and Is 53 is descriptive, not exclusive:
the life of the *one* Servant is offered for *many*, without
implying that there are others for whom it is not offered.)
Jesus' sacrificial life and death are called "ransom" (*lytron*:
this word only here in the New Testament, though equivalent
expressions are frequent) as a bold figure of speech that is
not to be pressed: a parable rather than an allegory. While
lytron was the money paid for the redemption of property
that had been pawned or forfeited, its metaphorical meaning
as applied to Christ's death is merely that by its means God
once more came into complete possession of his people. Therefore we do not ask what third party was "paid" this "ransom"
for the many, who it was that "owned" them before they
were "bought back." Ultimately the figure is based on Old
Testament types, according to which, for example, the God
of Israel "ransomed" his people from the slavery of Egypt
(Deut 7:8, etc.), not, obviously, by the payment of any price
to anyone but by the revelation of his power and grace.

Mk 10:46–52   The "journey to Jerusalem" of the
Mt 20:29–34, 9:27–31   Synoptic Gospels now brings Jesus
Lk 18:35–43   to Jericho, the city mentioned be-
                                     fore in the Gospels only as a detail
in the parable of the Good Samaritan (Lk 10:30). This was
not the famous Jericho of the Old Testament, which lay in
ruins, but a more recent city built nearby and embellished
by Herod the Great and his son Archelaus, some twenty
miles away from Jerusalem in the tropical Jordan Valley.
New Testament Jericho itself has long since disappeared,
but its site is contiguous with the modern town which still
bears the same name.

Mark and Matthew, as it happens, mention Jericho only to
dismiss it, since the event they describe along with Luke took
place, in their view, *as he was leaving Jericho with his*

disciples and a considerable crowd. Luke, who has a story to tell that took place in Jericho (Lk 19:1–10 below), prefers to set the scene *as he was drawing near to Jericho.* From a statistical point of view, there is scarcely any doubt that Mark and Matthew are correct. It would have been at the most frequented places, such as the Jericho-Jerusalem gate, that blind men would sit to beg, begging being the only means that such afflicted people had to gain their food. This is all the more likely if chronology is a real issue in this context, since the crowd which Mark mentions would probably have been the pilgrim throng making its way to Jerusalem and the Passover.

The other major discrepancy in the Gospel accounts involves the number of blind men who figure in the story. For Mark, followed by Luke, there is only one, whom Mark further calls by name, *Bartimaeus,* adding (he or a helpful scribe) the translation, *the son of Timaeus.* Matthew has two blind men. This is not, as we know (see above on Mk 5:1–20 and parallels), an isolated instance with the first evangelist. He omitted the previous story of a healing of a blind man in Mk 8:22–26. It is also possible that as, following Mark, he has made this episode the very last in Jesus' public life immediately preparatory to the triumphal entry into Jerusalem (see our next chapter), he has found it desirable to leave the testimony of *two* witnesses to Jesus as *Son of David* (vss. 30 f.) echoing in our ears as this part of the Gospel draws to a close. On the other hand, there seems to be no doubt that Mt 9:27–31, which also speaks of two blind men, is a doublet of this present passage, and therefore it may well be that Matthew depended on a tradition which differed from that of Mark. It may even be that it is more original than Mark's and that Mark's story has simply concentrated its attention on one of the central figures who was known by name to the early Church while the other had been forgotten. Matthew's earlier use of the story has been carefully integrated into the context of the Galilean ministry. There is a greater emphasis on the prerequisite of faith and

an injunction to silence about the miracle (which is ignored),
both of which are characteristics of the first days of the
ministry.

Mark's account has all the vigor and freshness we have
come to expect from the Second Gospel. We should probably
conclude that Bartimaeus was a young man from the description given of him by Mark. Persistent in his crying out to
Jesus after the crowd had tried to hush him up, at the
Master's call he throws aside his outer garment, springs to his
feet, and runs to his side. *Son of David* was a title which
Jesus never used of himself because of its nationalistic overtones. Here, however, it is plain that Bartimaeus uses it
without prejudice and that his faith, to which the healing
wonder is ascribed, is faith in the merciful dispensation of
God: restoration of sight to the blind is one of the works
expected of the anointed Servant of the Lord according to
the Greek text of Is 61:1.

Lk 19:1–10   Though Luke's is pre-eminently the Gospel
of the poor, and though he has some stern
things to say about the wealthy, it is interesting to see him
interrupt Jesus' journey at this moment to tell the story of
a man named Zacchaeus, a chief publican who was rich.
Probably he intends a topical association with the preceding
story: the *salvation* that comes to Zacchaeus' *house this day*
is the spiritual counterpart of the physical sight restored to
the blind man. The setting of such an event in Jericho is
quite understandable. Jericho was an important commercial
and trading junction on the main road between Judea and
Perea, and King Herod had built a winter palace there. As a
chief publican, Zacchaeus would have been in charge of the
taxgathering and collection of duties over the entire district,
having under his authority the various local publicans such
as Levi had been, sitting in his little toll booth in Capernaum
(Mk 2:13–17 and parallels).

There is something altogether charming about the story of

Zacchaeus, the little man who wanted to see Jesus in his own way just as the blind man had wanted to see in another. Forgetting his dignity as a prominent official, he clambers up into the low-hanging branches of *a sycamore tree,* doubtless not without being observed by the semi-hostile crowd which drew Jesus' attention to him, but hardly expecting to be singled out as in fact he was when the Lord called him by name. There is a touch of humor in Jesus' calling out to Zacchaeus to *hurry down* from the perch that he had just gained with a bit of breathless effort. But Jesus knew Zacchaeus better than the man knew himself. He recognized in him *a son of Abraham,* a true Israelite without guile (Jn 1:47), whose single-minded and ingenuous conduct was evidence of something that went deeper than mere curiosity, whatever Zacchaeus himself may have thought of it at the time.

Zacchaeus' words are probably to be taken as an evidence of his conversion, another vindication of Jesus' habit of consorting with sinners (cf. Lk 15:1f., etc.). The loose system of taxgathering made injustice almost an occupational hazard, and Zacchaeus is willing to concede the point without resort to casuistry: *if I have cheated anyone of anything*—as I doubtless have—*I restore it fourfold here and now* (fourfold restitution was traditional in cases of flagrant theft, cf. Ex 21:37; 2 Sam 12:6; but legally Zacchaeus could have been held to no such thing even if proof of a specific offense were possible). Furthermore, *I hereby give half of my possessions to the poor.* In a sense, Zacchaeus renounces his status as a rich man for the kingdom of heaven (cf. Lk 18:24–27); nevertheless, Jesus accepts at face value this voluntary commitment and does not require of him that he sell all that he has and give to the poor (see above on Mk 10:17–22 and parallels). Even Luke's Gospel does not regard possessions of themselves or any occupation of itself inevitable hindrances to the salvation of the kingdom. Of Luke's various references to the publicans, as a matter of fact (here and in 3:12, 5:27, 7:29, 15:1, 18:10), all have been favorable.

Lk 19:11-28   The parable with which Luke continues
may have been originally the same as an-
other told later in a different context in Matthew's Gospel
(see below on Mt 25:14-30). If so, however, the two traditions in which the parable was handed down have resulted
in a considerable difference of details, even though the
essential lesson still remains the same. In Luke's sequence
there is only a tenuous connection between the theme of the
uses of wealth as exemplified in Zacchaeus and the parable's
subject matter which also involves the use of wealth. This,
despite the fact that generations of homilists have understood the parable as an instruction on the right use of
personal gifts—the "talents" of Matthew's version. While such
an application of the story is not entirely foreign to its original
intent, Luke nevertheless makes it quite clear that it was first
uttered by Jesus *because he was near to Jerusalem, and
because they supposed that the kingdom of God was to
appear immediately*. It is a parable of eschatological decision,
of the immediacy of the kingdom of God.

It is true, there are certain allegorical elements in the
parable as reported by Luke, which were either in it from
the beginning or, as is perhaps more likely, were introduced
into it during the period of its oral transmission. The *certain
man* who is the chief protagonist of the story is qualified as
a nobleman who *went into a far country to receive kingly
power and then return*, whose *citizens hated him and sent
an embassy after him, saying, "We do not want this man to
reign over us,"* and who nevertheless did receive the kingly
power he had sought and ended by returning and putting to
death those who had rebelled against his rule. None of this is
really necessary to the parable, nor does it contribute anything to its lesson. It sounds very much like the story of
Archelaus, who journeyed to Rome in 4 B.C. after the death
of his father Herod to be confirmed as king of Judea and
who was opposed there, rather unsuccessfully, by a delegation of Palestinian Jews. Archelaus returned and reigned as
ethnarch of Judea for a few years, during which he added to
the splendor of Jericho, in the environs of which Luke has

placed this parable. It is easy enough to see why these details might have been added, therefore. They allegorize the parable by making its principal figure out as a king whose own natural subjects revolted against his rule and who were therefore punished: in Luke's eyes, the application to Christ and the Jews was obvious. This is an extension of the lesson that Jesus primarily intended, as we shall see in a moment.

What does the parable really say, first and foremost? The householder gives *to ten of his servants* each a like amount of money, *ten minas* for the ten, to each, therefore, a gold coin roughly the equivalent of twenty dollars. The amount is not important, nor is the number of the servants—that only three of them figure in the conclusion of the story shows how little interested it is in allegrical details. Neither, in all likelihood, is it significant to the story that one servant *by trading* has increased his master's money tenfold and another fivefold, and that they receive in recompense from this prince ten and five cities respectively (in vs. 25 the first servant's reward seems to be his master's money rather than authority over cities!). These servants appear in the parable only to underscore the slothfulness of the one who hid his gold piece *in a handkerchief,* who so much feared his master's wrath and the risk of loss that he did absolutely nothing with what had been entrusted to him. He thought to please his lord by preserving whole and entire exactly what he had received. But no, he has actually preserved nothing at all. Even what he thought he had is now taken from him. That it is given to another is a detail of the parable irrelevant to the main issue, except to the extent that it illustrates the parable of divine justice. In the parable it is given to the first servant, prompting the surprised exclamation (of the man's fellow servants? of those listening to Jesus?): *Lord, he already has ten minas!*

Thus the lesson of the parable: *To everyone who has, more will be given; but from him who has not, even what he has will be taken away.* Those who have prepared themselves for the kingdom will receive it, those who have not will not. And not to receive the kingdom means to lose everything.

Jesus has in mind the kind of Pharisee for whom the Old
Testament revelation was not a precious trust to be "traded"
in for the salvation of Israel and the world, but a fossilized
dogma to be hugged to sterile breasts in smugness and
complacency and legalistic exclusivism (see above on Lk
13:22–30). It is such men, who fondly think that they have
kept the faith pure and undefiled, who in reality are left
with nothing, since what was once given to them they have
stifled and smothered. The lesson of Jesus' parable, as should
be evident, is equally applicable to the Christian awaiting
Christ's coming for whom Luke wrote his Gospel. The
Christian, too, can retreat into a barren contemplation of the
truth which he possesses but which he will not allow to
possess him, and with a mean conception of God's mercy
and grace reduce his economy of salvation to a selfish kind of
bookkeeping which he calls "saving his soul." Risking nothing
in the mission field of the Church which is the world, he can
end by losing all.

Concluding the parable, one final time Luke holds up for
us his cherished view of the Christ of the Gospels *walking
ahead, going up to Jerusalem.*

Jn 12:1–8   It is now necessary, however, to interrupt
Mk 14:3–9   both the Lucan and the Synoptic sequence
Mt 26:6–13   for an episode which John places at this
              time, *six days before Passover.* Since as we
shall see later on, for John the Passover of Jesus' death took
place on a Sabbath day, he would be dating this present
event for us on the preceding Saturday evening, after
the Sabbath had officially closed with sunset. What is doubtless more important to him is that the anointing at Bethany
opens the "last week of the new creation" (see above on Jn
1:19–2:11). Jesus was crucified the day before Passover
(Jn 18:28, 19:31) and he rose on the following day following it (Jn 20:1); therefore this event occurs seven days
before the exaltation of Christ (cf. Jn 20:19–22). There
can be no doubt that this idea has influenced John in some
of the descriptive details of his narrative.

John's chronology is thus symbolical. It is, nevertheless, intrinsically more probable than that of the Synoptics, which has the event take place two days before the Passover (Mk 14:1 and parallel). The Synoptic dating has been determined by the significance that Mark, followed by Matthew, saw in the Lord's words concerning the woman at Bethany and in the relation which he placed between her gesture and the hasty burial of Jesus after the crucifixion. Mark, followed by Matthew, has consequently put this story into the most immediate possible proximity to the narrative of Christ's passion and death. Luke, who avoids even apparent repetitions or doublets, has omitted the story entirely because of his similar account involving the repentant action of a woman of Galilee (see above on Lk 7:36–50).

The Lucan story, as we noted at the time, has evidently picked up in oral transmission a few details that properly belong to the one that now lies before us. We also noted that the exchange was not entirely one-sided, and we can now find this contention verified especially in John's version of the story. The most striking discrepancy, when John's account is compared with the Synoptic telling of what happened at Bethany, appears in the use to which each says that the ointment of anointing was put. *She poured the perfume on his head,* say the Synoptics. Though the gesture was extravagant, as the story itself brings out, this sort of thing was also quite straightforward and comprehensible: the anointing of the head was and is in the Near East a customary and conventional thing. But John writes that *she anointed Jesus' feet.* This is as unlikely as the other is plausible; such an action would serve no assignable purpose, and there is no known precedent for it. Even more unlikely is what follows in John's Gospel, according to which *she dried his feet with her hair.* In the first place, why? Beyond this, it would have been unthinkable for a respectable Jewish woman to loose her hair in public for any reason. But these difficulties disappear if we assume that John has made use of a tradition in which some details from the Lucan story have been intruded. In that story both the feet of Jesus

and the hair of the woman figure both naturally and logically
—there it is the anointing that seems to be out of place.
Be this as it may be, John has taken the form of the narrative
as it came to him and has found in it his own meaning
which has enriched the message of the Gospel.

All the Gospels set the scene in *Bethany*. Somewhat unnecessarily John adds that it was here that *Lazarus was,
whom Jesus had raised from the dead*, connecting this
story with that of Jn 11:1–44 just as before he already
looked forward to what he is now about to describe (cf.
Jn 11:2). The presence of the resurrected Lazarus at the
banquet undoubtedly contributes, in John's eyes, to the
spiritual significance of what transpired there, helping to
determine its character as a "sign." Who gave the banquet for Jesus is not made clear in John's Gospel; neither
the fact that *Lazarus was one of those at table with him*
nor that *Martha was serving* (cf. Lk 10:40) would necessarily mean that the banquet was in the house of Lazarus
and his sisters, though this is often assumed. Matthew and
Mark say that it was *in the house of Simon the leper*,
who just possibly could have been a disciple of Jesus whom
the Lord had cured of leprosy. The banquet may well have
been a kind of civic affair.

Only John identifies the woman of the anointing as *Mary*,
who thus acts in the character assigned her in Lk 10:38 ff.
All the Gospels agree that she used an extraordinary quan-
tity of very valuable perfume, valued at upward of *three
hundred denarii* (Mark and John): roughly ten months'
wages! Presumably Mary would have stinted and saved for
a long while to be able to make this great gesture, which
would have recommended itself so highly to the Oriental's
love of display. All the Gospels, too, record the disciples'
initial displeasure at what has been done, their protest at
the extravagance on the practical grounds that the money
represented by it might better have been *given to the poor*.
(So Martha objected to Mary's devotion on practical grounds
according to Lk 10:40.) They also record Jesus' defense
of Mary's *beautiful deed* (Matthew and Mark). The acts

of love do not always respond to detached logic. Jesus yields to no one in his concern for the poor; however, there is more to religion—either as service of the Christ of the Gospels or the Christ continually living in his Church—than the alleviation of poverty. There is also room in religion for works which bespeak the heart rather than the mind, which are highly personal and uncalculated: *she did what she had to do* (Mark). John restricts the protest against Mary's action to *Judas the Iscariot,* meanwhile telling us for the first time that he kept the purse for Jesus' little band of disciples (cf. Jn 13:29). In ascribing it in his case to mean motives, however, we have the impression that, however justified the allegation may have been, John is attempting to lay the foundation for an explanation of Judas' treason that will not prove adequate to account for all its complexities.

All the Gospels have Jesus offer an interpretation of the woman's deed that has some relation to his burial. Mark and Matthew interpret his words to mean that this anointing must take the place of the embalming of his body that was later made impossible by the circumstances of the crucifixion and resurrection (cf. Mk 16:1; Lk 24:1). John's interpretation is more difficult to make out. What he seems to give as Jesus' words is: *Leave her alone, that she may keep it* [the ointment] *for the day of my burial.* He does not, therefore, see this action as an anticipated embalming of Jesus. In John's Gospel, as a matter of fact, the embalming of Jesus' body for the tomb was not omitted but carried out with all thoroughness (cf. Jn 19:39 f.). Rather, the "burial" of which John thinks is that spiritual burial of Jesus which is the source of life for the Church (see below on Jn 12:20–36). The anointing, in other words, has a continuing significance for the Christian who finds the living Christ in his Church. This interpretation does not altogether differ from that of those who believe that John looked on Mary's act as a symbolic anointing of kingship preparatory to his triumphal entry when (according to John's Gospel) he was hailed as "king of Israel" (see below on Mk 11:1–10 and parallels). In John's theology, Jesus' death and burial, triumph and glorification, are one and the same.

If we may understand "the day of burial" for which Mary was to "keep" the ointment as the period of the Church, then, just as John so often connects water with Jesus, doubtless thinking of its sacramental use in the Church which is the perpetuation of Christ in the world (see above on Jn 2:1–11), he may also be thinking of the Church's anointings in the same way (cf. Mk 6:13; Jas 5:14). Perhaps for the same reason he alone has stressed the large amount of the ointment which, poured on the Lord's feet rather than his head could then be wiped off with Mary's hair so that, as she walked about, *the house was filled with the odor of the perfume:* the ointment signifies the good odor of the Lord's presence in his "house" (cf. Jn 2:21, 14:2).

Jn 12:9–11   John concludes the Bethany scene by speaking of the crowds of Jews who were coming there from Jerusalem because of Lazarus, the witness in life to Jesus' life-giving power. He also repeats what was said in Jn 11:53 about the plot against Jesus being hatched by *the chief priests*—not "the Jews," who continue in this passage to represent the people in general—a plot which now extends, appropriately enough, to Lazarus as well. For the moment, however, they are powerless to do anything. The brief period of Jesus' public triumph is to begin on the morrow.

20. PALM SUNDAY

Mk 11:1–10   In the story of the anointing at Bethany
Mt 21:1–9   which we saw in our last chapter the
Lk 19:29–40   Johannine and Synoptic traditions came to-
Jn 12:12–19   gether in what up to now has been the
                rare exception to their rule of separate
ways. From now on, though the ways will still remain quite
distinct, they will be less and less separate, and four-Gospel
parallels will not be as unusual as in the past. This situation
reflects the unique character of the narrative of Jesus' passion, death, and resurrection (which, strictly speaking, John
has not yet begun), a narrative which by all accounts is
the most primitive of all the Gospel "forms," for which, in
varying ways and with different emphases, all that has gone
before in our literary Gospels serves as introduction (the
passion-resurrection narrative takes up almost the entire second half of John's Gospel), a form which enjoyed greater
rigidity and was less subject to variations than others in the
Gospel pattern. As we will see borne out in our remaining
chapters, while each of our Gospels retains its individuality
and makes its own contributions to what we discover to be a
mainly consistent and coherent common narrative, it is basically from three related but independent historical traditions
that the passion-resurrection story has been drawn. The

first of these is that of Mark-Matthew and, as before, it will
usually be obvious that priority in the use of the tradition
must be assigned to Mark. Luke, who has made use of
Mark's form of the tradition, nevertheless has one of his
own proper to himself, which may have been influenced in
part by the Johannine tradition. John's story, finally, continues to be uniquely his own, though in the opinion of most
scholars John also not only knew and made use of the common Synoptic tradition, but in addition was acquainted with
the peculiarly Marcan form of it.

If we follow John in thinking of this present event as
taking place on a Sunday, it is also because of his account
that we call it Palm Sunday. As John tells the story, Jesus,
accompanied by a crowd of Jews who had gone out to
Bethany and were witnesses of the resurrection of Lazarus,
was met by another crowd from Jerusalem enthusiastic over
the report of the miracle who *took palm fronds and went
out to meet him crying, "Hosanna!"* The Synoptics really
have nothing like this at all—neither do they ever explain
the sudden welcome which Jesus receives in Jerusalem, a city
with which they have shown him in no contact up to the
present. Now palm trees are about as common in Jerusalem
as they are in New York City or Chicago. Matthew says
that some of the people *tore down branches from the trees,*
olive trees, no doubt, which they strewed over the rutted
and miry road in Jesus' path; Mark has it even more
realistically that they *strewed reeds* (or rushes) *which they
had cut in the fields,* that is, making a matting of grass or
leaves; Luke includes nothing on this matter. It is difficult
to avoid the conclusion that John has further adapted this
story to the prophetic symbolism that already dominates it,
seeing in it an anticipation of the eschatological feast of
Tabernacles (cf. Zech 14:16–19). At Tabernacles, Hanukkah
("little Tabernacles," see above on Jn 10:22–39), and other
joyous occasions palm fronds, brought in from Jericho usually, were waved in sign of joy and messianic triumph
(cf. 1 Macc 13:51; Apo 7:9). The cries of the people, a
mingling of Ps 118:25 f. and other Old Testament allusions,

are taken by both John and the Synoptics as acclaim given
to a messianic king. Both Matthew (vs. 10) and Luke
(vs. 38) refer us back to their separate Gospels of the
Infancy (cf. Mt 2:3; Lk 2:14).

The same eschatological significance has been found in
the event by the Synoptics when they make the point that
Jesus began his procession *at the Mount of Olives* (cf.
Zech 14:4 f.), having passed from Jericho through Bethany
to *Bethphage* on the slope of the mountain facing Jerusalem.
John omits the story told by the Synoptics according to
which Jesus consciously fulfilled the prophecy of Zech 9:9.
As this is, seemingly, the only time in the Synoptic Gospels
that Jesus unhesitatingly identifies himself with the King-
Messiah of Jewish expectation (see above on Mk 1:22–28
and parallels), the incident deserves the closer attention
that we shall give it below. The story itself is credible
enough. Bethphage was a small village where everyone
knew everybody else. The people of Bethphage immediately
recognized Jesus' disciples and hence simply asked why the
colt he had sent them for was being loosed; they knew it
was not being stolen. Their answer, that Jesus wanted to
make use of it, was enough. The owners were probably
flattered to be of some help to the Master. The title *Lord*
used by and of Jesus in this connection, however, is probably
due to the later Christian transmission of the story.

Matthew's narrative is curious in that he speaks of two
animals rather than one and even seems to have Jesus
mount both of them, a rather evident impossibility. It seems
that he, who alone of the Synoptists quotes Zech 9:9,
wanted to stress an exact fulfillment of the prophecy even
at the sacrifice of the logical probabilities. The text that he
cited does, in fact, speak materially of two animals, but in
Hebrew parallelism wherein *she-ass* and *colt* refer to one
and the same beast. It is impossible to believe that Matthew
did not know this; rather than as evidence of the misreading
of a Semitic text by a Gentile evangelist (see page 37
Vol. I), what he has done corresponds to some of the
exegetical techniques of the rabbis. His adjustment of the

story to fit the text may also have something to do with his
fondness for two's (see above on Mk 10:46–52 and parallels).

John, who also quotes the prophecy, states that its meaning was not understood at the time, but only later by the
Church through the enlightenment of the Spirit (cf. Jn 2:22,
7:39, 13:7). At first such a remark seems strange. In the
same breath John records the despair of *the Pharisees* at
today's happenings, who utter another of the Johannine
prophecies: *See! the whole world has begun to follow him!*
This is in agreement with Luke, who shows the Pharisees
indignant over the messianic acclamation being showered
upon Jesus, but incapable of doing more in the face of it
than remonstrate with Jesus himself, calling on him to put
an end to the demonstration, which Jesus refuses to do.
Since the Gospels without exception have represented the
scene as a messianic proclamation, seemingly encouraged by
Jesus himself, John is obviously suggesting that there is a
messianic significance to the event that has not been grasped
by the applauding multitude. This may, again, be not too
far from what Luke means when he has the Lord tell the
Pharisees: *If these were silent, the very stones would cry
out!* The event, Jesus retorts, speaks for itself. The crowd is
of good will and is not to be discouraged; but neither does
Jesus necessarily accept its estimation of his present purpose
in Jerusalem.

Mt 21:10–11, 14–17   Perhaps some additional light is
Mk 11:11   thrown on the problem by Mat-
                     thew's sequel to the Palm Sunday
acclamation. When bystanders ask its meaning, they are told
by those who have been crying out to Jesus, *This is the
prophet Jesus from Nazareth of Galilee*. The thought of the
evangelist may well extend to the eschatological prophet of
Deut 18:18 (see above on Jn 1:19–24); but it is plain
that the Jerusalemites are now testifying of Jesus in much
less grandiloquent terms than they had used a few moments
before in their enthusiasm. A few verses further on Matthew
has a parallel to Luke's remonstration of the Pharisees when

he pictures *the chief priests and the scribes* shocked over *the children* who were echoing the messianic cry they had heard from their elders, *Hosanna to the Son of David!* Jesus cites Ps 8:3 both to accept the children's praise and confound those who opposed it. The full quotation is: "Out of the mouths of babes and sucklings you have fashioned praise *because of your foes, to silence the hostile and the vengeful.*" The main point is, however, that this is the praise of children, and for Jesus and Matthew children represent those who are open to the designs of God, who are prepared to receive his Messiah on his terms rather than their own (see above on Mk 9:33–37 and parallels; Mk 10:13–16 and parallels).

The most suggestive contribution to our reconstruction, however, is that made by Mark, who possesses what is without doubt the oldest tradition about the events of this day. Here we see a suddenly solitary Jesus walking about the Holy City in the company of his disciples, *inspecting everything*, returning to his friends at Bethany as the evening draws on. The "many" and the "others" who had followed and preceded him into Jerusalem (vs. 8) have now melted away and disappeared; just how many they were in the first place, we have never really been told. The messianic fervor of only a moment ago appears to have been very ephemeral indeed.

A possible explanation of all this is that while Jesus accepted the messianic acclaim of his Galilean companions and of the Jerusalemites who participated in it up to a point, he adhered throughout to his own unique interpretation of his messianic character and demonstrated it in the gesture that he performed fulfilling Zech 9:9. It is perhaps significant that John has Jesus perform the gesture *after* he had been proclaimed "king of Israel" by the crowd, not to provoke such a proclamation. Zech 9:9, though accepted by the rabbis as in the authentic tradition of Davidic messianism, which in the time of Jesus was almost invariably a highly nationalistic messianism, does not really conform to the triumphalist tone that is the characteristic of the other

Davidic oracles. Dependent on the exilic Isaiah of the Servant songs and on the other exilic and postexilic prophecies and experiences of Israel (especially, perhaps, on the prophecy of Zeph 3:14–17 which has also influenced the Lucan Gospel of the Infancy), Zech 9:9 pictures a messianic king who is less a conqueror than he is a sign of God's peace restored to his people. He is less a dispenser of judgment than he is the exemplar of God's saving mercy: he is savior not as a savior-king but as the leader of a saved people. He is called "humble," for he is first among the *anawim*, the poor of the Lord (see above on Mt 5:3–12 and parallel), and he enters the Holy City not on a war charger but on a lowly beast of burden. Such was Israel's kingly ideal as Jesus was prepared to fulfill it.

Once before Jesus had reacted to an attempt to proclaim him king by taking evasive action (see above on Jn 6:15 and Mk 6:45 f. and parallels). This time, the Gospels suggest, he did something much more positive and demonstrative. In both instances what he did was to repudiate a popular distortion of his mission, and in both instances he seems to have failed to channel the general enthusiasm in the direction toward which he had pointed.

Lk 19:41–44   It is in the vicinity of these events that the Synoptic Gospels, though variously, have located the story of Jesus' invasion of the temple, an action which, we have already noted, might better be placed in this context than in the one to which John has assigned it (see above on Jn 2:13–17 and parallels). Prior to this, however, only Luke records Jesus' lament over Jerusalem which bears out, on his part, the interpretation of the "triumphal" entry already ascribed to the other Gospels. Luke never, in fact, shows Jesus actually enter the city in procession, but has the Lord say to Jerusalem that *you did not know the time of your visitation.* Apparently awaiting its Peacemaker with open arms, Jerusalem in fact has not recognized what is God's peace. And because of this, Jerusalem would be destroyed (see below on Mk 13:14–20 and parallels). All that lay before his eyes—the great temple area with the beautiful temple of Herod, vast and priceless, the many towers of the city, the wide walls, the teeming buildings of Jerusalem the Golden—all would be leveled to the ground. *The days shall come upon you*—it was to be just forty years later—when enemies shall surround Jerusalem *and build a rampart about you.* This the Romans did with customary thoroughness. They laid total siege so that those within perished under miserable and degrading conditions; and when they had taken the city, they literally razed it to the ground so that nothing remained.

Mk 11:12-14   In a much more graphic fashion Mark and
Mt 21:18-19   Matthew convey the Lord's judgment on
Jerusalem by means of the story of the fig tree. The story causes all manner of difficulties out of any proportion to its size, and it is easy to understand why Luke chose to omit it. For one thing, this is the only instance in the Gospels in which Jesus is shown exercising his miraculous powers in a destructive way. Such an objection is not, of course, peremptory. The divine curse, anthropomorphism though it may be, is a corollary of the divine blessing, and the caricature of Jesus as a kindly do-gooder whose lips never moved except in benison grossly distorts the character of him who came to cast fire on the earth. The action is presented as a kind of parable, which certainly illustrates a genuine emphasis in Jesus' preaching of the kingdom of God. On the other hand, taken as a factual account, it comes uncomfortably close to picturing Jesus in the performance of an arbitrary and petulant action, especially given Mark's characteristically honest but none too helpful observation that *it was not the season for figs.* Figs in Palestine do not ripen till June, and the story is set in the early spring of the Passover season. To what purpose would Jesus have been looking for fruit from such an unlikely source? It is not surprising that many students of the New Testament believe that for this episode in his Gospel Mark depends ultimately on a parable of the Lord (see above on Lk 13:1-9) which

an early Christian tradition had transformed into a popular
and uncritical narrative about Jesus.

While Mark narrates the story with careful attention to
the detail in which it had come to him, Matthew tries to
get at the point of it without delay. According to his Gospel
the fig tree *withered up instantly*. There was ample prophetic precedent for the representation of Israel as figs or
a fig tree (cf. Jer 24; Hos 9:10) and for the threat of
divine judgment against it as the destruction of figs or of
fig trees (cf. Is 34:4; Jer 29:18; Hos 2:14; Mi 7:10).

Jn 12:20–36 John, too, in his own way, is going to
express the Lord's judgment on the unbe-
lief that has greeted his manifestation of the kingdom of
God (see below on Jn 12:37–50). Before doing so, however,
he concludes the history of Jesus' ministry with an event
and some sayings that both sum up its meaning and prepare
for the adverse judgment that is to be passed on the
unbelieving generation among which the Word of God had
appeared.

The *Greeks* who wanted to *see Jesus* were undoubtedly
Jewish proselytes or Gentiles otherwise well-disposed to Judaism who were accustomed to assist at its great feast days.
For John they undoubtedly represent the Gentile world
which will later fulfill the unconscious prophecy of the
Pharisees in verse 19, accepting the light which, for a final
time, the crowds about Jesus are to prove themselves blind,
the voice of God which they will not hear. Therefore the
pertinence of Jesus' present teaching: it is by means of
Christian faith that they will "see" Jesus. The Gentiles ap-
proach him through *Philip and Andrew*, the only two of
the twelve disciples who bear Gentile names, and these
consult together before speaking to Jesus in view of the
fact that hithertofore his ministry had been, as it continued
to be to the end, directed only to the Jewish world of
Palestine.

The hour has come. John is now on the point of beginning
the story of the passion, death, and resurrection of Christ,

when *the Son of Man will be glorified* (see above on Jn 1:14, 2:1–11). At long last, the "hour" of which he had spoken (cf. Jn 2:4, 4:23, 5:25) is upon him, when he will show forth in his own person the paradox of Christian faith, that death is the source of life. This, he says, is the law of sacrifice, a law which can also be seen mirrored in nature. *The grain of wheat* sown in the ground must sacrifice its existence as seed if there is ever to be a new shaft of wheat and spurs of new grain. If it were to insist on its continued existence as a grain of wheat, it would remain alone and fruitless. So it is with the renunciation of Christ, whose death will mean the life of the world.

To express the same truth he uses a saying which we have already seen in various Synoptic contexts (Mk 8:34–9:1 and parallels; Mt 10:37–39; Lk 17:22–37). What is nonsense when translated into this-worldly terms is Christian wisdom. One saves his life—the only life that truly matters —not by egoistically clinging to his separate identity as a good to be preserved at all costs, but by being willing to abandon and destroy it. This is the way of renunciation, of sacrifice, and of service which Jesus revealed as the genuine meaning of life, and this way of Christ must also be that of the Christian: *where I am, there shall my servant be*.

It is at this moment of his speaking of his sacrifice that Jesus undergoes in John's Gospel the experience which the Synoptic Gospels place in the garden of Gethsemane prior to his arrest and trial (see below on Mk 14:32–42 and parallels). *My soul is stirred:* the Greek verb is one used to express extreme mental and emotional anguish. The reference he has just made to his death and which seemed to be so lightly said, in reality cost him a great effort. *What shall I say?* We hear the voice of a Man seeking the consolation of the counsel of those who could never understand him. *Father, save me from this hour!* This is the alternative that was always open to Jesus, for the sacrifice asked of him had to be a free offering if it was to have any value, just as the commitment of Christian faith must also be free.

Jesus' cry appears merely to consider the possibility, however, not to entertain it. It is immediately followed by the reaffirmation of his first resolve: *it was for this that I came to this hour*. Thus his final words are an epitome of his entire life of dedicated obedience: *Father, glorify your name!*

As in the Synoptic stories of Jesus' baptism (Lk 3:21f. and parallels) and transfiguration (Mk 9:2–10 and parallels) *a voice from heaven* speaks the divine confirmation and interpretation of the event. The Father has already glorified his name by giving testimony to Jesus throughout his ministry of grace (cf. Jn 10:38, 11:40, etc.) by the many "signs" of the supreme glorification to be achieved in Jesus' triumph over death in his resurrection. It is typical of the crowd about Jesus that it cannot understand the divine voice (cf. Jn 8:43), even though Jesus says that it was directed to its ears rather than his own; he himself needs no reassurance, such is his oneness with the Father (cf. Jn 11:42).

Now is the judgment of this world. The glorification of Christ spells the end of the power of *the ruler of this world*, despite all the appearances there will soon be to the contrary. Through his death, when he is *lifted up* (cf. Jn 3:14), comes that triumph over evil whose enduring reality empowers the man of faith to escape divine condemnation while it condemns the unbeliever (cf. Jn 3:18). The people understand at least that he is talking of a going away. But he has said this of *the Son of Man*. This person can hardly be the Messiah, as they reason, since the messianic reign is to be everlasting according to *the Law* (that is, the Old Testament, cf. Jn 10:34: a typical reference would be Is 9:6f.). This kind of fatuous half-truth has characterized the Johannine dialogues all along and has provided the basis for much of their irony. But Jesus has now brought his period of instruction to a close. He merely states the issue of light and darkness one final time (cf. Jn 8:12, 9:4f.) and, as far as the Gospel of John is concerned, departs definitively from their presence.

Mk 11:18–19   The Synoptic Gospels have a rather more
Lk 19:47–48   complicated story to tell. John has previously connected the plot of *the chief
priests and the scribes* of which Mark and Luke now speak
with the aftermath of Jesus' raising of Lazarus, the "sign"
of Jesus which immediately precedes and occasions the hour
of his glorification (see above on Jn 11:45–57). The Synoptics join it to the story of Jesus' cleansing of the temple.
They also continue to stress the popularity which Jesus
continued to enjoy with the people at large, which prevented
any hostile action being taken against him immediately.

Mk 11:20–26   Mark and Matthew now conclude their
Mt 21:20–22   story of the withered fig tree, the denoue-
ment of which Mark alone has put *early
in the morning* of a following day. Actually, this passage
addresses itself not to the why of the fig tree's destruction, a
question which the Gospels allow the event itself to answer,
but to the how. Jesus discourses first on the power of faith,
in a saying which we have already seen in variant forms
in both Matthew and Luke (see above on Lk 17:3–6).
From faith the argument easily passes to the power of
Christian prayer: such works as Jesus has done his disciples
will also do provided their faith is unwavering. It is the
magnitude of the works, of course, that interests the catechetical purpose of the Gospels, not their specific nature.
Mark and Matthew here employ a saying of Jesus which
appears several times in John's Last Supper discourse, where
it contributes to one of the major themes developed by the
Fourth Gospel (cf. Jn 14:13 f., 15:7, 16:23). Finally, Mark
ends with a teaching of Jesus which Matthew placed in
the context of the Sermon on the Mount (cf. Mt 6:14):
not only confidence makes for effective prayer, but also a
pure heart free of enmities and disposed to the grace of God
which is the fruit of every prayer. (What appears as verse 26
in older translations of Mark is not in the better manuscripts,
but has been borrowed from Mt 6:15.)

Mk 11:27–33   Just as John showed a demand made on
Mt 21:23–27   Jesus by "the Jews" to give evidence of
Lk 20:1–8   the authority by which he had presumed
              to interfere in the temple's business (see
above on Jn 2:18–22), the Synoptic Gospels now tell of a
delegation which calls on him for the same purpose. The
delegation was composed of *the chief priests and elders of
the people* and, according to Mark and Luke, *the scribes.*
Here we have representatives of the three groups that spoke
for the three departments of Jewish life—though often with
some internecine rivalry—the religious and cultic, the national
and civil, and the legal and doctrinal. They were also the
three divisions of the Sanhedrin, and the present delegation
may well have been official. The concern, after all, was
legitimate, especially in the Synoptics' perspective of a first
visit of Jesus to Jerusalem. He had intervened in the temple,
his action had messianic overtones with possible political
implications, and *he was teaching the people in the temple.*

All the same, their demand was a most tiresome one, given
the total context of the Gospels. What Jesus had done in
Galilee had not been hidden in a corner, and even though
the Synoptic Gospels for reasons of their own have restricted
his ministry in Jerusalem to this one Passover visit, at times
they also reflect the viewpoint of John, namely that he was
no longer attempting to convince people who had proved
themselves to be incurably obdurate. Jesus, therefore, adopts
the rabbinical expedient of countering a question with a
question, shifting the initiative back to his questioners, and
at the same time presenting them with a dilemma which
they find insoluble. *Was John's baptism of divine or of
human origin?* They want to say it was human, of course,
for they were among those who had never accepted the
Baptist and had been thoroughly repudiated by him (cf.
Mt 3:7–10 and parallel). But they feared the consequences
of such an answer. John the Baptist was almost universally
regarded as *a prophet,* and doubtless all the more so now
that he was safely dead. Yet they could not bring themselves to concur in the popular opinion. For one thing,

their record was against them: *Why did you not believe him, then?* But more than this was involved. There was an uncomfortable parallel between Jesus and the Baptist, and the connection between the two was certainly known (see above on Lk 7:24–35 and parallel).

Jesus' hard question was not chosen at random simply to embarrass his adversaries. When these who claimed to be the spokesmen for Israel had to confess of the Baptist *we do not know,* they had placed themselves in the position of the Pharisees before the man born blind (see on Jn 9:1–34 above): "Why, here is a marvel!" Self-convicted of their inability to discern the presence of prophecy in Israel, they are as incompetent to judge the credentials of Jesus as they had been to judge those of the Baptist. It is the sign of Jonah all over again (see above on Mk 8:11 f. and parallels; Mt 12:38–42 and parallel).

Mt 21:28–32   In Matthew's Gospel Jesus quickly follows up his victory with a parable that underlines the lesson he has just made his enemies teach against themselves. The story is deceptively simple and utterly true to life, taking but a moment to tell. Suddenly another question is asked, and perhaps for a minute these leaders of the people were relieved because of the obvious answer that was expected, thinking that this time they could reply without incriminating themselves. *Which of the two sons did what his father wanted,* the one who was all promises with no performance, or the one who did after all what was asked of him whatever his first reaction? The answer was, indeed, obvious, and in giving it the hostile embassy to its dismay again finds itself self-condemned. All through their history they have been shouting "yes" to God, yet they have not obeyed him, while those whom they despise as sinners are inheriting the kingdom in their place. It had first been so with John the Baptist, and now it was so with Jesus (cf. Lk 7:29 f.).

Jesus pointedly acknowledges the unsavory reputation borne by many of those who had turned with repentance

to the preaching of the kingdom. Association with such
people had more than once been held up to him in reproach, but he glories in their titles the better to demonstrate
that the kingdom is the work of God's grace rather than of
self-righteousness. The catechetical lesson was not lost on the
Church, which in the time of the evangelists and sub-
sequently had to justify itself to the fastidious on some other
terms than as an exclusive club of the very best people.
That with God there is no respect of persons is an honored
Christian maxim that most respectable people find hard to
believe deep down.

Mk 12:1–12   The next parable, included by all three of
Mt 21:33–46   the Synoptic Gospels, is as complicated
Lk 20:9–19   as the preceding one of Matthew's was
                  simple. It contains numerous allegorical
elements, including a pointed reference to the death of
Jesus at the hands of the Jewish leadership, and largely
for these reasons many scholars regard it as a story told
by the Palestinian Church after the crucifixion rather than
an actual part of Jesus' teaching. However, while allegorical,
as is the parable of Is 5:1–7 on which it doubtless depends,
it remains a parable rather than an allegory: there are more
details that are not allegorical than those that are. If the
story were a Christian invention the presence of some of
these details and the lack of others would be hard to
explain—nowhere, for example, is there any hint of the resurrection of Jesus. If we concede that Jesus foresaw his death
as the end to which his course was inevitably leading, that
he unhesitatingly placed himself within the prophetic succession of Israel yet at the same time thought of himself
as in a special and unique way God's Son, there is nothing
in the parable that is incompatible with his teaching as we
otherwise know it. Its lesson is in large part that of
Mt 21:28–32. Finally, while we have the parable only in
its Marcan form as taken over by Matthew and Luke, it
would seem that its substance was also known to the Q
source utilized by these same two evangelists (see on the

Gospel of Matthew in Chapter 1), as evidenced by a saying we have already found in Lk 11:49-51 and which we shall find later in Mt 23:34 f.

The story is true to the Palestinian life of Jesus' time. The *hedge*, the *vat*, and the *tower* mentioned by Matthew and Mark all had their essential roles to play in a Judean vineyard (the details are in Isaiah; Luke omitted them probably because they would have been meaningless to his readers). The hedge was not a neat row of shrubbery but a wall of stones tightly fitted together designed to keep out animals and to protect the vineyard from the flash floods which, in the rainy season, quickly form in the valleys and sweep away any cultivated area in the open. The vat was a winepress as well, or rather, the two were usually found in conjunction: in Palestinian vineyards the grapes were pressed and the fermenting juice was stored right on the scene. The tower was simply a rough shelter of stone, cylindrical in form, covered over at the top with branches, if at all. It was for the use of those who were to watch over the vineyard and protect it from trespassers as well as to give the vines what attention they needed.

The system of sharecroppers or tenant farmers presupposed in the story along with an absentee landlord actually existed, together with the often attendant evils of the system. It was by no means unheard of that tenants would at times forcibly take over the land they worked and whose produce they regarded as their own rather than as belonging to a distant owner. The more distant the owner the greater their temptation and chance of success. In such a situation even the seemingly stupid idea expressed by the tenants that by killing the owner's heir they would "inherit" his vineyard makes some kind of sense. In Isaiah's parable it was the vineyard itself that was unproductive: Israel had not been faithful to the care which God had expended on it. In Jesus' adaptation it is rather the keepers of the vineyard who are condemned, who undoubtedly represent the Jewish leadership.

The *servants* whom the owner of the vineyard sends at

various times and whose fate is described with slight differences of detail by the three evangelists are beyond question the prophets sent to Israel by its God (cf. the Deuteronomic expression, "his servants the prophets," found in Apo 10:7, 11:18). At the end of the list the owner sends *his beloved son.* Here Jesus certainly means himself, but in the parable the son suffers precisely the same treatment as the others, neither more nor less. No attempt has been made to develop a christology from the figure, as later Christian theology would have tended to do.

A christology of sorts is developed, it is true, at the end of the parable, and this ending may very well be an adaptation made by the apostolic Church (cf. Acts 4:11; Rom 9:33; 1 Pt 2:6–8, etc.). The point of Jesus' parable is reached when he says (in Matthew, the listeners say it) that the owner of the vineyard *will come and destroy those vinekeepers and entrust his vineyard to others.* Were these "others" thought of by Jesus as another allegorical detail, or simply as a detail demanded by the logic of the story? Whatever may have been the original intent, the Gospels at least have taken it allegorically, Matthew most obviously of all, according to whom (vs. 43) *the kingdom of God will be taken from you and given to a people who will make it bear fruit* (cf. Mt 13:18–23): for Matthew more than for the other evangelists the kingdom has definitely passed to the Gentiles in the sense that the era of Israel is gone forever. All the Gospels insert at this point (in Luke it is a response to the *Not so!* of the crowd which has seen the application of Jesus' parable) a citation of Ps 118:22 f. which is obviously understood of Christ: he who was rejected by Israel has become the cornerstone of a new edifice of faith, the Church. Luke adds another thought topically related by the word "stone" and seemingly compounded from Is 8:14 and Dan 2:34 f., 44 (the parallel vs. 44 omitted in many manuscripts of Matthew is quite likely an intrusion from Luke): Christ is also a stone of stumbling for many, the occasion, all unwilling, of their destruction (cf. Lk 2:34).

The Gospels conclude with the note that those against whom Jesus had directed his parable understood it all too well. Matthew now joins the others in distinguishing *the crowds* with whom Jesus was popular from the leadership to whom he had become anathema.

Mt 22:1–14 Matthew, however, has yet another parable to contribute to this theme, one which we have already seen in a considerably different form in Luke's Gospel (above on Lk 14:15–24). Both versions of the parable have been adapted and developed in oral tradition, Matthew's probably much more than Luke's. The most striking adaptation which we discover in Matthew's story is the introduction of an entirely new parable at the end.

As Matthew tells the story, it was *a king* who invited guests to a *wedding banquet for his son*. The messianic significance is thus brought out much more definitely from the very beginning (cf. Apo 19:9). Not once only but twice he sends out *his servants* to summon the guests, and now the guests not only decline the invitation but end by killing those who have been sent. The resemblances of this story to the one that precedes it are obvious, but it is not entirely certain that these details should be taken allegorically. In the present perspective of the parable we are not dealing with guests reluctant to attend the social affair of a friend but with subjects in rebellion against the proclamation of a crown prince. Thus when the king *sent his army to destroy those murderers and burn their city,* there may or there may not be a pointed reference to the destruction of Jerusalem by the Romans in A.D. 70. In any case, the teaching of the parable is as before.

But at the end, there is another teaching. As in Luke's version of the parable, substitutes are found for those who were first invited and who refused the invitation, but Matthew observes that those who were brought in were *both bad and good*. We are reminded here of some of Matthew's classic parables of the kingdom, such as that of the weeds and of the dragnet (see above on Mt 13:24–30, 13:47–50).

The remark serves to introduce the additional parable that
continues and concludes the story, and which we should
read for its own proper lesson without expecting it to cohere
closely with the parable that introduced it. We do not ask,
for example, how someone who had been casually accosted
and dragged off to a celebration he had not anticipated
should be expected to appear in proper attire. The question
now is: Is it conceivable that anyone invited to a royal
wedding banquet should appear there and take his place
in his working clothes—blue jeans and a sweat shirt at a
White House reception, perhaps? The only thing to do
with such a misfit is to chuck him out: the parable slips
into its application as it specifies that he is to be cast into
the darkness outside where they wail and gnash their teeth
(cf. Mt 8:12).

Matthew (and Jesus) would not have us think that salvation consists solely in the acceptance of an invitation, as
some "saved" people seem to believe. It is, on the one hand,
God's free gift: no one can assure himself of it on his own
merits. But neither may he appear before his Judge empty-
handed. The guests *called* to the messianic banquet must
have their *wedding garment* to be among the *chosen*. By
"wedding garment" Matthew undoubtedly means not only
faith—the response to the invitation—but also the evidence of
that Christian righteousness which has been set forth especially in the teaching of the Sermon on the Mount. *Many*
and *few*, of course, are not intended as terms of mathematical
precision but as means of emphasis to warn the Christian
against an abuse of God's grace.

Mk 12:13–17   The three Synoptic Gospels continue the
Mt 22:15–22   interchange between Jesus and the Jewish
Lk 20:20–26   leadership of Jerusalem with this story of
                the question of tribute to Caesar. Luke
has it that the question was proposed as a trap by *spies*
sent by the scribes and chief priests, while Matthew follows
Mark in making the culprits *Pharisees and Herodians*. This
same unlikely combination we have seen before (cf. Mk 3:6),

and it is rendered plausible here by what Luke elsewhere tells us of the presence of Herod Antipas in Jerusalem for the Passover. However, as we have observed more than once, the Gospels are not always scrupulous in identifying and distinguishing the various elements that had made up the Jewish opposition to Jesus during his ministry.

It was not a particularly honorable means that had been chosen to get at Jesus, and the way it was gone about made it even less so. The spies pretended to be honestly troubled with doubts as to whether it was *lawful to pay taxes to Caesar,* whether such tribute went counter to their traditions and the Law of Moses. Scruples of conscience always have a claim of priority on any moral teacher, and his advice is consequently sought. The question was, without doubt, a genuine case of conscience for many God-fearing Jews, not simply a matter of reluctance to pay out money or of being forced to acknowledge the dominance of foreigners. In paying the tax to Rome and thereby acknowledging its government over the Jewish people, was one then denying the God who alone was ruler and Lord of Israel? Jesus was therefore being presented with a very live issue. The taxes would be paid in any case; Rome would see to that. But should they be paid? That Jesus saw through the feigned concern of his petitioners and brushed aside the fulsome compliments which they prefaced to their question did not make any less shabby their cynical exploitation of a truly moral problem. At the same time, because it was a truly moral problem the circumstances under which it was posed did not absolve him from giving his answer to it.

The dilemma was a real one. A simple reply that the tribute was lawful would have been odious to most of the people. A simple denial of its legality would have made him liable to denunciation to the Romans for sedition. But of course Jesus did not give a simple answer. *Render to Caesar the things that are Caesar's and to God the things that are God's* was his classic response.

It is to be noted that this answer was not only accepted as adequate by those about Jesus but that they even marveled at it. It was not, then, as some have later thought, merely a clever evasion which he was somehow allowed to get away with, to which no one thought to oppose the obvious sequel: what *is* Caesar's, and what *is* God's? His answer was, indeed, a good one, which evidently remained to guide the apostolic Church in its similar crises of conscience (cf. Rom 13:5-7; 1 Pt 2:13-17).

Jesus asked for one of the coins used in paying taxes, and of course he was handed a piece of Roman money, in this case *a denarius*. He asked *whose face and inscription* appeared on the coin, and of course he was given the obvious answer. By these dramatic gestures he had already forced his tempters to solve their own problem. Or rather, he had forced them to see what their real problem was, which they must now submit to their consciences. In submitting to the Roman state and in using its coinage as their own, they had both received the protection of Rome and had assumed obligations to it. It had been at the invitation of Jews that the Romans had first entered Palestine. Jews continued to derive considerable benefits from Roman rule, which for all its faults was infinitely preferable to the bloody anarchy it had replaced. Rather than question whether it was lawful to pay tribute, ought they not ask whether it was not required by conscience? Without abdicating his kingship over Israel God had used foreign princes before to further his designs on his people (cf. Is 44:28, 45:1; 2 Chron 36:22 f.; Ezra 1:1 ff., etc.); he was the Lord of all history, not merely Israel's, and by his authority kings ruled (cf. Dan 2:21, 37 f.; Prov 8:15 f.; Wis 6:1-3). Political reservations there might be in plenty over the circumstances of the Roman domination of Palestine, but Jesus was not being asked political questions. On moral considerations, it should have been perfectly clear to a Palestinian Jew what it was that belonged to Caesar.

It would be an exaggeration to propose Jesus' teaching in this passage, admirable though it was in its circumstances, as the Gospel's final word on Church and State. The Gospel, as it happens, has no theology of Church and State, nor has a Christian theology of Church and State ever been elaborated in the spirit of the Gospel. Jesus' saying about God and Caesar was an adequate principle for a Palestinian Jew or a first-century Christian, to both of whom the state was completely extraneous, at the best a beneficent irrelevancy which God used to protect his saints, at the worst an occasion for patience and endurance and the discipline of chastisement. It could and should be submitted to in good conscience as part of the order of things willed by God, but its laws and polities were no more a subject for determination by the Jew or Christian than were the laws of nature: another part of the order of things willed by God. By the time the Apocalypse of John was written the principle was already in trouble, as more and more it became impossible to honor a Caesar who now was firmly convinced that he was God. It was most unfortunate for Christianity that when Caesar became Christian he found it hard to break the habits of his fathers, and that the Church's conquest of Antichrist could be thought of as its conversion to the kingdom of God. The Christian men who now formed the state's laws and polities made them seem even more God's order of things, and there the Christian theology of Church and State rested. How little prepared the Church was to cope with the modern state which emerged from the great revolutions that swept aside once and for all the Roman ideas of law and authority, is part of our sad history. It is only in modern times that Christian thinkers have begun to take up realistically once more the problem which Jesus faced realistically in the context of his times. But that is another story, not the Gospel's.

21. BEGINNING OF THE END

Mk 12:18–27 In our last chapter we left Jesus in the
Mt 22:23–33 midst of controversy with the Jews of
Lk 20:27–40 Jerusalem, with hard questions being
asked on both sides. Here we find another
hard question asked in another controversy, this time in a
rare encounter of Jesus with *the Sadducees*. The connection
of this passage with the preceding is probably not incidental: of all the Jews of Palestine, the Sadducees had the
least difficulty in adjusting themselves to Roman rule, not
so much on principle, it is true, as on expediency, since as
largely representatives of the propertied class and the in-
stitutional side of the Jewish religion they had a fierce
instinct for maintaining the *status quo*. Their question
was aimed as much against their enemies the Pharisees as
it was against Jesus, who in their eyes was merely a Pharisaical rabbi, but it obviously raised issues that remained actual
for the Church of the Gospels as well.

The Sadducees *hold that there is no resurrection*, says
our text. Extremely conservative in religion, the Sadducees
accepted only the Law of Moses as divine revelation, rejecting alike the prophetic literature and later writings of the
Old Testament and the oral tradition on which the Pharisees
depended to integrate and explain the whole. Perforce they

rejected belief in a resurrection or in any kind of real survival after death, both of which ideas developed in postexilic Judaism and are never taught in the Torah. Cases such as the one they proposed to Jesus it was their delight, as true believers rejecting the traditions of men, to use to bedevil the orthodox rabbis. The case is on a level with one that a village atheist might use today to ridicule the faith of the godly. Jesus eluded their trap in the only way possible to him, by repudiating the fundamentalist naïveté that is identified with orthodoxy by Sadducees, village atheists, and the godly.

The Sadducees refer to Deut 25:5–10, the so-called levirate or brother-in-law provision of the Torah (whether it was ever a strict law, may be debated), designed both to preserve the name and memory of a man who had been so unfortunate as to die without an heir and to prevent family property from being alienated through his widow's marriage outside the clan. It seems to have been the intention of later laws like Lev 18:16, 20:21 (dating from a time when women as well as men could inherit property and pass it on) to do away with this ancient and somewhat primitive provision, but levirate marriages appear to have continued among the Jews even into Christian times, and this Gospel passage probably indicates that they existed in the Palestine of Jesus. The Sadducees' story stretches the long arm of coincidence in supposing seven so unlucky brothers, but still it was always possible. How, then, does the rabbi answer? If there be a resurrection, whose wife would the woman be?

Belief in the resurrection, in the time of the Gospels or in this twentieth century, is belief in the creative *power of God*. This, Jesus replies, is precisely what the Sadducees do not understand. The idea of a resurrection appears childish to them because they have never thought of it except in childish terms, as though it meant the reanimation of corpses which would continue the human process of eating and drinking, loving and hating, giving in marriage and taking wives. The resurrection, however, means first and foremost our translation into a new mode of existence (cf. 1 Cor 15:51–53), when we shall be *like the angels* or, as Paul would later write to the Corinthians, possessing spiritual rather than fleshly bodies (cf. 1 Cor 15:42–50). The power of God which can call men back from death is not limited by the materiality of man's ability to conceive of it. The reference to the angels is, of course, another slap at the Sadducees, who denied the existence of a spiritual order (cf. Acts 23:8).

The Sadducees also *do not know the Scriptures.* Jesus cites Ex 3:6, the passage about Moses and the burning bush, because this was Scripture also received by the Sadducees. That God identified himself to Moses as *the God of Abraham and the God of Isaac and the God of Jacob* might not occur to us as a proof of survival after death; however, it was evidently an argument that was significant for the Jews. And, as a matter of fact, there is more to it than meets the eye. *He is not the God of the dead but of the living.* The experience of the living God was what had given pious Jews their first groping thoughts about immortality, the conviction that somehow the vital contact would be preserved, that this God would never wholly abandon those whom he had made his own (cf. Pss 16: 8 ff., 49:15 f., 73:23 ff.).

Mk 12:28–34 Luke (vs. 39) concluded the story of the
Mt 22:34–40 dialogue with the Sadducees by noting
the approval of *the scribes* who were standing by, and as Mark tells the following story of Jesus' conversation with *one of the scribes* we have a friendly dialogue by honest enquiry. This fits somewhat strangely in the present context of controversy, and it is likely that Mark has brought it in from some other time and place simply to complete the sequence: Pharisees and Herodians, Sadducees, and now scribes. Matthew has adjusted the story to its polemical surroundings: in his Gospel the question of *the lawyer* is a test inspired by the Pharisees. Luke's earlier version of the

story (see above on Lk 10:25–28) did not make it altogether clear in what spirit the question was asked.

Jesus is asked *what is the greatest commandment.* The question is posed in a legalist sense. As the rabbis analyzed the Law, it was made up of 613 distinct commandments, 248 of them positive (the "do's") and 365 negative (the "don't's"). They distinguished between great commandments and small, and even very great and very small. Jesus replies, however, by giving as the greatest commandment the spirit of what Matthew knows as *the Law and the prophets* (see above on Mt 5:17–20). Though he himself distinguishes two commandments, it is obviously only for the purpose of showing how they coalesce in one and are inseparable one from the other. He begins with the *Shema,* the words of Deut 6:4 f., in which other high-minded rabbis had found a summation of the Law's spirit, and to this he adds Lev 19:18, the precept of the love of neighbor. It is disputed whether in the time of Jesus Lev 19:18 was already recited as part of the *Shema;* at all events, it is true that some of the rabbis regarded it as the greatest of the Law's commandments. The greatness of Jesus' teaching does not consist simply in his association of these two precepts and in the radical connection that he perceived between them, but also in the new dimension that he gave to both. If love of God above all is to be the motive and form of every act, and if experientially this love is to find itself in the love and service of the neighbor, it obviously matters very much who the neighbor is perceived to be (see above on Lk 10:29–37). Reciprocally, the dimension that is given to "neighbor" determines existentially who the God is that is loved and served in him.

In Mark's story Jesus discovers a kindred spirit in the scribe, who paraphrases his response with approval, recognizing in it the authentic voice of Israel's prophets (cf. 1 Sam 15:22; Hos 6:6, to which he alludes). In turn, Jesus tells him that he is *not far from the kingdom of God,* and we have every reason to hope that he followed him there.

Mk 12:35–37a   In all three Gospels Jesus terminates this
Mt 22:41–46   series of interchanges by proposing a final
Lk 20:41–44   enigma for solution. The device appears
                 to have proved eminently successful, since
commentators on this passage have remained puzzled
ever after. The question is, how would Jesus himself have
answered what his adversaries are unable to answer? This is
what the Gospels do not tell us, for what seems to be the
quite sufficient reason that they did not know. The enigmatic
quality of the passage makes it another of those about whose
authentic connection with Jesus' teaching we have the least
doubt in reading the Gospels. A saying of this kind, of
whose meaning no one is exactly sure, is hardly invented,
though it is most easily remembered.

Whose son is the Messiah? The answer to that was easy,
and it is given unhesitatingly. "The son of David" was
doubtless the most commonly used title for the Messiah
among Palestinian Jews. As we know, it is a title that Jesus
never applies to himself, not even in John's Gospel where
his teaching so often is phrased in the language and concepts of a developed Christian theology. His own view of his
role in the economy of divine salvation was far too complex
to be expressed by a simple identification with the Davidic
Messiah. There was a sense in which he was the Messiah,
and to this the Gospels and all of the New Testament
testify. There was a sense in which he definitely was not,
and it was this that necessitated the "messianic secret" (see
above on Mk 1:22–28 and parallel). Certainly he was not
the Messiah in the sense in which doubtless most of his
contemporaries thought of the Messiah.

It seems that in this story Jesus tried to suggest some of
the complexities of the messianic question as he knew it
but which were bypassed in the conventional messianic thinking of Palestine. He quotes Ps 110:1, as it was commonly
accepted among the Jews of his time, as a verse written
by David under divine inspiration in referring to the Messiah:
The Lord said to my Lord . . . If the Messiah is rightly
called David's son, nevertheless how can David speak of him

not as one whose greatest glory it will be to re-create the Davidic age as his worthy successor, but as his own Lord indeed? The paradox is brought out at its clearest in the Greek version of the Old Testament cited by the Gospels, where the same word *kyrios* is used to translate the first "Lord" (the God of Israel) and the second (the Messiah). However, much the same effect would have been produced by the use of the Hebrew text or an Aramaic translation, since it is the second "Lord" that poses the problem. Given the accepted meaning of the verse about which there was no dispute, in it David spoke of the Messiah as someone far more exalted than himself.

Jesus' question is left hanging in the air. It is answered neither by his audience nor by the Gospels. Since it is plain, however, that he asked it neither for curiosity's sake nor merely as a clever conundrum to discomfit his enemies, we may presume to find in it an attempt at self-revelation. In this passage we can discover, however obscurely, another of the Synoptic testimonials to Jesus' awareness of divine sonship that is the commonplace of John's Gospel.

Mt 23:1–14 The following discourse is somewhat em-
Mk 12:37b–40 barrassing both in its length and in its
Lk 20:45–47 harshness, but it must be faced up to
both as an historical record and as part of the Gospel message. It comes appositely enough at the conclusion of a series of controversies with the Jewish leadership, and doubtless it does represent some kind of terminal judgment of Jesus on his scribal opposition. The few verses of Mark and Luke have been replaced in Matthew by a schematic arrangement that extends over nearly an entire chapter, but the longer version is scarcely more bitter than the shorter. For the First Gospel, as we have observed more than once before, the question of Jewish opposition was still a much liver issue than it was for the Christians for whom Mark and Luke wrote: this explains both the length of Matthew's treatment and the fact that he has broadened the condemnation into a diatribe against both *the scribes*

and the Pharisees, against normative Jewry, in other words. Nevertheless, it is not simply anti-Jewish. It can even be conceived as a kind of defense of the Jews, among whom must be counted Jesus and his first disciples and the earliest Christian tradition on which the discourse depends, against those whom it regards as their betrayers and false guides: Jesus speaks *to* the people *about* the scribes and Pharisees. Neither is it a condemnation of all the scribes and far less of all the Pharisees. It is a repudiation of certain of their tendencies that certainly existed, that were prevalent enough to be taken as typical, and which were symptomatic of all that was opposed to Christ and Christianity. The discourse should neither be exaggerated beyond its intentions nor minimized because of them.

The scribes and Pharisees have taken their place on the chair of Moses, Jesus begins. This is no blanket rejection of Pharisaism or of rabbinical Judaism, the legitimacy of which Jesus did not question. By and large, Jesus himself would have been regarded by his contemporary Jews as a Pharisee and a scribe, though in neither instance a professional. The Lord addresses himself to matters of practice, and immediately we are reminded of various passages in the Sermon on the Mount. Luke has also included some of the examples in his record of Jesus' denunciation of Pharisaical piety (see above on Lk 11:37-54). New is the reference to the widening of *phylacteries* and *tassels*. Phylacteries, still used at times of prayer by conservative and orthodox Jews (by whom they are called *tefillin*), were little boxes containing bits of parchment on which were written various verses of the Law, which were bound with straps to the left arm and on the forehead and worn in literalist obedience to Deut 6:6-8. The "professional" Pharisee would wear them all day long and be sure that they were large enough to be seen. So would they do with the tassels which all good Jews wore (see above on Mk 5:21-43 and parallels) in obedience to the Law (cf. Num 15:37-41; Deut 22:12).

Jesus mentions three titles in which these religionists took particular pride: *rabbi, father,* and *teacher.* Properly, these

were all titles borne by the scribes, and essentially they
amounted to the same thing. They were honored names
bestowed by a people who reverenced learning and who,
by using them, intended less to glorify the learned than the
learning itself, which was the knowledge of the Law, the
word of God. They were applied, at various times, to Jesus
himself, who never rejected them. And of course, there was
nothing wrong in them. What made them wrong was their
being taken seriously, as titles of personal excellence, as
though those whom we entitle "your honor" or "excellency"
or "lordship" or "eminence" and the like should suddenly
translate these honorifics of office to their own human selves
as somehow setting them apart from other human selves.
You, says Jesus, must *avoid* such things. The "you," there
can be no doubt, is the Christian Church. The Church
avoids what Jesus was talking about not by determining the
nomenclature of office but by raising up doctors who know
the difference between ministers of Christ and the lords of
the Gentiles (see above on Mk 9:33–37 and parallels; Mk
10:35–45 and parallel).

In verse 13 Matthew begins a series of seven "woes"
against the scribes and Pharisees, the first of which is a
parallel of Lk 11:52. The second does not appear in verse
14, which on the manuscript evidence is an addition to his
text from Mk 12:40 and Lk 20:47. It is no less a reproach
to be brought against the scribes and Pharisees, however,
who in any case *devour the savings of widows and recite
long prayers to keep up appearances.* What seems to be involved in this change is that, contrary to the spirit of the
laws of Num 27:5–11, 36:5–9 (which in principle guaranteed inheritance through female as well as male descend-
ants), the Pharisees had decided that widows could not
inherit from their husbands but rather must contract another
marriage in order to guarantee their economic and social
identity. They had even decreed that daughters could not
inherit directly from their fathers but only through their
sons. Contrary to such rules the early Christian Church

regarded widows as a category of persons apart, possessed
of rights on the whole community and to be honored in
their own estate (cf. Acts 6:1, 9:39, 41; 1 Tim 5:3–16;
Jas 1:27).

Mt 23:15–22   The second and third of Matthew's "woes"
are proper to his Gospel. The *converts*
of whom Jesus speaks were undoubtedly proselytes to Judaism out of paganism: in the first Christian century Judaism was an immensely successful proselytizing religion. It
is not proselyting that is condemned here, but the "pharisaiz-
ing" of proselytes, evidently. What is meant by the proselytes
becoming *sons of gehenna twice as bad* as the scribes and
Pharisees is not specified, but it is well known that converts
to a system are usually its staunchest supporters. The casuistry over oaths we have seen discussed in the Sermon on
the Mount (above on Mt 5:33–37) and in respect to practices like the *korban* (see above on Mk 7:1–13 and parallel).

Mt 23:23–36   The remainder of the discourse is closely
paralleled as to content in Lk 11:37–54.
In Matthew's fourth "woe" Luke's "mint and rue and every
herb" has become *mint and dill and cumin,* and Matthew
has included the expressive saying about those who *filter
out a gnat while swallowing a camel whole*—one of those
inspired impossibilities like leading a camel through a needle's eye. A more serious difference with Luke appears in
the fifth "woe" concerning those who *clean the outside of
the cup and the dish* (Matthew used another word for the
latter vessel, which is unimportant). Luke's version contrasted
the Pharisees' zeal for the cleanliness of things with their
lack of concern for their own interiors. Matthew's use of the
saying turns it into a parable in which the cup and dish
stand for the scribes and Pharisees themselves: outwardly
they are clean, for they take great care to surround themselves with the signs of piety, but within they are guilty

of all uncleanness. *Cleanse the inside of the cup so that the outside may also become clean* means, obviously, that if they would be sincere in their piety and practice genuine righteousness the externals would take care of themselves.

Luke spoke of the Pharisees as "hidden graves" by which men are contaminated unawares. Matthew's sixth "woe" varies the figure: they are like *whitewashed tombs*, nice to look at from the outside, but containing in themselves corruption. Tombs were customarily painted white so that they would be clearly visible even at night and thus the more easily avoided. The last of the "woes" is an expansion of one that Luke directs against the scribes, in which the Christ of the Matthaean Church speaks, condemning not only the murders of the past but also those that are to come, when he will send other *prophets and wise men and scribes* to be hunted down and crucified by these killers of the prophets. These titles should not be seized on as offering any indication of the constitution of the apostolic Church, however, since they are simply the applicable Old Testament terms extended into New Testament times. The most curious of the variants in Matthew's text is the identification of the *Zechariah* of 2 Chron 24:20–22 (whose father's name, according to the same passage, was Jehoiada) as *the son of Barachiah*. This is the result of a confusion with another, more famous prophet Zechariah (cf. Zech 1:1), and for this reason the phrase has been omitted in some of the manuscripts of Matthew's Gospel.

At the conclusion of this discourse Matthew has Jesus utter the words over Jerusalem which we have already seen placed in a somewhat better context by Luke (above on Lk 13:34 f. and parallel).

Mk 12:41–44
Lk 21:1–4
Possibly because of the somber tone achieved in the discourse on the scribes and Pharisees which is to be sustained in the eschatological discourse that follows, Matthew has omitted this little story about the widow and her gift which

Mark and Luke have told. Though it has not always been given its proper place of honor in the Church, the evangelists surely intended that churchmen should reflect on it when considering to whom it is that the Church owes the most for the support of itself and its works. Most churchmen, whether or not they follow out its implications, know it to be a story that is profoundly true.

The treasury was in the temple courtyard, where there were thirteen chests for donations, each marked for a separate purpose. Particularly at the time of the great feasts there would be considerable activity about the treasury as the many pilgrims came to make their offerings. The Gospel does not necessarily imply that the wealthy were making a show of their large donations; generous giving was accepted as a matter of course. Jesus' saying simply regards the relative value of the gifts, depending on the sacrifice involved. The rich gave much because they could afford to do so, but the poor widow gave everything that she had. What she gave, in absolute figures, the Gospel calls *two lepta,* undoubtedly using the *lepton,* the smallest Greek coin in circulation, as the equivalent of the Palestinian *perutah:* two *perutoth* was the smallest offering accepted. Mark further translates the sum for his Roman readers as a *quadrans* which, as the name indicates, was the fourth part of a Roman *as,* a copper coin worth about one cent.

Jn 12:37–50   We are about to take up the Synoptic eschatological discourse, which in the three Synoptic Gospels represents Jesus' final words of teaching before the beginning of the passion story proper. Before we do this, it will be just as well that we see the corresponding section in John's Gospel, which appears immediately before he begins his story of the passion. There is little resemblance on the surface, yet a line of connection exists between the two endings in the two traditions. If it is with an eschatological message that the Synoptics leave us, John also concludes on a note of eschatology, the "realized" eschatology that is the emphasis of his Gospel.

But first, as John brings to a close the first half of his Gospel, his "book of signs," he offers his answer to a question that plagued the early Church more than did many others, namely, the scandal of Jewish incredulity. This Jesus Christ in whom a now largely Gentile Church believed as its risen Lord and so confidently proclaimed in Old Testament terms as Messiah, Son of God and Son of Man, the Word of prophecy incarnate, why had he ended by being rejected, generally speaking, by the people of the Old Testament? Why had it been that he came unto his own and his own received him not?

John insists, first of all, that the rejection of Jesus was foreseen by God and included in his plan of salvation. This was one of the earliest affirmations of the Church, that in his shameful death and repudiation Jesus had fulfilled the prophetic role of the suffering Servant of the Lord (cf. Acts 2:23, 3:13; 1 Cor 15:3; and Rom 10:16 which also cites Is 53:1 along with John). If this was the case, then in their unbelief the Jews were only bringing to pass God's prophetic word: *they could not believe*. In this connection, and to the same purpose, John quotes Is 6:10 which the Synoptic Gospels use to explain Jesus' lack of success with his parabolic teaching (see above on Mk 4:10–12 and parallels). John adds that *Isaiah said this because he saw his glory and spoke of him*. It was the glory of Yahweh, the God and King of Israel, that Isaiah saw in vision (cf. Is 6:3). However, for John the glory of the Father and of the Son are one and the same (cf. vs. 28 above), and he doubtless thinks of the pre-existent Christ as active in the Old Testament. In announcing the failure of his own prophetic ministry Isaiah also spoke of Christ's, for they are two phases of the same word directed to the same recalcitrant people.

But why was this prophetic word uttered? Why did God have to include this obduracy in the construction of his economy of salvation? John can only say that *they loved the glory of men rather than the glory of God* (cf. Jn 5:44). We are left with the impression that John recognizes the inadequacy of this explanation, however true it may have been. In Rom 9–11 Paul explores the mystery of Israel more deeply than this, from the same standpoint of Jewish unbelief. But neither did Paul emerge with a definitive answer. The relation of Judaism to the Church in the final working out of God's kingdom is a matter on which the New Testament has uttered no ultimate word, and with it Christian theology continues to grapple.

In verse 36 John brought Jesus' public teaching to a close with the note that he now retired from the sight of men. It is doubtful, therefore, that the evangelist intends the concluding verses of this chapter of his Gospel to represent a new discourse, which in any case would be quite anticlimactic after his own peroration. Rather, they appear to be a summation drawn from the preceding discourses of the "book of signs" to allow John to portray dramatically and for one final time in the Lord's own words the light of revelation whose rejection he has just described. No new theme is introduced by these verses. Appropriately, the here-and-nowness of God's eternal judgment is brought to the fore, and we are left with the figure of the Christ of faith continuously present offering himself as eternal life for man's acceptance or refusal.

Mk 13:1–2 The Synoptic eschatological discourse begins
Mt 24:1–2 in all three Gospels with Jesus' prediction
Lk 21:5–6 of the destruction of the Jerusalem temple,
a prophecy that was to be fulfilled some forty years later, on August 9, A.D. 70, to be exact. That Jesus actually made such a prophecy, in view of his consistent eschatological teaching on the soonness of a divine visitation on Jerusalem and Judea, his conviction of the decisiveness of his own role in the workings of salvation history, and his reading of the temper of the times, there is absolutely no reason to question. His words are in the tradition of Israel's prophecy (cf. Jer 7:1–15; Ezek 24:15–23) and have not been simply made up by Christian

writers in the light of later events. For one thing, the
temple was not pulled down stone by stone, as a literalist
interpretation of the prophecy would suggest, but was destroyed by fire against the orders of the Roman commander
by the soldiers who were enraged at Jerusalem's having
held out so long against their siege. One of the charges
made against Jesus at his trial was that he had spoken of the
destruction of the temple (cf. Mk 14:58 and parallel).

The occasion of Jesus' prophecy is the exclamation of the
disciples over the grandeur of the temple and its annexed
buildings. Even today when one first looks over the temple
area from the Mount of Olives he cannot fail to be struck by
the impressiveness of what he sees. However, the singularly
beautiful mosque called the Dome of the Rock which now
dominates the area could hardly be compared in any way
with the sight that greeted the eyes of him who looked
down on Herod's temple. The whiteness of its massive stones
and the gold of its façade made it one of the known wonders
of the world, and no Jew could look upon it without feeling a
natural surge of pride in his race and his religion. Thus the
shock, such as we can hardly imagine, that must have been
caused by Jesus' words. Who could conceive a world without
the temple? The end of the temple would mean the end of
sacrifice, and surely sacrifice would end only with the world
itself.

It is this association of related ideas that is reflected in
Matthew's version of the discourse as it continues, according
to which the disciples ask the time not of the destruction of
the temple but *the sign of your parousia and the end of the
world*. This is much more precise than their question as it
appears in Mark and Luke. All the Gospels, of course, are far
more concerned with the eschatological question as it affected the Christian of the first century than as it would
have presented itself to a pre-Christian Jew. Matthew, therefore, besides mentioning explicitly the two ideas that were
associated in the minds of the disciples, has also phrased
their question in Christian terms.

Mk 13:3–8   The two ideas, end of the temple and end of
Mt 24:3–8   all, continue to be associated in the discourse
Lk 21:7–11   that now follows as the Gospels tell of Jesus'
             answer to his disciples—only Mark notes that
these were *Peter, James, and John,* his three chosen intimates,
together with *Andrew,* Peter's brother. Certainly in the
thought of the evangelists the destruction of Jerusalem and
its temple—an event which, for Matthew and Luke at least,
had by now already taken place—was the first act in the
drama of the end-time in which the Church was now living,
the last act of which would be the Lord's glorious *parousia*
(see above on Lk 17:20 f.). In this view the New Testament
is one. Even in such a work as the Gospel of John with
its strong emphasis on "realized" eschatology that we know
so well, the expectation of an eventual end of this present
order and beginning of a new age in a final judgment and
resurrection remains accepted doctrine. The only appreciable
difference among the New Testament writings in their views
on the *parousia* and its aftermath is as regards when all this
will take place, quite soon or in the indefinite future? This
difference has no more complicated explanation than the
process of continuing history, as the *parousia* was more and
more "delayed" and as this or that "sign" that had been
thought of as pointing to its coming proved to be no
sign at all. Of course, the "delay" of the *parousia* had
enormous influence on the development of New Testament
theology, especially the theology of the Church. No one is
disposed to bother much about organizing or theorizing on a
Church that will at best be in existence for only a few
months or years. It is a vastly different matter when the
Church must think of itself, finally, in terms of becoming one
of the semi-permanent institutions existing in this world.

But what of Jesus himself? Did he make the same association of ideas as did the early Church? Many today think
that he did not, that the idea of a *parousia* and an end of
this present world has been imposed on his teaching by an
apocalyptically minded Church for reasons of its own contrary to, or at least not in accord with, his original in-

tentions. (This is the exact reversal of a theory of a half-century or so ago, which wanted to explain everything in Jesus' teaching as derived from his obsession with the imminent end of the world.) According to these scholars, Jesus either believed that with him the kingdom of God had come into the world once and for all, with nothing more to follow, or that, at the most, the kingdom would be definitively brought in through some soon to come historical crisis, such as the end of Jerusalem. The Church apocalypticized Jesus' simple message either to explain away inconsistencies that had not yet become apparent in his lifetime, or merely because most of the early Christians thought in apocalyptic categories whereas Jesus had not.

Such a theory does violence to the New Testament evidence and to reason. Our first contact wth Christian literature is from about A.D. 50, in Paul's first letter to the Thessalonian church. From this writing it is evident that the expectation of the *parousia* was already an "ancient" Christian doctrine, so much so that it had been made the occasion of a good deal of peripheral and bootless speculation about details and nonessentials. From then on, concern about it as a pressing event tends to decrease rather than increase. All this had occurred, independently of Jesus, within a period of some twenty years of his death? Suppose that it had: whence did it come? There was no precedent for it in Judaism—though both the word and the concept of *parousia* seem to be present in Dan 7:13—for the perfectly adequate reason that Judaism knew of no dying and resurrected Messiah, and therefore of no reason that he should return. It makes far better sense to credit the idea to Jesus than to anyone else. And why not to Jesus? That he believed that the kingdom of God had, in some fashion, begun with his preaching in Galilee, the Gospel seems to tell us on every page. That he also foresaw an imminent judgment of his own people, as we have just said, also seems to be inescapable. But that he should have made no pronouncement on his *parousia* is simply incredible. He knew that his death was necessary for the kingdom. But if death, resurrection; and if resurrection, *parousia*.

Otherwise we find incomprehensible one of the affirmations on which all four Gospels are in the most solid agreement: that Jesus identified himself above all and by preference with the eschatological Son of Man, the judge and savior.

All this is said not to deny that here as elsewhere the evangelists have given us the Lord's words in the interpretation of the Church from which they had received them. In this passage which begins to speak of the time of the end of Jerusalem, Mark, followed by Matthew as usual, has responded with the doubtlet of a passage which he later uses in verses 21–25 where the reference is obviously to the last times; with his customary tidiness, Luke has avoided most of the repetition. What must be insisted upon is that the apocalyptic mentality reflected in these Synoptic passages and elsewhere in the New Testament was one in which Jesus shared. Apocalyptic, despite its to us at times bizarre imagery, was a way of thought with a high and serious purpose truly rooted in the Old Testament revelation. It was a way of thought that could get out of hand, obviously, as can any other. Jesus could not be called an apocalyptist in the sense that apocalyptic dominated all his thinking, just as he could not be called a legalist merely because he upheld the Law. But apocalyptic had a part in his teaching even as did historical and realized eschatology. It is part of the religion of Christianity. Remove it, and the vital New Testament concepts of prophetic witness and sacrifice are removed along with it. Apocalyptic affirms that this world is under judgment. Remove it, and the city of man becomes the city of God by its wishing so, while the transforming word of Christ is reduced to a "social gospel." The world is not evil, as some apocalyptists thought of it or think of it now, but it is the mission field of the Church in view of the kingdom of God, and there is a real sense in which it must come to an end and be changed.

Speaking of the "signs" that will precede "these things," Jesus refers to the *many* who *will come in my name*, pretending, in other words, to be the Messiah. There were,

in fact, various persons who assumed this character before
the fall of Jerusalem. The Acts of the Apostles names several:
a certain Theudas and a Judas of Galilee (Acts 5:35–37)
and an unnamed Egyptian Jew (Acts 21:38); and undoubtedly there were others. The times were filled with
messianic hope, and it was inevitable that messiahs would
come forward to satisfy it. However, this as well as the
other warnings about *wars and rumors of wars, earthquakes,*
and the like, borrow from standard apocalyptic imagery
relating to the last times. *This is the beginning of the birthpangs:* this term and concept is borrowed from prophetic
texts like Is 66:7–9; Hos 13:13. "The birthpangs of the
Messiah" referred to the travails that must be undergone by
the world or by the messianic people as a condition for the
birth of the messianic age.

Lk 21:12–19	From the general trials of the messianic
Mk 13:9–13	times Jesus descends to the specific suffer-
Mt 24:9–14	ings to be undergone by his disciples.

Both Matthew and Luke have already partly
paralleled this section in telling of earlier instructions and
warnings given to the disciples (see above on Mt 10:16b–25
and parallel). It appears most likely that the original purview
of Jesus' words had to do with what the disciples might
expect in Jerusalem and Judea in the troubled times of
the Jewish Church immediately following his crucifixion and
resurrection, the period covered in the first chapters of the
Acts of the Apostles. Luke and Mark tend to preserve
this prospect, with its references to the *synagogues* and local
Jewish *courts* into which the first Christians would be haled
to give account of themselves (cf. 2 Cor 11:24). In verse 10,
however, Mark has what is probably his own comment on the
discourse which has adapted it to the later viewpoint of the
Church to which the Gentile mission had been revealed: *but
first the Gospel must be proclaimed to all the nations* (cf.
Rom 11:11 f., 25 f.). In verse 14 Matthew repeats and ex-
pands on this idea, and in keeping with it describes the

persecutions as emanating more from Gentiles than from Jews.

Mk 13:14–20   Jesus now speaks of the destruction of
Mt 24:15–22   Jerusalem as a pre-eminent sign of the last
Lk 21:20–24   times. *When you see Jerusalem being surrounded by an army* in Luke is doubtless
a free paraphrase in more prosaic terms of the Semitisms of
Mark and Matthew, the paraphrase of a tradition that had
been the fulfillment of the Lord's prediction (see also on
Lk 19:41–44 above). Mark and Matthew quote Jesus as
designating the sign by what has been traditionally translated
the abomination of desolation (that is, an abominable thing
which destroys) *standing where it ought not* (Matthew
specifies, *in the holy place*). The reference is to Dan 9:27,
11:31, 12:11, and what was meant there was the desecration
of the temple in 167 B.C. by the Syrian king Antiochus IV
Epiphanes (cf. 1 Macc 1:54, 6:7), who had erected in it an
altar and statue of the Olympian Zeus. Antiochus' terrible
persecution of the Jews eventually led to the wars of the
Maccabees and the establishment of an independent Jewish
kingdom that was to exist until internal dissensions brought
in the power of Rome. *Let him who reads take note!* means
that what had occurred in Maccabean times will once more
be a sign, and when the abomination of desolation again appears, *those who are in Judea should flee to the mountains.*
Their flight must be precipitous and unhesitating, Jesus
adds. Woe to him who has any kind of encumbrances!
Simply pray that it be not necessary to flee *in winter,* when
travel was virtually impossible, *or on the Sabbath,* when
those bound by the Law were forbidden to travel.

Whatever may have been Jesus' precise intention in proposing "the abomination of desolation" as a sign, it appears
that Luke's interpretation of it was commonly held by the
Christians of Palestine. In A.D. 66 the first great Jewish revolt
against the Romans broke out, and in the following year the
Roman legions were already surrounding Jerusalem, occupy-
ing the rebellious towns of Galilee and Judea one by one. A

reliable tradition has it that at that time the Christian popu-
lation migrated across the Jordan to Pella in Perea (by some
Pella was counted as part of the Decapolis), not to return to
Jerusalem till after it had been seized and sacked by the
Romans in A.D. 70.

Mk 13:21-27   Already in their references to the *shorten-*
Mt 24:23-31   *ing of the days* of travail in favor of God's
Lk 21:25-28   *elect,* lest all living creatures should perish,
                the Gospels have shifted their view from
the beginning of the last times to their continuation as leading to the final appearance of *the Son of Man.* The highly
apocalyptic description of the last times that now follows in
Mark has been somewhat heightened by Matthew and toned
down considerably by Luke. It is a mélange of prophetico-
apocalyptic allusions from the Old Testament (cf. Is 13:10,
27:13, 34:4; Ezek 32:7 f.; Dan 7:13 f.; Joel 2:10; Hab 1:8,
etc.): such an "anthological" style is one of the prime
characteristics of apocalyptics as a literary form, as can
easily be seen from its best exemplification in the New
Testament Apocalypse of John, a book which is literally a
tissue of such allusions.

It is conceivable that even in an apocalyptic passage of
this intensity the Gospels, or perhaps Matthew and Luke,
have historicized and realized the prophetic vision in events
that had already taken place in the emergence of the
Church, thus returning apocalyptic to its own origins, which
were the prophecy of contemporary historical deeds and
occurrences. Luke ends his description by the note that all
these things are signs that *your redemption is near.* "Redemption," found only this once in the Gospels, is eminently a
Pauline term which is usually, though not always, eschatological: the redemption of Christians is the object of their present
hope, the consummation of God's kingdom in the resurrection of the just. Taken eschatologically here it makes admirable sense. It is just possible, however, that by it Luke
means the liberation of Christianity from Judaism. The
cataclysm of A.D. 70 was a sign of the eschatological age—it

manifested, in some way, the kingdom of God—because out of it the Church came forth on its own, never more to be taken by anyone (as it had been taken in the beginning by outsider and insider alike) as merely another Jewish sect. It was now freed for the conquest of the Gentile world—*they will assemble his chosen ones from the four winds,* Matthew says. It might be considered, therefore, that in some real sense the Son of Man had in this event already been made manifest in his glory to the world, in the same kind of realized eschatology with which we are familiar from the Gospel of John.

Mk 13:28–32 Such an interpretation, if the Gospels were
Mt 24:32–36 patient of it, would remove all difficulties
Lk 21:29–33 from the verses that follow. Though it is
not necessarily entirely wrong, however, neither is it adequate of itself alone to elucidate the fullness of Jesus' teaching as the Gospels seem to have understood it. Jesus evidently intends, now and finally, to respond to the disciples' initial question as to when "all these things" would come to pass. "All these things," as we saw, were not only the destruction of Jerusalem, but also the Lord's *parousia* and the end of the world, all of which together formed a single concept, in the mind of Jesus as well as in the mind of the disciples.

If *parousia* and the coming historical crisis formed a single concept, nevertheless it is not true to conclude that they were simply identified. All through his public preaching Jesus has been rebuking the Palestinians for their failure to read the signs of the times (for example, see above on Mk 8:11 f. and parallels), to recognize, in other words, that on historical grounds an intervention of God was inevitable and coming soon. This is also the lesson of *the parable of the fig tree,* which has been carefully chosen as a sign of things to come. In Palestine, where most of the trees are evergreen, the fig tree's sudden leaving into green indicates, as other trees do not, *that summer is near.* Luke accommodates the parable to a non-Palestinian audience when he simply equates the fig tree with *all the other trees*. So, Jesus applies the parable, *when you see these things happening, you will realize that he is near, standing at your door,* or, as Luke paraphrases, *the kingdom of God is near*—the "he" being the Son of Man, the eschatological judge and savior.

The difficulty is not only that Jesus seems to be speaking of the predictability of what in the next breath he says is unpredictable, but also that it is hard to know what is the antecedent of "these things." The apocalyptic "signs" in the moon and sun and stars, and so forth, of the preceding context are not thought of as indicative of the proximity of the *parousia* but rather of its presence as a *fait accompli;* by its very nature, an apocalyptic inbreaking of God into history and ending history is unpredictable, as indeed Jesus goes on to say. By now, however, it should have become plain that the eschatological discourse is a composite work in which not every verse now stands in its original historical context. As far as the Gospels are concerned, it is likely enough that their authors took the historical crisis to be a sign of the soon coming *parousia* and interpreted this verse accordingly, preserving the outlook of the primitive Christian community. It is equally likely that Jesus first uttered the verse in reference to the coming historical crisis itself, in keeping with the sense of the parable and in the pattern of his other similar utterances. In the same way we should probably understand his further word that *this generation will not pass away before all these things come to be.* The following saying on the passing away of heaven and earth has been obviously adapted to this context for topical reasons (cf. Mt 5:18; Lk 16:17).

We are not saying that Jesus could not have looked on the coming destruction of the temple as an immediate sign of the *parousia,* but that he does not seem to have. If there is a series of words ascribed to him in which the kingdom of God is presented as coming quite soon or, indeed, as already present in some fashion, there is an even more impressive series in which its suddenness and unexpectedness is the theme: such is the message of practically all of the "parables

of the kingdom." We have discussed this situation before
(see above on Mk 8:34–9:1 and parallels; Lk 17:20f.).
The final words of Jesus recorded by Mark and Matthew in
this section belong to this last series and even explain it:
*Concerning that day or its hour no one knows, not even the
angels of heaven, nor even the Son, but only the Father.*

Once more we are reading one of those absolutely convinc-
ing sayings of Jesus that no one can imagine the early
Christians having made up: "nor even the Son" is missing
from a significant number of important manuscripts of Matthew's Gospel and that evangelist may in fact have omitted
the words; Luke certainly omitted the whole saying. It is,
nevertheless, a most precious contribution to our understanding of the historical process of God's revelation in Jesus
Christ. At the very least, we are given to know that the time
of the *parousia* was not a part of what Christ had come to
reveal concerning God and his designs. But the text says
more than that. In his incarnational state Jesus did not play-
act as man but freely took upon himself the limitations of
the human condition that he embraced (cf. Heb 2:17, 4:15).
Of what he did not reveal he himself had no effective
knowledge. Theoretically at least, he too could have shared
the Church's expectation of an early *parousia*.

Mk 13:33–37   Mark and Luke conclude the eschatologi-
Lk 21:34–36   cal discourse analogously but not in parallel. Mark's emphasis is on vigilance in
view of the uncertainty of the time of the Lord's coming,
and in the process he tells a parable which we have already
seen in more developed form in Luke's Gospel (above on Lk
19:11–28) and will see again in Matthew's (below on Mt
25:14–30). Luke, too, insists on vigilance, but in Pauline
terms (cf. 1 Thes 5:1–11), moralizing the eschatological
message as he has done before (see above on Lk 3:10–14).

Mt 24:37–44   It is Matthew who has done the most with
the same theme, for he has made the eschatological discourse the fifth and last of his major dis-

courses over which he has mainly divided the teachings of
Jesus. He continues, therefore, with a series of sayings and
parables, the first collection of which we have already seen
at two places in Luke's Gospel with no appreciable difference
in meaning (see above on Lk 17:22–37, 12:35–40). The
parable with which he concludes his chapter 24 we have also
already considered (see above on Lk 12:41–48 and parallel).

Mt 25:1–13   The following parable, however, is proper
                 to Matthew's Gospel, aside from what may
be a few echoes of it here and there in Mark and Luke. As in
the preceding story, a point is made of the *delay* in an
expected coming, a factor which serves to sharpen the stress
on constant vigilance and preparedness for an eschatologically
minded Church.

The parable tells of *ten virgins who took their lamps and
went outside to meet the bridegroom* (not "and his bride":
this is an addition in some manuscripts made by someone
who did not understand the background of the story). The
wedding customs of Palestine have not changed greatly over
the centuries. The festivities extended over several days, and
their solemn conclusion took place when the bridegroom
and his friends came in procession to the home of the bride,
who was surrounded by her friends, the virgins of the
parable; all then went into the wedding feast together. The
circumstances of the story lend themselves readily to Jesus'
message, and there is little if any allegorizing. The delay of
the bridegroom's coming was the most natural thing in the
world: among a people not notorious for their punctuality a
bachelor is having a last fling with his male friends. The
bride is not mentioned because she is irrelevant to the
lesson: not the bride, but the virgins in the story represent
the Church. They are not rebuked for sleeping—all of them
sleep—but for being unprepared to meet the bridegroom on a
moment's notice. In real life, of course, the improvident
virgins could hardly have bought *oil for their lamps* in the
middle of the night, nor, probably, would their more prudent
sisters have shrugged off their plea so casually; these are

devices to get the foolish virgins out of the way so that it can
be made more evident how only the vigilant will enter into
the kingdom: *watch, therefore, for you know neither the day
nor the hour*. It is pointless to look for symbolism in the sellers
of the oil, the oil itself, the number of the virgins, their
relative division into wise and foolish, and so on.

Mt 25:14–30   The parable of *the talents* in Matthew
has been allegorized, as has its companion
piece in Luke (see above on Lk 19:11–28); it is not likely,
however, that separate traditions had elaborated these
lengthy stories out of any common source that we can now
discern in the Gospels, certainly not the brief little comparison
of Mk 13:34 which we saw above, though as regards the
one basic point of vigilance against the coming of the kingdom it can be called the same parable.

In both Matthew's and Luke's telling of the story the
lesson concerns the eschatological kingdom, stressing the
need of both vigilance and preparedness. The original polemical direction of the parable against Pharisaism can perhaps
be more readily perceived in Luke's version, however. Matthew has more obviously adapted it to the situation of the
Christian awaiting the *parousia:* the master returns suddenly
and *after a long time,* and he demands accounting from
each servant for what has been committed to him *according
to his abilities.* Furthermore, the reward awaiting the vigilant
and deserving servant is not simply the kingdom itself, conceived as something that he has not previously possessed,
but *greater things* of the same order as the *smaller* in which
he has proved faithful: this it is to *share your lord's joy.*
This teaching we have seen before (above on Lk 12:41–48
and parallel). The monetary terms used in Matthew's and
Luke's separate parables are in striking contrast. The talent
was a weight, not a coin. A talent of silver would have been
roughly the equivalent of sixty *minas.* A talent of gold would
have been simply a fabulous sum of money.

In keeping with the perspective which the parable has in
Matthew's Gospel, significance is seen in the deprivation of

the profitless servant of one talent and the further enrich-
ment of the one of ten talents. The former has not simply lost
his chance for what he never had; he is truly deprived of
what he did possess. Thus there is a new point to the saying
that *everyone who has will receive more and possess in
abundance, while he who has nothing will be deprived of
even what he has.* At the end the symbolism of the story is
dropped, and the punishment of the useless servant is
described in terms of the well-used figure of *the outer
darkness where they weep and gnash their teeth* (cf. Mt
8:12, 13:42, 50, 22:13, 24:51; Lk 13:28).

Mt 25:31–46   These same ideas are continued in the
                   magnificent passage with which Matthew
concludes the eschatological discourse, a passage which fit-
tingly takes the last judgment as its subject yet which is far
more concerned with the here-and-now life of the Christian
than with the ratifying judgment of the last day. The passage
is not precisely a parable, though it contains a small and
incidental parable of the sheep and the goats to which the
elect and the condemned are compared. It is a parabolic
story told by Jesus—its Aramaic origin shows through in more
than one place—in which, however, the details of the story
are not so much applied or allegorized as they are representa-
tional.

Several important lessons are included in this story. First
of all, *the Son of Man,* the eschatological judge and savior,
is recognized as *the King* and Lord because he has ascended
the throne of his glory: the apocalyptic vision of Dan 7:9–14
is simplified in that it now becomes evident that the Son of
Man is identical with Israel's God and Savior (cf. Is 6:1–5).
Early Christian theology used the royal and divine title Lord
of the resurrected Christ in testimony to this faith, for even
though the *parousia* was not yet, his glory had been proclaimed in the resurrection; the Gospels have even, at times,
applied the title to Jesus in their treatment of his early life.
This understandable development, another aspect of realized
eschatology, is here given a paradoxical twist. We are now

called on to recognize the exalted King and Lord present in
the world as Son of Man still. And he is present not only as
Man and in man, but in the most wretched and miserable of
men.

Paul's doctrine of the Church as the Body of Christ as
something to do with this teaching: in part it was dependent
on a revelation like this one (cf. Acts 9:4 f.). However, the
teaching is broader than the various ecclesiological applications to which Paul put it. We are confronted by an
eschatological picture in which *all the nations will be as-
sembled before* the God of all. It is not only the reprobate,
but also the elect, who have failed to recognize who were
these least of my brethren in whom Christ was deserted or,
all unknowingly, was served. Jesus is not merely reiterating
the venerable prophetic doctrine that religious people find it
so hard to learn, and so perplexing to them, that God is less
impressed by what they do for him than by what they do for
one another (cf. Is 58:3–7). He not only singles out the poor
and the wretched as objects of his special solicitude, he
identifies himself with them. Before he had taught that the
total dimension of "neighbor" is "man" (see above on Lk
10:29–37). Now he teaches that he who serves man serves
Christ.

Matthew is writing for the Church. It would not be foreign
to his purpose to explore the implications of Jesus' teaching
for those who lie outside the Church's pale, but it would be
beyond it. The message for the Church is quite enough to
concern us. Christian apocalyptic does not abandon this
world that is passing away and that must be changed. Rather
it serves it, and in serving it serves Christ. The kingdom of
God that comes unexpectedly comes, however, through the
prayers and the works of the saints (cf. Col 1:24; Apo
8:2–6). The Church has, not as an avocation but as its
highest and most essential calling, the duty to serve man in
all of his needs spiritual and physical, and to fight all his
ancient enemies—ignorance, poverty, disease, injustice, big-
otry, death of body or soul. It is this whole man that Jesus

became and remains forever. It is the wise virgin, the profit-
able servant, who makes the Church's vocation his own. He
who does not deserves no name of Christian, and the Lord
has said that this name will be taken from him at the last.

22. A LAST SUPPER

Lk 21:37–38 Luke offers a summary statement on the Lord's practice while in Jerusalem for the days of the Passover (cf. Jn 8:1 f.). Actually, the statement refers to the days preceding rather than those that will follow. Jesus' practice was doubtless dictated by prudence, to avoid the attentions of his enemies, but also by convenience: on *the Mount of Olives* he could find solitude and privacy. As this was in the direction of Bethany, it is not unlikely, too, that he enjoyed the hospitality of the house of Martha and Mary.

Mk 14:1–2 The Synoptic Gospels now open the story of
Mt 26:1–5 the passion with a date; at least Matthew
Lk 22:1–2 and Mark do, while Luke contents himself with saying that *the feast of Unleavened Bread called Passover was drawing near.* Matthew's and Mark's *two days before,* for that matter, is not without its ambiguities, in view of the Jewish practice of reckoning a new day's beginning from sunset and of counting any part of a day as a full day. Presumably they mean that this was Wednesday of Holy Week, since for them the Passover meal was eaten by Jesus and his disciples on a Thursday evening after sunset. Matthew first makes his customary

transitional ending to the eschatological discourse (see above on Mt 7:28 f.). In all the preceding instances this formula introduced a change of place in Jesus' mission. In this case there can be no question of such a thing, and instead Jesus speaks of his coming passion and death that are to terminate his mission (see above on Mk 8:31–33 and parallels).

The Gospels go on to speak of a conspiracy of *the chief priests and scribes* (for the latter, Matthew substitutes *the elders of the people*) against the life of Jesus. There is nothing new in this (see above on Mk 11:18 f. and parallel; Jn 11:45–57), though Matthew now has it for the first time. It is also he who places the meeting at the house of the high priest *Caiaphas*. We have no reason to think that for this reason the conspiracy had any official status, however. It was simply a meeting of some of Jesus' powerful enemies who were taking up an old item on their agenda. Fear of the people persuaded them to be cautious. To act against Jesus during the feast might provoke a riot, and a riot could easily bring in Roman martial law. They planned to defer any overt action till after the Passover, therefore, when the thousands of Galilean and other pilgrims would have left the city. What changed their plans to one of immediate action was the treason of Judas, the next act in the Synoptic drama (interrupted in Mark and Matthew by the story of the anointing at Bethany: see above on Jn 12:1–8 and parallels).

Mk 14:10–11
Mt 26:14–16
Lk 22:3–6
It was pointed out above (on Jn 12:1–8) that the Gospels' scanty information on Judas Iscariot allows us no adequate basis for an appraisal of his character and motivation, or rather, that what little they do say could easily lead to a superficial and distorted assessment. Judas was, obviously, a source of extreme embarrassment to the early Church, which consequently thought about him and remembered about him only the little that was required by the statistical facts: that he had been a member of the Twelve and that, nevertheless, he had betrayed the Lord.

That as one of the Twelve he should have made no
particular imprint on Christian tradition is not, in itself, an
isolated phenomenon (see above on Mk 3:13–19 and parallels); we know relatively little about most of the Twelve
as regards their distinct personalities. In Judas' case there
was positive cause to forget him as soon as possible, and
when at last it became necessary to set down about him
what had been remembered, it is not surprising that that
was not very much nor entirely coherent.

Luke states that Judas did what he did because *Satan
entered into* him, and with this judgment John agrees (Jn
13:2, 27; cf. Jn 6:70 f.). This is, however, a theological
evaluation, not an historical explanation. John (cf. 12:6) has
already called him a thief, an assertion which may depend
on a creditable tradition yet which sheds little light on the
matter at hand: it is doubtful that any of the Synoptic
Gospels intend to suggest that the money which Judas
received constituted the sole motive of his betrayal. Only
Matthew mentions a specified amount, *thirty pieces of silver*,
a paltry sum which has a symbolic value for him (cf.
Zech 11:12) and to which he will return later. At all events,
Judas could hardly have been paid a great deal. If we
accept John's information that he was the treasurer for the
apostolic band, we would have to conclude that even
though their resources were not great he could without
doubt have had at his disposal more than these few coins at
almost any time during his period of service. Besides, he had
already resolved on Jesus' betrayal when he approached the
chief priests; the money was an afterthought and incidental,
perhaps a matter of some haggling but definitely not a mov-
ing cause, for no one had sought Judas out to bribe him.

Perhaps we might reconstruct the succession of events as
follows. Judas could easily have heard the *temple police*
(Luke) discussing the troublesome reformer who had run
afoul of their masters, whose popularity, however, had them
baffled as to what action they could take. It was to these
that Judas could first have offered his services, guaranteeing
to find a way to turn Jesus over to them in secret before the

people could know. The temple police would hasten to bring him before *the chief priests,* all too happy at this unexpected opportunity. Judas was given his token payment, and it remained for him to find his chance.

Because of this incident, the Wednesday of Holy Week has been traditionally known as "Spy Wednesday." There are all kinds of spies, it is true. Some serve for money, some for thrills, and some, probably the greater number, out of conviction. Judas' action, here and later, reads like that of a man who has changed sides. It is possible that Mark and Matthew have had some inkling of its meaning by placing his betrayal immediately after the story of the anointing at Bethany, when Jesus had spoken so forcefully about his coming death and burial. To think that Judas had first associated himself with Jesus from an erroneous persuasion of his messianic mission is to assert little more about him than has to be asserted about the Twelve in general (see above on Jn 6:5–15, 16–17a). That Jesus must suffer and die, that his messianic proclamation of the kingdom would, to all appearances, end in an ignominious anticlimax, had been an incomprehensible scandal to the Twelve (see on Mk 8:31–33 and parallels). They refused to accept it, and, as subsequent events will show, their refusal continued through the very events themselves, as Jesus had foretold them. It is conceivable that Judas took Jesus' words more seriously and at their face value than the rest of the Twelve did. As Peter thought on occasion, so did Judas: here was a Master who no longer talked like a Messiah, who was no longer pointing to a triumphant kingdom but to a miserable defeat of every messianic hope. The great difference, of course, is that Peter could believe without understanding or that his faith in Jesus' person could transcend the mystery of Jesus' words, while Judas' faith was not adequate to cover a prospect that boded only ignominy and shame in exchange for the life he had once committed to a great cause. The end of such a course could only be despair, disillusionment, and bitter resentment against one who had fed his hope in vain. Aside from hints and surmises like these, it has not been given to us to penetrate more deeply into the soul of Judas Iscariot.

Mk 14:12–17 Mark's and Matthew's *first day of the*
Mt 26:17–20 *Unleavened Bread*—Luke's *the day* is less
Lk 22:7–14 precise, but means the same thing—indicates the following day in the Synoptic chronology. It also seems to indicate that for them this Thursday was the fourteenth day of the month Nisan, that is, the Preparation day for the Passover, which began with sunset; as the text goes on to show, the Synoptic Gospels quite definitely treat the Last Supper of Jesus and his disciples as a Passover meal. Though originally the Passover and the Unleavened Bread were separate observances, throughout most of Israelite and Jewish history they were celebrated as one feast, with all the accumulated rites interpreted in relation to the circumstances of Israel's exodus from Egypt under Moses (cf. Ex 12:21–27, 37–42, 43–49, 13:4–10). On the Preparation day all leavened bread was removed from the house, for only unleavened bread was to be eaten during the entire week of the Passover. It was on this day, too, that the lambs were sacrificed which served as the *pièce de résistance* for the Passover meal. In the time of Jesus, with the scribal interpretation of the Torah as a unified and normative body of law, the lamb of the Passover meal was considered to be a sacrifice that could only be immolated in the Jerusalem temple, and for the same reason the Passover could be eaten only in Jerusalem (cf. Deut 16:1–8). In the evening, the slain lamb having been brought home from the temple and the other preparations made, the Passover was celebrated as of old, as a family feast of joy and freedom, on the beginning of the fifteenth of Nisan (the month also called Abib in the Old Testament).

Already we have entered upon one of the most fretted of New Testament questions and what is without doubt the most significant of the chronological discrepancies of the Gospels. Insistent as the Synoptic Gospels are on the Last Supper as a Passover meal, John is no less intent on showing that it was no such thing. All the Gospels agree that there was a Last Supper and that it was celebrated on a Thursday evening; all the Gospels agree that Jesus suffered and died on the following day, a Friday. For John alone, however, that Friday was the Preparation day, and it was not until that evening that the Passover was celebrated, therefore on the Sabbath. For John the Last Supper could not have been a Passover meal, and he does not present it as such.

Both chronologies are theological. While the Synoptics make much of the Last Supper as the origin of the Christian Passover, the Eucharist, John is understandably silent on this aspect of the meal. Instead, he finds it most significant and appropriate that Jesus should have died at the very time that the Passover lamb was being sacrificed. St. Paul in 1 Cor 5:7 seems to follow John in this.

If both are theological, obviously both cannot be equally historical. It is not true, incidentally, though often asserted in this connection, that the tradition of Western Christianity has favored the Synoptic chronology and the tradition of the East the Johannine, as though this followed from their separate disciplines of unleavened and leavened bread in the celebration of the Eucharist. In the oldest Western tradition leavened bread was used indifferently with unleavened, and though unleavened bread later became normative it may have begun as an innovation. Furthermore, though unleavened bread doubtless came to be used because of the supposed circumstances of the Last Supper as described by the Synoptics, there was never any serious attempt in the Church to make the institution of the Eucharist as annually celebrated coincide with the time of the Jewish Passover. Holy Thursday has always been observed as a Christian feast because of its relation to Easter, never as a continuation of the Jewish Passover. Always, that is, apart from some late patristic allegorizing.

All in all, the Johannine chronology has the most to recommend it historically. As we shall see, not only as told by John but also as told by the Synoptics the passion story makes good sense only on the assumption that the Passover feast had not yet begun. John's chronology, for that matter, has never caused any problems at all for the reader of the Gospels, except for the conflict that it creates when juxtaposed with the Synoptic story of a Passover meal. It is probably safe to say that the majority of scholars both past and present have always opted for the Johannine over the Synoptic chronology in this respect, and it is this option that we also shall take, without, obviously, being in any position at this time to do any kind of justice to the weighty arguments that have been and still are being proposed on both sides of the question, which remains a live one in New Testament studies. Accepting John's chronology as historical, we are probably able to assign with fair accuracy the date of Christ's crucifixion, in satisfying harmony with the few other meager indications we have of the time of the ministry of Jesus (see above on Lk 3:1 f.; Jn 2:18–22). The Passover, or fifteenth day of Nisan, coincided with a Sabbath, a Saturday, in the year 30 according to our reckoning, on April 8 to be precise. If this computation is correct, then Jesus who was born sometime after 8 B.C. (see above on Lk 2:1–7) died something in advance of his fortieth year.

What, then, are we to make of the Synoptic accounts which not only characterize the day of the Last Supper as the beginning of Passover, but add that Jesus *sent two of his disciples* (*Peter and John*, according to Luke) *into the city* of Jerusalem to prepare for their eating a Passover meal? There have been various attempts to harmonize their story with John's uncompromising chronology. Could not the Galileans have celebrated the Passover on a day differing from that of the Jerusalemites? Since the counting of the days of the lunar month depended on the observation of the new moon by the naked eye, might there not have been a difference of opinion on when the fifteenth day occurred? Might not a confluence of Sabbath and Passover call for special and variable rules and practices? All these are possibilities—there are few things that are not possible—but there is evidence for none of them, and much reason to deem them all improbable. Could there not have been a calendar

dispute among the Jews of the first Christian century, as
there is among so many other religions, the Christian included, which resulted in the observance of the same feast on
different days? In recent years it has been discovered that
there was indeed such a dispute. At least, it seems that the
Qumran people followed a more ancient calendar than that
in use by the official Jewry of the time, a solar calendar
attested by both the Old Testament and by some later
Jewish apocryphal literature, which may, as a matter of fact,
have had some influence on early Christian practice. The
Essenes of Qumran did keep the Passover on a different
day from that of the Jerusalem hierarchy. Unfortunately for
the hypothesis, however, it was on a day that has nothing to
do with the Synoptic story of the Last Supper; as far as
we can tell, this sectarian calendar was unknown to the
Gospels.

It is extremely unlikely that in the Jerusalem of A.D. 30
any Passover meal could have been eaten except on the day
officially recognized for it and without the lamb that had
been immolated for it on the one day set aside for this
purpose. It is equally unlikely that Jesus himself would have
countenanced any such grave departure from the practice of
normative Judaism. The Last Supper, therefore, could hardly
have been a real Passover meal. It is worthy of note that
though the Synoptic Gospels treat it as a Passover meal,
they are strangely silent about what would have been its one
main component, the Passover lamb, and that when they do
speak of another of its important features, the bread, they
use the common word *artos* rather than the technical term
azymos, unleavened bread, which alone was permitted during the Passover season. Of most of the other rites proper to
the celebration of the Passover there is also no trace in the
Gospels.

What appears to have been true is that during this
Passover time Jesus ate a farewell meal with his disciples
which under the circumstances had the overtones of a Passover meal and partook of some of its elements. Because of
these circumstances it was remembered as a Passover meal

and is so treated in the Synoptic Gospels. We must treat it in the same way when studying them, for these elements which were no doubt intentionally present when Jesus instituted the Eucharist enter into their theological portrayal of this all-important event.

Matthew greatly summarizes the story told in more detail by Mark and Luke. The disciples were instructed to follow a man *carrying a water jar* and to ask for the master of the house which he entered. The servant would have been conspicuous: men ordinarily transported water in skins slung over their shoulders and left it to women to carry it in jars balanced on their heads—a graceful sight still quite familiar in the Near East, though gasoline tins have now generally replaced the earthenware jars. The disciples doubtless watched for the servant at the pool of Siloam and by this prearranged sign were led to the house with whose owner Jesus had spoken for the use of his *guest room*. The Passover retained its character as a family meal, even though in the vast concourse of pilgrims celebrating it together in Jerusalem the "families" would be rather temporary, and it was eaten in privacy. The *upper* room which the disciples found prepared might have been hired for the occasion, but it may also have been simply set aside by a pious Jewish householder for the use of some "family" of pilgrims during the Passover season. The upper room of a Palestinian house was not usually connected with the rest of the rooms of the building but was reached by an outside stairway only. The traditional site of the upper room of the Gospels, the Cenacle, can be seen on the map of Jerusalem, in what is now part of the Israeli sector of the city. The tradition is not particularly ancient and respects only the site occupied by the present building, which before the partition of Palestine between Jews and Arabs was a mosque.

Lk 22:15–18   The various accounts of the Last Supper are selective and not always mutually coherent. It is necessary, therefore, to perform a certain amount of suturing and reconstructing. On the assumption

that the meal embodied some of the Passover ritual, however,
Luke's introduction makes admirable sense. Wine was drunk
at four different times during the Passover. At the beginning
a blessing was invoked, the *kiddush,* and a cup of wine
was then drunk in silence. This is no ordinary Passover meal,
of course, and Jesus breaks the silence to determine the
meaning of what is being done. *I have greatly desired to eat
this Passover with you* and *I shall not eat it . . . till the
kingdom of God comes* have been interpreted in many ways.
Coupled with Jesus' injunction that the disciples *divide this
among yourselves,* it appears that he is explaining his own
abstinence from a meal to which he is attaching eschatological significance. As he is about to present the bread and wine
of the meal as a memorial of his own body and blood, he
himself does not partake of the meal. It is to be noticed that
the Gospels speak of Jesus and his disciples as *reclining* at
table. Though they sometimes did it at other times as well
(see above on Lk 7:36–50), at Passover time the Jews made
it a point of honor to dine in the reclining position introduced
by the Romans. This was the position of free men, and the
Passover was above all a celebration of freedom.

Lk 22:24–30   Though Luke topically connects the institution of the Eucharist with the inaugural cup
that he has just described, his own choice of material makes
it logical that we consider this following episode next. Jesus'
mention of the kingdom could easily have provoked one of
those childish disputes of which we have already seen one
example above on Mk 9:33–37 and parallels. Or perhaps the
question of precedence at table rose among them (see above
on Lk 14:7–11). Once more Jesus must patiently remind
them of what kind of Master they are disciples and of the
scale of values that ought to govern his kingdom. For all
practical purposes the words of Jesus that we read here
have already been recorded in separate contexts by Matthew
and Mark (see above on Mk 10:35–45 and parallel; Mt
19:27–30).

Jn 13:1–17   As is so often the case, John comes forward
with a parallel to Luke in distinction to the
other Synoptic Gospels. And what a parallel this is! What
Luke has by precept, John records in action, an action which
completely sums up the dedication of Jesus' life to be the
servant of all. Laying aside his outer garments, he wraps a
towel about him and proceeds, basin in hand and on his
knees, about the outer circle of the reclining disciples, washing their feet one by one. It is well to recall that among the
Jews not even a slave (if he was a Jew) could have been
legally compelled to perform this act.

John keeps his distance from the Synoptic tradition: this
took place *before the feast of the Passover.* Nevertheless, this
supper was no less important to him than it was to the
Synoptics. Hence his solemn exordium and his insistence that
this great symbolic act took place *during a supper. Having
loved his own who were in the world, he loved them to the
end* doubtless is John's way of characterizing this entire
evening: the sign of the foot-washing is merely the prelude to
the great discourse that will follow.

We are left to imagine the stolid silence in which Judas,
whose presence John has just emphasized, received the
Lord's ministrations. Characteristically, it is Peter who finds
something to say, recognizing the incongruity which Jesus
himself points out in a moment. However, it is precisely
this incongruity, this reversal of the roles of master and
servant, that is folly to the world and wisdom to the Gospel.
What Jesus now exemplifies is his own life, indeed, and also
the life of every true Christian, but especially what must be
the regimen of his Church: *What I do you do not now know,
but later you will understand.* Peter, who definitely does not
yet understand, responds naïvely in the pattern of the
Johannine dialogues. First he will have nothing to do with
his unseemly washing, then, when it is forcibly presented to
him as the Lord's mysterious will, he would literally bathe in
it!

Unless I wash you, you have no part with me obviously
regards the Christian duty to share in the sacrificial life of

Christ: the *command* of verse 15. It is from this command, *mandatum* in the Latin liturgy, that the name Maundy Thursday was derived. John with his habitual liking for multiple senses, may very well have intended Jesus' words to signify also the necessity of Christian baptism. Jesus' other response to Peter is more difficult to interpret, apart from its evident surface meaning. The text itself is not certain, but probably it should read: *he who has bathed needs only to wash his feet, then he is clean all over.* The disciples were not dirty; one of the virtues of rabbinical Judaism was the personal cleanliness on which it insisted. Before reclining at table they had thoroughly washed their face and hands from the dust of the street. But undoubtedly there is a spiritual and Christian depth to this state as there is to the former. Over and above baptism ("he who has bathed": various forms of this verb are used elsewhere in the New Testament to designate baptism, cf. 1 Cor 6:11; Eph 5:26; Tit 3:5; Heb 10:22), something else is required of the Christian if he is to be perfect. He must also have entered into the Lord's "washing" effectively, in work and performance, as well as having given assent to its high ideals. That "clean" does, indeed, have a spiritual meaning in this context, is shown by Jesus' contrast of Judas with the rest of the disciples.

Jn 13:18–30   That Jesus denounced the traitor on this
Mk 14:18–21   occasion is the testimony of all four Gospels.
Mt 26:21–25   Mark and John have him quote Ps 41:10,
Lk 22:21–23   to the same effect of the statements as-
                      cribed to him by Matthew and Luke: one
of the Twelve, one of his familiar friends now sitting at table with him in this family gathering, will betray him. The Gospels do not bother to explain the source of Jesus' knowledge; they simply take it for granted that he could and did know.

The action which involved *dipping into the dish* which now follows in Matthew and Mark on the one hand and in John on the other looks to be two variant recollections of the same event. In the Synoptics the action merely serves as a dramatic reinforcement of Jesus' assertion that one of his table-fellows will betray him. Doubtless even as he spoke several hands were in the common bowl together, and certainly all had been or soon would be there. On the assumption that this meal was following the Passover order, the dish may have been that of the *haroseth,* a sauce compounded of crushed fruits, spices, and vinegar whose color and consistency were supposed to make it a reminder of the clay from which the Israelites had moulded bricks during their slavery in Egypt (cf. Ex 1:13 f.). Into this bitter herbs were dipped and eaten as an hors d'oeuvre preliminary to the main Passover meal. Even in Matthew's Gospel where the traitor is at least identified to himself the result is ambiguous. To Judas' protestation, *Surely, rabbi, it is not I?,* Jesus' answer is, *As you say.* Did Matthew consider Judas' question to be one of sheer hypocrisy, or an indication that he was still wrestling with himself over his desertion?

In John's Gospel the situation is rather different. Judas is designated as the traitor, but only to *the disciple whom Jesus loved,* whom we generally assume to have been John the son of Zebedee, by the familiar gesture of a host's offering one of his guests a dipped morsel of food. The Gospel presupposes Jesus and the disciples reclining at the three sides of the low table or in a semicircle about it, with the beloved disciple on Jesus' right, almost literally *in his bosom* (in view of Jn 1:18, this expression is undoubtedly significant). In turn Peter would have been on John's right and Judas, presumably, on Jesus' left. In the mind of the evangelist it was at this moment that Judas made his irrevocable decision, spurning Jesus' final gesture of love and grace.

John alone tells us that Judas left the Last Supper. *What you have to do, do quickly* are important words for the evangelist, who wants to show Jesus always in control of the situation during this hour of his glorification: not even Judas can act against him till he has received "permission." The interpretation put on Judas' departure by the rest of the disciples indicates both their ignorance of the identity of the

traitor and the assumption of the Gospel that the Passover
feast had not yet begun, since during such a time all the
shops would have been tightly closed. *It was night,* adds
John: the time of darkness has come at last (cf. Jn 9:4).

Mk 14:22–25   We come now to what for the Synoptic
Mt 26:26–29   Gospels is the supreme moment of the Last
Lk 22:19–20   Supper and has constituted it forever the
               Christian Passover. The Passover ritual it-
self, to whatever extent it was really followed that evening,
has long been forgotten in view of larger realities; within the
format of a Passover meal, the institution of the Eucharist
would in all likelihood have coincided with the drinking of
the third ritual cup, after the meal proper had been concluded (cf. Luke's *after supper* introducing the consecration
of the cup): this would not conflict with the *while they were
eating* of Matthew and Mark, since in the large sense the
meal continued until the final blessing and drinking of the
fourth ritual cup of wine.

Anyone who reads the Gospels attentively will see immediately that the Synoptic tradition has preserved two
distinct Eucharistic formulations which agree substantively
but also differ in some important details. For all practical
purposes, Matthew and Mark present one and the same text,
from which Luke diverges. He diverges even more if we
accept the so-called shorter Lucan formulation that appears
in some manuscripts (the omission of vss. 19b–20), which is
held by many modern scholars to represent the original text
of Luke. But while it is true that the tendency of scribes
was to expand their text rather than to contract it, and that
therefore longer texts are rightly held suspect when there is a
shorter variant in the manuscripts, in this instance the shorter
text is best explained as the result of deliberate omission on
the part of someone who misunderstood the function of the
first, non-Eucharistic cup in Luke's story and who took this
means of harmonizing it with the other Gospels. Luke's formulation is in substantial agreement with that of 1 Cor

11:12–25, the fourth traditional account of the institution of the Eucharist given us by the New Testament.

At the outset we should recognize that all the formulations, the Marcan-Matthaean on one side and the Pauline-Lucan on the other, have without doubt been conditioned by liturgical usage, which varied somewhat from local church to local church, just as in some respects it still does today. Even Matthew, who has reproduced what Mark has almost verbatim, seems to have done so not because he was copying Mark but because he was in possession of his own Eucharistic narrative that was very nearly the same as Mark's. Luke follows Paul closely, but not precisely. Paul explicitly states that he was following ecclesiastical tradition, and the same affirmation is implicit in everything that we know about the Gospels and their formation.

Secondly, we must recognize that these formulations without exception are those of Gentile churches. One import of this factor we have already observed when treating of the Eucharistic doctrine of John (see above on Jn 6:51b–59). John, who reproduces no Eucharistic formulation of his own, nevertheless quotes the Lord as speaking of his *flesh* rather than his *body*. It is altogether likely, in fact, that "flesh" is the word Jesus himself used to designate his Eucharistic presence under the sign of bread. Neither Hebrew nor Aramaic—in one of which Jesus must have spoken—possessed an acceptable word for what we understand by "body," for the simple reason that the Semites did not distinguish the body from the self. "Flesh" is about the only word that Jesus could have used. But "flesh," as we know, also possessed some undesirable connotations, more so for the Greek, but even for the Semite as well: it is this fact, we saw, that made Jn 1:14 such an astounding utterance. It is not surprising, therefore, that the Gentile churches soon took advantage of the greater flexibility of the Greek language to substitute the more neutral term "body" for the earlier "flesh" of the Eucharistic formulations.

These twin considerations regarding the transmission of

our Eucharistic narratives probably prove somewhat pointless a good deal of the discussion that has gone on in the past
concerning the "very words" used by Jesus in the institution
of the Eucharist as recoverable from the Gospels. Here
perhaps more than anywhere else in the Gospels the teaching
of Jesus comes to us refracted through the language of
apostolic Christianity. Whether such and such a specific expression can or cannot be "retranslated" into Aramaic neither
proves nor disproves that Jesus did or did not say it or
something substantively like it. It only indicates, as the
variant traditions themselves already indicate, how the
Church of the Gospels found meaningful ways of transmitting
what it knew and testified to in the Spirit that Jesus had
taught. It is very doubtful that any scholar will ever be able
to reconstruct to the satisfaction of any other scholar the
ipsissima verba of Jesus at the Last Supper. The only test
that we can apply is what the words of the Gospels say. By
that test we hear only Jesus speaking in all of the Eucharistic
formulations, in all of their variations. This we must now try
to show by examining them.

It is sometimes wondered why John, with his known
sacramental interests, should have done nothing with the
story of the institution of the Eucharist. We are by now
familiar enough with his Gospel, however, to realize that it is
not his way with the sacraments to have done what the
Synoptics did. His sacramental doctrine, while pervasive, is
communicated by indirection. Or rather, the direction it
takes is to focus our attention on their here-and-now ecclesial
significance and power instead of on their historical origins,
on their realization of history instead of their evocation of it.
There is also a special consideration in respect to the
Eucharist. For John—and not, it seems, for the Synoptic
tradition, for all its insistence on the Last Supper as a Passover meal—the sacrifice of the Passover lamb was a type of
Jesus, who was put to death at the moment the lamb was
being immolated. To describe the origin of the Christian
Passover, the sacrament of Christ's death and resurrection,

anterior to the Passover sacrifice might not have been impossible, but it would have been artistically awkward.

The first basic agreement of the Eucharistic narratives is that Jesus *took bread*—whether it was the unleavened bread of the Passover or leavened bread is immaterial—*and broke it* (so also in the Synoptic stories of the miracle of the loaves: cf. Mk 6:41 and parallels; Mk 8:6 and parallel; while John together with the Synoptics uses the Eucharistic word *klasmata:* see above on Mk 6:34–44 and parallels); this bread he then identified with himself: *this is my body.* With the cup of wine he did the same, identifying it with his blood. These elements, in other words, are the signs of his being and presence: "flesh and blood" are the sum and substance of the human person (cf. Mt 16:17; Gal 1:16, etc.).

But Jesus is not merely present in the bread and wine, he is present in a very special way. The body, says Luke, *is given for you* (Paul says simply, "is for you"). This may also be translated "will be given for you," but the difference is not too important. Jesus will die on the morrow, thus completing his atoning sacrifice for the sins of man, but his death will be only the termination of an entire life that has been and is now consecrated as this sacrifice (cf. Phil 2:7 f.). All the Gospels say of his blood that it *is* (or "will be") *poured out for you:* Matthew and Mark substitute here *for many* (Is 53:10 f.: see above on Mk 10:35–45 and parallel). Matthew adds, perhaps unnecessarily, *for the forgiveness of sins:* this was the traditional function of the spilling of blood (cf. Lev 17:11; Heb 9:22). Thus we find the first significance of this new Christian Passover. The Passover of the Jews commemorated the saving act by which God freed his people from the bondage of Egypt. The Christian Passover commemorates and signifies the sacrificial and saving act by which the Servant of the Lord has freed man from the bondage of sin. The broken bread and separated cup of wine, therefore, not improbably portray the broken body and shed blood of Christ's death (cf. 1 Cor 11:26). "Broken body" and "shed blood" remain, of course, within the order of conventional terms for death: technically, crucifixion was a bloodless form of execution, and according to John, Jesus' body was not broken (cf. Jn 20:36).

Jesus further specifies that his blood—his death—is the inaugural rite of a new covenant between God and man. In Mark and Matthew we read *this is my blood of the covenant*, which may be a Semitism for "this is the blood of my covenant"; Paul and Luke have *this cup is the new covenant in my blood*. The allusion here is to Ex 24:8 (cf. Zech 9:11), the story of the ratification of the covenant of Sinai by Moses, who sprinkled the people and the altar of God with the blood of bulls to signify the blood-bond established by Yahweh's saving act and Israel's acceptance of his law (cf. Heb 9:18–22). Just as the Jewish Passover rejoiced in a covenant enacted in blood, so the Christian Passover is the joyful covenant meal (cf. Ex 24:9–11) of a new covenant (cf. Jer 31:31–34), again enacted in blood, this time the blood of the atoning Servant of God (cf. Is 53:11 f.). Under this aspect of covenant meal the Eucharist is sacrificial not in virtue of the Old Testament type—for the blood of the bulls was not sacrificial—but in virtue of the sacrifice of Christ which it represents.

The aspect of covenant meal, however, makes already implicit in all the Gospel accounts the rubric stated explicitly only by Luke and Paul: the command to repeat it *in my memory*. This "memory" (*anamnēsis*) is an active word; the Eucharist does not merely call to mind, commemorate, the saving act of Christ, it also re-presents it, makes it present in the sacrament of his body and blood. It thus continues for the Christian the meaning that the Passover has for the Jew when he recites at its beginning: "We celebrate tonight because *we* were Pharaoh's bondmen in Egypt, and the Lord our God delivered *us* with a mighty hand." By the same token it is eschatological, a present sign of a future reality: what God has done is the best guarantee of what he will do. Matthew and Mark bring in at the end the same eschatological saying which Luke has attached to the drinking of the first Passover cup. As St. Thomas said of all the sacraments, the Eucharist "is a remembrance of what once took place, its manifestation in the present, and a forecast of what is to come."

23. THE TRUE VINE AND ITS BRANCHES

Jn 13:31–35   With Judas now removed from the scene, John begins his own great contribution to the Last Supper story, the last discourse of Jesus which verbalizes so much of what the Synoptics have implied in their descriptions of the institution of the Eucharist. Here even more than elsewhere in the Fourth Gospel it is the *glorified* Christ who speaks to his chosen disciples, who are at one and the same time every Christian and the appointed leadership of the Church. These he now calls *little children*, a term found only here in the Gospel but which is characteristic of the First Epistle of John. The glorification of the Son of Man which is also the glory of God (cf. Jn 12:28, 14:13) comes *immediately*: for John the culmination of Christ's glory (see above on Jn 1:14) is his passion-death-resurrection, the basis of the realized eschatology which is the stress of his Gospel.

As I told the Jews. It is a technique of this discourse that in it statements from the earlier polemical discourses (here from Jn 7:33 f., 8:21) are taken up either to be reversed or employed in another sense. The disciples cannot follow Jesus as yet, for he refers now to himself as the principle and author of the Christian life, who must first return to the Father and prepare a place for them (Jn 14:2). How they

will then "follow" him (cf. Jn 14:3), he immediately adds:
a new commandment I give you. Love of neighbor is not
unique to Christianity, nor does John suggest that it is. What
is new is the dimension of both love and of the concept of
neighbor as revealed in Jesus Christ (see above on Mk 12:
28–34 and parallel; Lk 10:29–37): *as I have loved you, you
must love one another.* The love of Jesus, which is supreme
(cf. Jn 15:13), is both the model and the principle of
Christian love, and because of this it is a sign of the abiding
presence of Christ, the witness of the pilgrim Church to what
God has done. It is rightly called a new commandment in
virtue of this character it confers on the Church.

Jn 13:36–38   Luke follows John in putting in this context
Lk 22:31–34   of the Last Supper Jesus' prediction that
Mk 14:26–31   Peter will deny him before the night is out.
Mt 26:30–35   The same episode occurs next also in the
               Gospels of Mark and Matthew, but for these
evangelists only *after* Jesus and his disciples *had sung a
hymn* and *returned to the Mount of Olives.* The first two
Gospels have now done with the Last Supper; the "hymn"
to which they refer, in keeping with their perspective of the
supper as a Passover meal, would have been the second part
of the *Hallel,* that is to say Psalms 115 through 118, which
was sung after the fourth and last ritual cup of wine concluding the Passover. Luke and John still have more to tell
about the supper, and John a great deal more.

In John the occasion is one of those typical misunder-
standings that haunt the Johannine dialogues. Peter has
heard Jesus say that he is going away. Where can he
possibly be going that his faithful disciples cannot follow, as
they ought? The misunderstanding is not complete: in some
vague way Peter realizes that the subject of death is in the
air. I *will lay down my life for you!* Jesus does not deny the
possibility (Peter's vehement assertion may be one of John's
unconscious prophecies), but sadly foretells his threefold
denial before *a cock crows.* The third watch of the night,

the period from midnight till about three A.M., was known as "cockcrow."

In Luke it is Jesus who takes the initiative, in one of those passages by which all the Gospels consistently testify to Peter's priority among the disciples. *Satan has petitioned* (and obtained permission) *to sift you,* the plural: all the disciples, *like wheat,* Jesus tells Peter. It is God's will that they will soon undergo a severe test of faith. But to counter Satan's influence Jesus has *prayed* (successfully) that Peter's *faith may not fail;* so that, once Peter has *turned back* from a deviation he is about to take, he will again be a source of strength for his fellow disciples. The prediction recognizes Peter's pre-eminence, but it also speaks of his defection. Thereupon Peter protests his loyalty and is told what is to happen, substantially as we read it in John.

In Matthew and Mark more is made of the coming general desertion of Jesus by the disciples, seen as an illustration of Zech 13:7, and coupled with this prediction is another of the post-resurrection reunion of Master and disciples in Galilee, an important element in Matthew's Gospel (it is possible that in Mark this part of Jesus' saying is an interpolation from Matthew). All the disciples are offended at Jesus' lack of confidence in them, Peter most of all. According to Mark Jesus looks for Peter's denial *before a cock crows twice.* This would have designated the end of "cockcrow," or around three o'clock in the morning, and probably the other Gospels have the same time in mind.

Lk 22:35–38 Luke continues with another saying of the Lord which he doubtless sees in relation to the foregoing. The "sifting" that the disciples are soon to undergo is one aspect of the greatly changed conditions to which they must reconcile themselves in the time that lies ahead if they will remain faithful to their calling. In former days, Jesus reminds them—though in words which Luke previously attached to the mission of the seventy(-two) disciples rather than of the Twelve (see above on Lk 10:1–12)—things had been relatively easy for them.

When he had sent them forth they had taken nothing with them, relying on a hospitable reception in which they had not been disappointed. Jesus was in favor and they had shared in his popularity. Now they will again have to share the lot of their Master, and a vastly different one it will be. He is to be condemned as a common criminal, fulfilling once more the role of the Servant of the Lord (Is 53:12). They will be taken for nothing better. Henceforth they must shift for themselves as best they can, and fear for their lives in the bargain.

The disciple is advised to *sell his cloak and buy a sword*. Jesus employs a parable derived from the holy war, an institution that had once been deadly serious in Old Testament times and which remained something more than figurative for the Jewish zealots and the sectaries of Qumran, but which in the New Testament is a metaphor (cf. Mt 10:34 and parallel; Rom 13:12; 2 Cor 6:7; Eph 6:11–17). The Christian mission, he says, will be a battle in which not clothing or like possessions but survival itself will be at stake, and for this the disciple must prepare himself. The saying, therefore, has no relevance pro or con to the question of defensive warfare against persecution. Jesus' teaching on this matter has been expressed elsewhere (see above on Mt 5:38–42 and parallel). It is probably also implicit here in his reply to the disciples who triumphantly produce two real swords: *It is enough!* The disciples had reacted to his words without understanding as they so often do in the dialogues of John's Gospel, and Jesus' answer is appropriately ironical. The lesson will be completed when they see to what extent he permits the use of the sword in his own defense (cf. Lk 22:51 and parallels). The disciples' swords were doubtless not military weapons but long knives which served other utilitarian purposes than defense in the troubled Palestine of those days.

Jn 14:1–14 John now resumes the Lord's discourse, taking up from the point where Jesus had referred to an imminent departure. This must not sadden the disciples, he now adds, and immediately gives the reason. *As you believe in God, so you believe in me:* the Son and the Father are a common divine and personal principle of salvation (cf. Jn 10:30). It is this Christian faith in Jesus as divine Savior that explains what is entailed in his going away. He goes *to prepare a place* for them in the *Father's house.* There are *many rooms* in this house, therefore they must not fear that no place can be found for them—if such had been the case, he would have warned them of it. When he has prepared the place for them, he will *return* and take them along with him, so that *where I am you will also be.* Thus unlike that of the Jews (cf. Jn 13:33), their inability to follow him is only temporary.

All of this is said in the traditional language of Jewish and Christian eschatology. In John's realized eschatology, however, the language takes on new meaning. The inadequacy of human speech to convey divine realities is likewise clearly brought out. Jesus' "return" and their "joining" him are only two ways of saying the same thing; if they will be where he is, he could with equal ease tell them that he will be where they are, since the "places" in the Father's "house" are the Christians who together make up the resurrected body of Christ, the true house of God (cf. Jn 2:20f.). St. Augustine correctly perceived John's meaning when he commented that Jesus' going was not so much to prepare places as to prepare those who were to occupy the places. Hence the further significance of Christian faith. Faith in the glorified Christ not only identifies the objects of Christian hope as future realities, it is also the way whereby they become present here and now. In this sense, *the way to where I am going is known to you.*

The questions of *Thomas* and *Philip* afford the opportunity, as usual, for Jesus to explain his meaning more thoroughly. Whoever in faith knows and sees Jesus, whoever experiences the life of grace and is witness to Christ living and acting in his Church, has already achieved the heavenly goal, which is to know and to see God: *henceforth you know him and have seen him.* This is true because of the

oneness of the Son with the Father, so that in Christ one
finds *the way and the truth and the life*. The best commentary on these verses is John's own rhapsody on Christ
as the Word of God which we treated in our Chapter 2.

Faith, then, is the key to all Jesus is now saying. And
just as faith in the historical Jesus as God's Son rested
upon his words and his works—which testified to him because they were really God's words and works (cf. Jn
7:16, 8:28)—in the same way faith in the Christ of the
Church rests on the works of the Christian faithful which
are really Christ's. Jesus speaks of them as *greater works:*
his own historical ministry was sharply circumscribed by
the circumstances of time and place, but in the Church his
word will also gather in the sheep once lost to Israel (cf.
Jn 4:35–38) and be heard throughout the entire Gentile
world (cf. Jn 10:16 f., 11:52, 12:20 f.). They remain, of
course, his works, since it is he who works in his Church:
whatever you ask in my name I will do. This is not a
blanket guarantee of infallible efficiency to every prayer of
every Christian; "in my name" firmly grounds the promise
in the condition of a communion of faith which leaves the
initiative with Christ (cf. Jn 1:12). That the things of
which he has spoken are possible, Jesus repeats, is due to
his death and resurrection: *because I go to the Father*.

Jn 14:15–26   From the relation of the Son to the Father
and the faith by which the Christian also
enters into the relationship, Jesus now passes to the Spirit
and to the love which is the working of the Spirit. Love
itself, he has already said (Jn 13:34 f.), is the great commandment by which the living presence of Christ is experienced by the Christian and made known to the world.
Let no one be deceived, however, by what merely calls
itself love and is not. True love shows itself in its works:
if you love me, you will keep my commandments. Where
this true love is present, there is the Spirit of God: *I will
ask the Father, and he will give you another Paraclete.*
The meaning of "Paraclete" we shall see better below; the

Spirit is called "another" Paraclete because the Son himself has been the first (cf. 1 Jn 2:1). It is through the Spirit, Jesus goes on to say, that *I am coming back to you*. The presence of Christ will be invisible to the world, visible to the eyes of faith which will see him in the working of the Spirit. Just as the Son was sent into the world by the Father to reveal God's saving presence, so the Spirit will be sent to continue this revelation. In the possession of the Spirit will the Christian recognize that a trinity of personality in the Godhead is not simply an abstraction devised for the contemplation of the theologian, but the effulgence of a divine love in which he has been caught up and of which he is now a part: *in that day you will know that I am in my Father, and you in me, and I in you.*

A further question, this time by *Judas* the son of James (see above on Mk 3:13–19 and parallels) mentioned now for the first time by John, leads to a restatement of the work of the Paraclete, *the Holy Spirit,* in realized eschatology. In addition, mention is now made of his role in completing the Christian revelation by enlightening the Church in its understanding of Christ's teaching. The discourse which we are now reading in John's Gospel is, of course, one of the prime examples of the results of the Spirit's activity which has moulded the tradition on which the Gospel depends.

Jn 14:27–31 Jesus concludes the discourse with the classic Jewish word both of farewell and of greeting (cf. Jn 20:19), *Peace*. The basic concept of "peace" (*shalom*), in the Semitic sense, is that of harmony, completeness, integration. Peace was the effect produced by covenant, thus the blessing bestowed by the God of election (cf. Num 6:26), and thus, in an eschatological and messianic dimension, virtually the equivalent of "salvation" (cf. Is 9:6). Eph 2:14 speaks of the Christ in whom Jew and Gentile have been made one as "our peace." Here it sums up the entire dispensation of saving divine love which produces the new society of the Church, the final acts of which are about to be played through in Jesus' passion, death, and resurrection, the occasion of this leave-taking. *The Father is greater than I* is in the category of similar soteriological statements we have encountered in John's Gospel (see above on Jn 5:16–30): in the economy of salvation the Son is in the world to do the will of the Father.

The final words of this little section doubtless indicate that at one time it was the conclusion of the Last Supper discourse: bringing his remarks to a close, Jesus announces the imminent overthrow of *the ruler of the world* in the events of his glorification, and summons the disciples to depart with him from the banquet room. As John originally designed his Gospel, therefore, it is highly likely that what now appears as chapters 15–17 did not form a part of it. These chapters are, however, every bit as much the work of the evangelist as the rest of the Gospel; they are not additions to the Gospel but rather supplementary and parallel versions of Jesus' teaching brought in by the evangelist when composing the definitive edition of his work. Some of the parallels, though in part repetitious of much that has gone before, are precious in their own right, and the Gospel would be the poorer without them.

Jn 15:1–17   Precious indeed is the allegory of *the true vine and its branches* with which Jesus begins his discourse afresh. As has taken place in other instances—involving the shepherd and his sheep, for example, or the growth of a seed of life—here an Old Testament figure for the people of God (cf. Is 5:1–7; Jer 2:21; Ezek 15; Ps 80:9–16), which in the Synoptic Gospels Jesus takes up in one or another of his parables of the kingdom (cf. Mk 12:1–12 and parallels, for example), appears in a Johannine discourse simply identified with Jesus by one of his magisterial "I am's." Jesus *is* the eschatological Israel. On the sense in which he is the "true" vine, see above on Jn 1:9–13. The allegory, which is pellucid, strikingly illustrates the community of life shared by Christ and the Christian as well as the dynamic quality which is the character of this life: it must *produce much fruit*.

The comparison occasionally breaks down, of course. There is no exact correspondence between the pruning work of a *vine-dresser* and the fruit which the Father produces by tending the vine which is Christ and his Church. Neither would the injunction to *remain in me* apply to the prime analogue: unlike the branches of a vine which have no choice but to remain where they are, the followers of Christ must make their participation in his life the object of a deliberate commitment. As Jesus has been the instrument through whom God has reconciled the world of man to himself, his historical continuity in the Church remains the locale of the divine activity working in man. Remaining in Jesus the vine means adherence to his *words* by which his disciples are *clean*, well-tended branches capable of bearing fruit (cf. Jn 13:10): Jesus' words are all that has both taught and done as the prophetic Word of God, revealing the Father (cf. Jn 5:24).

Once again the theme of Christian life as an overflowing and communication of God's love is introduced: the parallel with the discourses in Jn 13–14 is close. Love has constituted the union of Christ and Christian, and by love the union will be maintained. This love, as previously said, is proved by the keeping of Christ's commandments, even as by fulfilling the will of his Father he proved his own love. By keeping his commandments the disciples will not only show their love for Christ, they will continue to be loved in turn by him, and thus their union will be maintained.

This irrefutable conviction of God's love ought to be the source of a great *joy* which should pervade all of Christian life. Even if this life be one of privation and suffering, as Christ's was, there should be joy, for in the revelation of the divine love in Christ suffering and sacrifice have been given meaning. Jesus' command that the disciples *love one another as I have loved you* takes on its fullness now that he refers to his death: *to lay down one's life for one's friends* is the ultimate extension of love. Once more the newness of his commandment of love is brought out (cf. Jn 13:31–35). Only the Son of God could make such a demand which is dictated by no natural law of life and which no other religious teacher would dare assert on his own authority. It is such a concept of the duty of the love of neighbor that is part of the folly of the Gospel (1 Cor 1:23)—a folly, we must add in all honesty, of which very few Christians are prepared to be found guilty. Folly and paradox though it be (see above on Jn 12:20–36), it is a law of life and death revealed in the Christ-event and thereby constituted the law of Christianity (cf. 1 Jn 3:16). Though by this-worldly standards it is a self-defeating principle, in fact it has proved to be the source of all life. To accept it as such, to live by its norm, requires great faith; but any faith that falls short of it is of necessity something less than Christian.

Whoever can share in this love revealed in Christ is ennobled by it. If God has loved us so much, if his love truly abides in us, then we must be worthy of such attention, we must have been elevated by it beyond our merely creaturely condition. He has *chosen* us. No longer is the title *servant* applicable, honorable though it may be (cf. Jn 12:26, 13:16). We are now *friends*. Friendship with God is the result of God's love, and the love of friendship is mutual, a love that is exchanged. We enter into the intimate life of God and share it. We are introduced into familiarity with him. No longer servants whose duty it is to obey simply because it has been commanded, we return God's love in obedience to his will because it is the desire of a friend. To *remain* in Christ's love can thus be seen not only as the greatest but also, in a way, as the only commandment. Jesus tells us what should be and what can be, not necessarily what will be. To the extent that what can and should be does become reality for any of us, to that extent we have remained in his love, and to that extent only.

Jn 15:18–16:4a   As he does in the Synoptic Gospels (see
above on Mt 10:16b–25 and parallel; Mk
13:9–13 and parallels), Jesus now warns his disciples of the
world's hatred and of coming persecutions. In John's context
this warning appears as a further dimension of the way
in which the Christian is assimilated to Christ in the life
which God has been pleased to share with him. The Church's
endurance of persecution and its rejection by the world,
foreshadowed in Old Testament types (*they have hated me
without cause:* Ps 69:5), are a continuation of the experience
of Jesus; they are additional ways in which his prophetic
witness to God's truth is lived out. This doctrine was also
St. Paul's (cf. Rom 8:17, etc.). All the Gospels, and Paul
too, for that matter, speak of hostility and persecution exclusively in Jewish terms. In the formative days of the
Church that produced and shaped the Gospel materials
the pressures brought against Christians—who, for all practical purposes remained identified as a Jewish sect even when,
as speedily happened, Gentiles began to join them in great
numbers—were measures taken by their fellow (but non-
Christian) Jews. It is for this reason that we have such a
prevalence of Jewish conflict stories in the Gospels (see
page 27 f. Vol. I), that in John's Gospel "the Jews" so often
means nothing more or less than "the world," and even that
the Gospels can at times exchange the terms "Pharisee,"
"Sadducee," "scribe," and the like, without too much bother
about statistical accuracy. Historically, the first opposition to
Christianity had come from the Jews. Later—but too late for
most of the New Testament—it would come from the far
greater world of the Roman empire, a world of much vaster
resources of ruthlessness and the will to make use of them,
as the second half of the Apocalypse of John bears witness.

Jn 16:4b–22   The discourse continues with what becomes
ever more obviously a reprise of the discourse
of Jn 13:31–14:31. While in Jn 13:36 and 14:5, however,
the disciples did ask Jesus, *Where are you going,* here he
reproaches them for not asking the question. Actually, these

are two variant dialogistic devices to bring out the same
teaching. The disciples have not yet asked the question
rightly, namely by showing an awareness of the real meaning of Jesus' "going away" in terms of the history of salvation, the realization of the last times in the Church. This he
now proceeds to explain once more, practically as we have
seen it above. This time, however, much more is said in
detail of the role of the Holy Spirit as *Paraclete*.

Both the Greek word *paraklētos* and its companion term
katēgoros were available as loan words in the Palestinian
Aramaic of Jesus' day. Borrowed from the language of the
courts, they referred to what we would designate respectively
as "defense counsel" and "prosecutor." In the jurisprudence
of the Mosaic law, however, these functions were both assumed by a single person, the "witness." The witness who
testified against someone did so primarily as a witness *for*
that which the accused was alleged to have violated; there
was no such thing as a disinterested witness. In a capital
case a witness for the prosecution quite literally testified to
the truth with his life, since if his testimony were proved
false by the acquittal of the accused it was he and not the
defendant who would undergo death. Thus it is that while
the Holy Spirit is called *paraklētos* and never *katēgoros*—
the latter term was the equivalent of the native Hebrew
and Aramaic *sātān*, "accuser," and is so used in Apo 12:10
—we should not be surprised when we find that his function
is seen to be as much prosecutor of the world as it is
defender of the Church.

The term is juridical, but the juridical background is
not much stressed. Rather, in the Fourth Gospel the concept
of the Spirit as Paraclete continues and completes a pattern
of *prophetic* witness which is one of its stresses. This
witness to truth, light, and life, against falsehood, darkness,
and death, the perennial witness of the prophetic word
(cf. Jn 1:1–4), has been the testimony of prophets like
Abraham (Jn 8:56), Moses (Jn 5:46 f.), Isaiah (Jn 12:38–
41), and John the Baptist (Jn 1:19 ff.). It reached its apex
in the incarnation of the prophetic Word, in Jesus Christ.

But now Christ, about to withdraw his visible presence from the world, leaves behind the prophetic Spirit of God to continue the testimony, the Spirit of prophecy itself now "incarnate" in his Church.

For it is in this "incarnational" state, as the "soul" of a Church of living men, that the Holy Spirit *will convict the world of sin, and of justice, and of judgment*—a conviction that is simultaneously a vindication of Christ, a witness to him. Of sin, first. Who was guilty of sin, Christ who was put to death or the world which condemned him? The lives of Christians, living by the power of the Spirit of God, must be such as to demonstrate that nothing of Christ can have any part in sin; their belief, then, must be the proof that it is with unbelief that sin lies: *because they do not believe in me.* Next, of justice. Who was just, Christ or the world? The just lives of Christians must show that it was and is Christ who lives in them invisibly present in his Spirit: *because I go to the Father and you see me no longer.* Finally, of judgment. Who has been truly judged and condemned in the crisis in which Jesus was engaged with the world? The lives of Christians, once more, must show that not Christ but *the ruler of this world has been judged.* The work of the Paraclete, therefore, is to inspire the Church as a body of prophetic witness which, in the words of the Fathers of the Second Vatican Council, "shares in Christ's prophetic office by spreading abroad a living witness to him by lives of faith and love, and by offering God the sacrifice of praise, the fruit of lips that confess his name." The witness of the Spirit and the witness of the Church is one and the same: "Those who bear witness to Jesus have the spirit of the prophets" (Apo 19:10). From which it also becomes plain that realized eschatology as we find it in John's Gospel is not simply the Church's re-evaluation of the realities of its hope, but is at the same time its most profound recognition of its call to holiness, a call which has been heard by everyone who has believed.

Jesus also refers to the Paraclete as *the Spirit of truth* (cf. Jn 14:17, 15:26) *who will lead you into all truth,* bringing to completion, as a witness to Jesus, the witness which Jesus himself has given to the Father. The sense of this form of the Spirit's testimony we have already noted in Jn 14:15–26 above. It, and all other aspects of the life of the Church (cf. Jn 14:13), *glorifies* Jesus even as Jesus glorified and was glorified by the Father, as evidence of the saving divine presence still active in the world.

The disciples now do engage in a discussion like that of the questions of Jn 13:36 and 14:5, over the *little while* of which Jesus speaks, the parallel to which we have seen in Jn 14:18 f. above. Jesus' illustration of the woman in labor, apt in itself, may also be an allusion to the Jewish concept of "the birthpangs of the Messiah" (see above on Mk 13:3–8 and parallels). In this connection, the temporary sorrows of the disciples will herald the messianic age as realized in Christ's resurrection and glorification.

Jn 16:23–33 Jesus concludes with a final series of effects that are to be attributed to the work of the Paraclete. First of all, he tells the disciples, *in that day you will ask me about nothing.* The meaning of this is picked up by his comparison of their present understanding of his teachings—*in parables*—with the understanding that they will have "in that day" when he speaks to them—through the Holy Spirit—*plainly.* Further, he refers again (see on Jn 14:13 f.) to prayer *in my name,* that is to say, to prayer that will be addressed to Jesus as Lord of the Church, reigning over it by his Spirit as the triumphant Son of God who has *come forth from the Father* and *again* has *returned to the Father.*

All at once the disciples desert their somewhat studied obtuseness to take a spectacular leap into overconfidence. Though Jesus had just told them that the time for plain speech was coming and was not yet—the one thing out of his discourse that they might have been expected to hear plainly—they think they know their Master well enough to take from him in their own time what he has promised to give in his own. Their assured statement is a fine example of Johannine irony. Parroting Jesus' own formulations as though this were all of Christian faith, they merely reinforce what he has said about his words being parables to them. This forms the occasion of Jesus' prediction of the general defection of the disciples, an event which, as we saw at the beginning of this chapter, Matthew and Mark have also recorded. Yet withal, he ends on a note of consolation.

Jn 17:1–8   The final part of the Last Supper discourse of Jesus takes the form of a prayer, but in it his instruction certainly continues. We can imagine him and his disciples now standing, in the classic Jewish attitude of prayer, as *he raised his eyes to heaven* and began to address the Father. This passage has long been called Jesus' High Priestly Prayer, and rightly so, since in it he presents himself as consecrated for his great sacrifice of love and obedience; as both the victim and the priest of this sacrifice he prays for all the fruits that will derive from it. The prayer is for the consummation of all that he has been speaking of to the disciples, of the union between them and himself, the union which consists in faith and in the love of the disciples for him and the Father. So first of all he prays for himself, and for himself in union with the Father, the union which signifies and makes possible the unity of the Church with Christ. As *the hour has* now *come* for his passion, he prays that the Father may indeed *glorify* him, exalt him, that in his glorification he may bring with him into God's presence those who are united with him. The glorification of the Son, we know, likewise means the glorification of the Father. He has glorified the Father by the words and deeds of his earthly life, and now he will continue to glorify him in the extension of his person, in the Church, in the lives of those whom he will bring to sanctity.

This characterization of Jesus as a specifically priestly mediator is not one of the major stresses of the Gospels; in the New Testament it is almost a unique emphasis of the Epistle to the Hebrews. There may be a hint of it, however, in Jesus' own designation of himself, first in his "enigma of the Messiah" (see above on Mk 12:35–37a and parallels), later in his reply to the high priest (see below on Mk 14:62 and parallels). In both of these passages he applies to himself Ps 110 which, taken messianically, called the Lord of whom David had written "a priest forever, like Melchizedek." It is the same typology that the author of Hebrews exploits. There was a strand of Old Testament thinking which spoke of soteriological expectation in priestly terms, but in the normative Judaism of Jesus' time no way could be seen to combine in one person the royal figure of a Davidic Messiah and a priestly figure who, it was thought of necessity, must be Levitical. Some elements in Judaism solved this problem by looking for two Messiahs, one a king and the other a priest (the Qumran sectaries had an idea resembling this), or by featuring an eschatological high priest who would anoint the Messiah (it is possible that there is a trace of this idea in Luke's insistence on the priestly ancestry of John the Baptist). As the author of Hebrews perceived, however, he could apply to Jesus the Messiah a text that was an embarrassment to Judaism precisely because of the clean break which Christ's priesthood had effected with the Levitical priesthood of the Old Testament. Jesus' own use of Ps 110, his depreciation of the temple in respect to himself (Mt 12:6), his substitution of himself for the temple (Jn 2:19; the over-all theme of Luke-Acts), and the priestly prayer that we are now reading, appear to point in the same direction. That direction is definitely away from any attempt to find precedents for the priesthood of Christ in the priestly legislation of the Mosaic law, despite the persistent efforts of some Christian writers to do just this. Christ's priesthood was and is a new thing, uniquely his in virtue of his unique consecration by the Father, and like Melchizedek's precisely because Melchizedek's priesthood was not that of Moses and Aaron. Significantly, the New Testament never applies the biblical (Old Testament) word "priest" (Greek *hiereus*=Hebrew *kōhēn*) to those who exercise the priesthood of Christ in his Church, though one of the words it does use, *presbyteros* (elder, translating the Hebrew *zāqēn*), became "priest" in English and other European languages under Christian influence.

Jn 17:9–19 Jesus' prayer now embraces the disciples, those whom the Father has given him. In praying *not for the world* he does not exclude the world from his prayer, since he will pray that his followers be consecrated for the service of the world; he does insist, however, that the disciples must be preserved from the world if they are to be preserved for it. Not only are they *in the world,* they are *sent into the world* even as the Son was sent into the world by the Father; but even as he, they must remain *not of the world:* the world is not its own salvation. They must be kept in God's *name,* with the *word* and life which Christ has bestowed on them; they must *be one even as we are one,* preserved in a love that has as its measure the love of the Father for the Son.

Not only is the relation of Father and Son the model of the disciple-and-Christ relationship, it is its principle. They must be *consecrated* with a priestly consecration, not, however, with anything less than the consecration of the Son himself, of *truth* and the *word. As you sent me into the world, so I sent them into the world:* the mission of Christ and the apostolic mission of the Church are one and the same, drawing their resources from the same source, with the same authority and powers.

Jn 17:20–26 Finally, Jesus prays for the Church of all time, for those who will believe through the preaching of his immediate disciples, *that they may be one, even as you, Father, in me and I in you.* In this unity of faith and love the world is to find a sign, and thus unity is by the divine will the great imperative for the Church's mission. The basis of this oneness is variously described as knowledge, recognition, faith, love, glory, but as the object of prayer it is *that where I am they may also be with me.* The prayer has subsumed the whole of the Last Supper discourses; in the world the Church communes with its heavenly Savior and finds realized in itself the divine presence even as Christ incarnated the divine Word through his communion with the Father.

24. AGONY

Mk 14:32a
Mt 26:36a
Lk 22:39
Jn 18:1

Now that both John and Luke have completed their stories of the Last Supper, they join Mark and Matthew in taking Jesus and his disciples *across the valley of the Kidron* (John) *to the Mount of Olives* (the Synoptics) *to a place called Gethsemane* (Mark and Matthew). Luke and John (vs. 2) tell us that it was a place of ordinary resort for Jesus (cf. Lk 21:37), and John speaks of it as *a garden*, evidently an enclosed garden (vs. 1, *he entered;* vs. 4, *he went out*). Our sources converge independently here in an obvious reference to a site that was well known. It was doubtless the private garden of a friend containing an olive grove and the oil press (*gath shemane* in Aramaic) for which it was named. The Gethsemane of modern Jerusalem, a place of pilgrimage from ancient times, can hardly be far removed from the garden that the Gospels locate so precisely.

Mk 14:32b–42
Mt 26:36b–46
Lk 22:40–46

The scene that follows, traditionally called "the agony in the garden" (from the word *agōnia* in Luke's account, vs. 43), is entirely omitted by John (who, however, seems to refer to it in vs. 11); in the Fourth Gospel the

entire passion story from beginning to end is represented as
Jesus' triumph and exaltation, and episodes of this kind are
bypassed. In truth, John would have found it difficult to
incorporate the story in any way into his Gospel, though as
we have seen (on Jn 12:20–36 above), he does have something like it in another context. Here we are shown a Jesus
most nakedly human, bewildered, torn by conflicting emotions, moved almost beyond endurance; and of course, this
is as authentically a Gospel portrait of Jesus as is that of the
sublime and serene Teacher that John likes to paint. The
implications of the account in respect to the psychological
consciousness of the historical Jesus of Nazareth are for the
theologian to draw and to incorporate into his christology.
We are concerned at the present merely with what the
Gospels say and why they say it. About the implications
the New Testament writers, we may be sure, were far more
tranquil than later Christians have been. The author of
Hebrews, for example, for whom Jesus is without doubt
the unique Son of God and celestial High Priest, completely
sinless (4:15, 7:26, 9:14), was very likely thinking of this
very story when he wrote: "In the days of his earthly life
he offered up prayers and supplications, with loud cries
and tears, to him who was able to save him from death . . .
Son though he was, he learned obedience through suffering,
and, once perfected, became the source of eternal salvation
for all who obey him, being designated by God high priest
in the order of Melchizedek" (5:7–10). For the Gospels
this event is, before it is anything else, Jesus' priestly consecration (cf. Jn 17:19). From it he emerges with his
sacrifice interiorly completed; the details of the passion that
then begin to unfold he has already anticipated and accepted: they fulfill but do not constitute the offering that
he has now made.

Luke's account differs considerably from that of Mark-
Matthew. In the latter story only are the favored three
disciples featured (see above on Mk 9:2–10 and parallels)
as witnesses not of Jesus' agony itself—the Gospels agree

that all were asleep during this—but of its most important
prelude which Luke does not even mention explicitly. Matthew himself has somewhat toned down what Mark has
written to describe this. *He went into a state of shock*
would not be a translation too wide of the mark. What
we are being told is that now Jesus experiences as a proximate reality the meaning of the destiny he had voluntarily
assumed, to be the Servant of the Lord and to suffer an
atoning death for the sins of man. It is one thing to embrace
a vocation firmly and unequivocally with all its consequences
clearly foreseen, and then to meet those consequences no
longer as future abstractions but in the concrete present: in
this instance to face an imminent death by torture. Yet
even now more is involved than mere human repugnance
to suffering and death. Jesus is fully aware of the vicarious
nature of his suffering, which makes it not easier but all the
more difficult to bear. All at once it is brought home to
him how utterly alone he is in a world for which he is
prepared to die and in which there is not another single
person who can or will afford him the slightest consolation.
For this reason he withdraws from the company of even
the disciples of his choice and speaks with the Father who
alone can understand him.

It is important to recognize that Jesus' agony is one of
fear and horror, not of despair. *My heart is ready to break
with sorrow*, his words to the disciples, evoke Pss 42:6,
12, 43:5, which is a psalm of confidence in God. Kneeling
in the presence of his Father he prays not that he may be
dispensed from his lot, nor does he rail against it; he only
asks whether another way might yet be decreed by the one
to whom all things are possible. And in his prayer he finds
the strength he needs to go forward resolutely: *not as I will,
but as you will.*

How long Jesus' prayer continued, the Gospels do not
indicate. Luke does not prolong it over three stages as do
Mark and Matthew. Luke makes his own contribution, however, both in personifying the divine consolation in the pres-

ence of *an angel from heaven* and in his graphic portrayal
of the agony of Jesus in which *his sweat became like great
drops of blood falling down upon the ground*. Whether this
last he intends us to take quite literally or as an expressive
figure of speech—the literal experience of bloody sweat seems
to be an established pathological fact—in any case we cannot fail to grasp from it the reality of the agony itself. These
two verses in Luke's account are missing in many of the
early manuscripts. It is much easier to conceive of them as
having been deliberately omitted, however, than as being a
scribal invention; in all probability they formed an original
part of Luke's text.

The sleeping disciples appear in ironic contrast to the
Jesus who has just successfully survived his soul's crisis.
Luke says that they were *sleeping for sorrow*. Although
he had nothing about their witness of Jesus' shock and fear,
he doubtless intends to suggest that they had had some
surmise of it. Catching something of Jesus' mood they too
experienced sorrow and, perhaps, depression. Unlike Jesus,
however, they found prayer a task to which they were
unequal, and thus they slept. Luke is quite as charitable as
Jesus himself in interpreting their motives. The *temptation*
against which they have been warned is, as in the Lord's
Prayer (see above on Lk 11:1–4 and parallel), the hour
of trial for the elect at the ushering in of the messianic
age. In Matthew and Mark Jesus can tell the disciples, not
without gentle sarcasm perhaps, that they may now sleep
on and enjoy their rest, for the trial has been met and
overcome by himself alone. And now the hour is at hand.

Mk 14:43–52   The story of Jesus' arrest is told dramatically
Mt 26:47–56   by all the evangelists, but with the kind of
Lk 22:47–53   simple drama that appears to appeal to lit-
Jn 18:2–11   tle more than an ultimate eyewitness recol-
                    lection. There have been a few embellish-
ments acquired in oral tradition and through theological
meditation, but it is not difficult to reconstruct the event to

the satisfaction of an historian, at least in its essential details. Of capital importance, however, is a detail on which our three passion-sources are not in agreement and which has considerable bearing on what is to follow. From Mark-Matthew we would judge that those who arrested Jesus were simply a hired mob—the kind of democracy in action never hard come by in any society at any time—sent *with swords* (or simply "knives") *and clubs* by the cabal of his inveterate enemies among the Sanhedrin which had plotted against him and bargained with Judas (see above on Mk 14:10 f. and parallels). Luke mentions, as he has before, the involvement of *the temple police,* one of whom may have been *the servant of the high priest* who figures in the accounts of all four Gospels. There is no reason to question Luke's datum, which for that matter is confirmed by John. The temple police could have hardly been officially involved, it is true, for the Sanhedrin itself was not now acting officially. At the same time, they were the minions of those who had sent the mob, and it is not uncharitable to suppose that they included in their number men who were no better than their masters.

John's modification of this picture is most surprising. There was also present, he says, *the cohort.* He uses the Greek word normally employed for this Roman military unit of six hundred men (though this full muster was not necessarily normal), and by the article he evidently intends to say that they were soldiers of the Roman garrison at Jerusalem. Later (vs. 12) he adds that they were commanded by their *chiliarchos:* the term which designated a Roman *tribune*.

It is easy to say that John has, for theological reasons, magnified the array of worldly powers engaged in the arrest of Jesus: in an earlier age of Gospel criticism a judgment of this kind would have been routine. On the other hand, the introduction of Roman troops at this stage of the proceedings makes a good deal of sense in respect to the historical background of the passion story. John, be it noted, has no advantage to serve in inculpating the Romans of the events of this night. Neither was this a Roman arrest, according to John or any of the other Gospels. The Romans —most of whom, incidentally, were without doubt Syrians recruited from the neighboring province—could have been present only as "advisers." But that there were Romans privy to the plot against Jesus is not only not unlikely but almost inevitable. To mention only one thing at this time, it is hardly credible that any armed band of any size would have been permitted to pass through Jerusalem without prior Roman knowledge and approval. At the Passover season the Roman authorities were especially nervous about such things, but at no time did they look on unauthorized assemblies with a kindly eye. The Gospels have more than once included among the conspirators against Jesus certain Herodians (cf. Mk 3:6, 12:13; Mt 22:16), and the Herodians were Romanophiles. Suborning Roman officials in the provinces was neither unusual nor particularly expensive. All in all, there is ample cause to believe that the arms carried by the band that arrested Jesus were borne by Jewish and Roman soldiers, just as John tells us.

John's chronology of the Last Supper is likewise supported by this story and the ones that follow. It is hardly credible that any such thing could have taken place on the actual day of the Passover feast.

All the Gospels put Judas at the head of the arresting mob, even John's which has no account of the prior arrangement between Judas and Jesus' enemies. The Synoptics have the story of Judas' betrayal *with a kiss;* in Mark-Matthew the point is made that this was a prearranged signal. It is Luke who brings out the dreadful incongruity of the gesture, which, however, was a normal enough greeting between disciple and rabbi. In the dark of the garden—only John has thought to mention the *torches and lanterns* carried by the crowd—some identification of this kind was needful. Besides, most of those present did not know Jesus by sight; they were just simple mercenaries earning their pay with no especial interest in who was being arrested or why.

John omits the story of Judas' kiss and substitutes another which definitely does seem to be theologically motivated. In this account Jesus himself takes the entire initiative, while Judas stands helplessly by. The soldiers, awed by Jesus' commanding presence, arrest him only after he has identified himself and given them leave, and only after he has protected to the end those whom the Father has given him (cf. Jn 6:39, 17:12).

It is John who identifies the one who cut off the ear of the high priest's slave, and for good measure names the slave as well; neither identification causes any difficulty, and the first we might have suspected in any case. All the Gospels except Mark ascribe some saying to Jesus on this occasion, each of which is appropriate, and Luke tells us that he healed the wound; but the silence of the Lord is just as eloquent as his words. In the Synoptic Gospels he further rebukes the crowd for its armed hostility, seemingly presupposing his having been often in Jerusalem, as we know from John's Gospel.

The final lines in Mark's account are fascinating because of their obscurity and because Mark, who we know is not in the habit of wasting words, is the only evangelist to have kept the story. Theologically, it is pointless; it can only be the recollection of an eyewitness which Mark thought important enough to record. But why? Who was the *young man wrapped in a linen cloth*—apparently a sheet snatched from the bed by someone rudely awakened—who *fled away naked leaving the sheet* when an attempt was made to apprehend him? Perhaps the owner of the garden where the arrest took place, who suddenly found his villa invaded by a rabble of armed men. Perhaps Mark himself, who belonged to a Jerusalem family comfortable enough to support a town house (the upstairs room of the Last Supper?) and a garden on the Mount of Olives (cf. Acts 12:12). The possibilities are endless. At all events, whoever he was, he took the course of the rest of the disciples, surprised and dismayed as they were at the turn events had now taken. *They all deserted him and fled.*

Jn 18:12–14   We probably do well to be guided by John
Lk 22:54a   in the sequence that follows. He alone tells
Mk 14:53   us that after his arrest Jesus was taken *first*
Mt 26:57   *to Annas, for he was the father-in-law of*
               Caiaphas, who was high priest that year.
In saying that Caiaphas was high priest "that year" John
undoubtedly intends only to identify the high priest of the
fateful year of Jesus' crucifixion, not to insinuate that the
high priesthood changed hands every year—though as a
matter of fact, between Annas and Caiaphas there had been
a quick succession of three high priests, none of whom had
lasted more than a year. John reminds us that it was
Caiaphas who had uttered the cynical "prophecy" of Jn
11:50.

Annas himself had been high priest from A.D. 6 to 15,
at which time he had been deposed by Valerius Gratus,
Pontius Pilate's predecessor as governor of Judea during the
years 15 to 26. He was patriarch of one of the half dozen
families among which the high priesthood circulated, and
himself appears to have had five sons, one grandson, and a
son-in-law who at one time or another filled the office.
There is no doubt, then, that he was the grey eminence
behind the high priesthood throughout this entire period,
and therefore it is not surprising that Lk 3:2 and Acts 4:6
speak of him as high priest. Probably in the minds of many
Jews he was the legitimate high priest, since the Jews never
quite reconciled themselves to the Roman governor's asserted
right of deposing and appointing high priests at will, or, as it
usually happened, for a bribe. Joseph Caiaphas was high
priest from A.D. 18 to 36. He was deposed at just about the
same time Pilate himself fell from favor and was removed
from office, and the connection is probably more than casual.
The Annas-Caiaphas family appear to have had an "arrangement" with the Roman governor, a fact which may help to
explain the presence of Roman troops at the arrest of Jesus.
It was certainly a fact that did not endear them to the
great mass of Palestinian Jews. The Gospels are by no
means alone in giving bad marks to these men. By the

great majority of Jews of the time they were regarded as unworthy of their office and as more interested in perpetuating their political power than in preserving the faith of Moses.

At all events, that Jesus should have been taken to the house of Annas as John maintains is quite believable. Furthermore, it is most likely to Annas that Luke refers when he also narrates that Jesus was taken away *to the house of the high priest*. Luke agrees with John, therefore, when he is read apart from the other Synoptics. Luke further differs from Mark-Matthew in describing no trial of Jesus on this occasion; the trial, Luke insists (vss. 66–71), took place only on the following morning, and in the council chamber of the Sanhedrin, the proper place for a trial. All the historical probabilities are on Luke's side. The Sanhedrin could not pass judgment at night or in secret. Neither would the browbeating of a prisoner as the Gospels describe the treatment of Jesus have been tolerated in a regular and legal session of a Jewish court. What happened to Jesus this night after his arrest was not a trial by the Sanhedrin, but harassment at the hands of the Jewish conspirators and their lackeys who were detaining him against his trial in the morning. John, for his part, tells of no trial either at night or in the morning. In his view it is not Jesus but the world that is on trial during Jesus' passion-glorification.

But the Mark-Matthew narrative does describe the night detention of Jesus as containing a trial; furthermore, Matthew speaks of it as taking place in the house of Caiaphas rather than Annas. At the same time, both Gospels do later on join Luke in recording an arraignment of Jesus before a full session of the Sanhedrin on Friday morning. What seems to be our best conclusion is that this narrative of the passion has telescoped the events of Thursday night and Friday morning into one account, even though it retained a memory of the separate Friday trial, since it was far more interested in the drama of the story than in its correspondence with Jewish legalities. Though two separate "high priests" were involved in it, Annas in whose house

Jesus was abused by his captors and where Peter denied
his Master, Caiaphas under whose presidency Jesus was
tried, Mark simply refers to *the high priest* throughout.
By the time the story had reached Matthew, who thought
it necessary to call the high priest by name, it had doubtless
been forgotten that in the historical sequence of events two
high priests had figured in it in two different capacities,
and in the First Gospel, as a consequence, we find only the
name of Caiaphas, the official high priest. Having subsumed
the sequence of events under the one heading, the Mark-
Matthew narrative does nothing with the actual trial except
to refer to it summarily.

Jn 18:15–27   Following the reconstruction just
Lk 22:54b–65   proposed, we shall consider the
Mk 14:54–61a, 65–72   four accounts as they lie before us,
Mt 26:58–63a, 67–75   extracting from the Mark-Matthew
                         narrative only the solemn adjuration
and question put to Jesus by the high priest, which served
as the basis of his judicial condemnation and which we
shall see better where it belongs in parallel with Luke.
What remains is the story of the abuse of Jesus during the
night of his detention and, coinciding with this, the story
of Peter's denial of his Lord. As we shall have already
surmised, John is interested in telling only the latter story,
not at all the former.

It is John who offers an explanation as to how Peter
came to be in *the high priest's courtyard,* an explanation,
when we come to think of it, that is really necessary. The
arrest of Jesus, after all, was still secret and unofficial,
and it was not in the interests of his captors to admit just
anyone to the scene of their machinations. By the same
token, Luke's and John's portrayal of the arrest as the work
of hired soldiers makes very good sense. Only John has it
that besides Peter *another disciple had followed Jesus* after
he had been taken. This cryptic anonymity from an evangelist
who is otherwise free with names makes us suspect that
the disciple is deliberately unnamed and that he is that

"disciple whom Jesus loved" (cf. Jn 20:2), presumably John the son of Zebedee, the ultimate source of John's Gospel. At any rate, it was through this *other disciple known to the high priest* that Peter gained access to the high priest's house. "Known to the high priest" need not mean anything more than that he was known in the high priest's household, that is, among his servants, as, indeed, the story itself seems to suggest.

It is without doubt pointless to try to harmonize completely the Gospel accounts of Peter's multiple denial of Jesus. The Gospels agree that Peter denied Jesus three times, and on the circumstances of the first denial they are in fair agreement also. As for the subsequent denials, there are discrepancies both as to the circumstances and as to the precise individuals who put the question to Peter. These variations are such as would be expected to have occurred in separate oral transmissions of events that had been made known through hearsay—for certainly none of the evangelists was witness to them. Far more important than any attempt to reconcile stories that simply had in mind to relate the fulfillment of what Jesus had foretold (see above on Jn 13:36–38 and parallels) is it to make note of certain details in the stories that have something definite to tell us about the Gospel narrative, whether or not these were consciously thought of by the Gospel writers.

First of all, the character of Peter's denials should be properly understood. He was not, as Jesus was, being asked to declare himself before the world for its acceptance or rejection; he was probably being asked to do little more than satisfy the curiosity of uninvolved bystanders. While the curiosity was not precisely friendly, neither need we presume that it was especially hostile. These were the questions of servants milling about the high priest's courtyard, as much surprised as anyone else over the turn of events that had brought the man Jesus to their master's house. Peter's was a sin of cowardice and human respect (see above on Mt 12:31 f. and parallels). For the rest of it, matters like the open fire built against the cool of an early spring night, the persistence of the girl at the courtyard gate, Peter's Galilean accent which grated on Judean ears, seem to go back to eyewitness recollections all the more credible as such for having got somewhat mixed up, as eyewitness recollections generally do.

The only indignity which John allows to be shown to Jesus is in conjunction with the high priest's exploratory interrogation about his disciples. As an old political schemer himself, Annas could hardly think of anyone having messianic pretensions except in terms of political rebellion. Such thinking coincided with the interests of Rome, which Annas had long served for his own ends and which he would continue to exploit over the body of Jesus. Both in his disdainful reply to Annas, however, and in the mild but imperturbable reproof he administers to his sycophantic police officer, Jesus' dignity is shown enhanced all the more. It is he who controls the situation, not his captors exploring mare's nests for evidence and proving by their violence that they have run out of arguments.

What the Synoptic Gospels also describe is a searching for evidence against Jesus and the coaching of witnesses, not a formal presentation of a case that would hold in court. The abuse that was showered on him undoubtedly was intended as much to provoke some indictable response as to serve as an outlet for frustration and contempt. The one usable piece of evidence that was forthcoming, according to Mark-Matthew, was Jesus' prophecy of the destruction of the temple (see above on Mk 13:1 f. and parallels). That Jesus had not only made such a prophecy, but had connected himself intimately with the event and its consequences, is amply testified in the New Testament: once again by Mark-Matthew (Mk 15:29; Mt 27:40); by Luke not here but in Acts 6:14; for John's interpretation, see above on Jn 2:18–22. Therefore it is surprising that Mark insists that in bringing these words of Jesus against him *they testified falsely*. Evidently he means that they were quoting the prophecy in a garbled form and contrary to the spirit in which Jesus had uttered it, as though the temple

were of no account except to serve as the occasion of a
vulgar show of magical power. At any rate, whatever evi-
dential value such a statement may have had seems to have
vanished because of the faulty memories of those who had
heard it: *even here their testimony was not the same.* To
convict under the Mosaic law the agreed testimony of a
minimum of two witnesses was required (cf. Deut 19:15).
It may well be, however, as the Gospels suggest, that it
was the implications of this saying of Jesus that led the
high priest to put to him the question by which he became
incriminated in the eyes of the Sanhedrin, and that it was
the same that influenced the Sanhedrin to regard Jesus'
answer as incriminating.

Lk 22:66–71   John has already said (vs. 24) that
Mk 14:61b–64, 15:1a   following the interrogation of Jesus
Mt 26:63b–66, 27:1   at his house, *Annas sent him bound
                         to Caiaphas the high priest.* Though
John has no intention of describing any trial of Jesus, his
next passages will presuppose that such a thing has, indeed,
taken place, and it is this that is now depicted for us by
Luke, *when day came,* the only time that a trial could
legally take place. Mark and Matthew, though they too
preserved a tradition of a morning meeting of the Sanhedrin,
now that they had already anticipated the judicial sentence
of death passed on Jesus during the events of the night
before, were somewhat at a loss what to do with the
redundant session. At least Matthew was; Matthew is always
more sensitive to such problems than Mark. Mark's source
had it that *early the next morning . . . the whole Sanhedrin
reached a verdict.* Though this might have given him pause
in view of what he had already written about the verdict,
he simply put down what he had and went on to the next
matter, the delivery of Jesus to the Roman governor. Matthew solved the difficulty by understanding the "verdict"
as a new decision of the Sanhedrin to hand Jesus over to
Pilate; this decision, however, would have been implied in
the beginning in any sentence of death.

It is not much that the Gospels tell us about the trial of Jesus. We are left to imagine the title under which the Sanhedrin was convened, the nature of the charges that were proffered, how the seizure of Jesus and his harassment were legalized, and much else. Certainly Jesus was not friendless even among the Sanhedrin (cf. Jn 12:42 f.), to say nothing of his more general popularity with the people at large. His enemies were powerful and strategically placed; nevertheless, to accomplish what they did must have entailed much more maneuvering than we are able to follow in the Gospels. Of plots and plans we have been told, but without much detail. Of course, many of the details would have been unavailable to the Gospel sources.

One of the problems encountered by any commentator on the passion narrative is the time element. Events have moved very swiftly leading up to this Good Friday morning, and they will move even more swiftly hereafter. So swift is the tempo, in fact, many students of the Gospels refuse to believe that it can correspond to historical fact. They find it difficult to believe that Jesus could have eaten the Last Supper with his disciples, that he could then have gone to Gethsemane, have been arrested, carried off to detention and abused, have been tried and condemned, remanded to the Roman governor, sentenced, crucified, that he should then have breathed out his life, have been taken down from the cross and buried, all within the space of less than twenty-four hours; and from the list we have omitted several other episodes that the Gospels pack into this long day. An apparent way out of the supposed impasse has been found by some in the Qumran solar calendar which we mentioned above in connection with the date of the Passover (see on Mk 14:12–17 and parallels). If Jesus and his disciples did, indeed, keep the Passover according to the Qumran rule, the Last Supper would have taken place on a Tuesday evening, such being the peculiarity of its calendar. If the Last Supper occurred on a Tuesday and the crucifixion on a Friday—for the Gospels are at one on this—

then we are afforded a more realistic time distribution for
the events of Holy Week.

Though in the abstract this solution may have something
to commend it, however, in fact it comes up against the
Gospel chronology which knows nothing of such a possibility.
This would not be a peremptory objection, it is true, but it
is also true that there are many good reasons to believe
that Jesus would never have followed the heterodox Qumran
calendar. Furthermore, the very unlikeliness of the Gospel
chronology may be the best proof of its authenticity and,
perhaps, may help to explain the secret of the success of
Jesus' enemies. If we take it at its face value, probably
by the time that the news of Jesus' arrest had become
known in any general way in Jerusalem he would have
been already inexorably committed to death, beyond the
hope of any remedial action by his friends and supporters.
His powerful enemies had the advantage of surprise, they
controlled much of the machinery of law in their own
right, and they knew how to oil the machinery that they did
not control but needed. What the Gospels describe is not
impossible; it is simply obscure, and for the usual reason,
that neither the Gospels nor their sources have bothered
very much, if at all, with a great deal of what the modern
historian considers to be of prime importance.

Another question that the Gospels do not solve concerns
the legality of the sentence of death passed on Jesus by the
Sanhedrin. Whether, indeed, the entire Sanhedrin was involved in the process is not certain—the Gospels' references
to "all the chief priests," "all the elders of the people,"
"the whole Sanhedrin," and the like, have obviously not
drawn on the official minutes of the supreme Jewish tribunal.
We have argued above that Jesus' trial was held in the
morning rather than at night for legality's sake not on any
a priori basis, but because our sources for the passion-history,
John, Luke, and even Mark-Matthew for that matter, indicate that such was the case. Psychologically considered, it
makes very good sense that such should have been the
case. A semblance of legality was needed by men who

stood for the Law and the temple if they were to condemn
Jesus in the name of the Law and the temple. But only a
semblance was needed: no really successful criminal makes
the mistake of violating obvious and easy laws which cost
nothing. There remain many elements in what little of the
trial we know about whose legality the scholars will long
continue to debate. Was it lawful for the high priest to put
a self-incriminating question to the accused? What precise
legal ground was the basis for declaring Jesus' answer a
"blasphemy"? In some part we are hampered by a lack of
information concerning judicial procedure of the first Christian century, to what extent it corresponded with later Jewish jurisprudence that is better known. Was it lawful, for
example, to pass sentence on the same day that judgment
had been rendered? In later times, it certainly was not. But
again, we ponder such questions without much help from
the Gospels.

The Synoptic Gospels give us little more than the crucial
question which the high priest asked of Jesus, together
with Jesus' answer, on which the Sanhedrin passed its verdict. And even these they give us somewhat differently.

The high priest's question was: *Are you the Messiah?*
This was to be, as we shall see, the title under which
Jesus was handed over to the Romans as worthy of death
and the title under which he was executed. In Roman eyes
it was high treason to claim messiahship. But it was not
a Jewish crime. Many in the Sadducean-dominated Sanhedrin might have been disposed to view it as a dangerous,
even pernicious quixotism that could only bode disaster for
the *status quo* of Roman Palestine (the sense of Caiaphas'
"prophecy" in Jn 11:49 f.); but it was not against the Law.
The Pharisees present would certainly not have been much
moved by the question as such. To claim falsely to be the
Messiah might indeed be a cause for condemnation; but
in that case the question was poorly phrased. They themselves had on more than one occasion required of Jesus
testimonials to his messianic character, and he had always
refused. They were doubtless not loath to see removed on

any pretext one who had challenged their traditions and ridiculed their religiosity as hypocrisy. Still, on what pretext of Law? From the standpoint of Law Jesus was unassailably an orthodox Jew, and all the more so for his faith in messianism.

All the Gospels at one place or another make synonymous with Messiah in this passage the title *Son of God* (*Son of the Blessed One* in Mark's version has a more authentically Jewish ring to it). Students of the New Testament continue to dispute whether in pre-Christian Judaism this title was commonly used of the Messiah. Whatever may be the answer to this question, the Gospels evidently do consider it to be a messianic title (see above on Mk 8:27–30 and parallels), even though the evangelists quite obviously know of a deeper sense in which Jesus Christ was and is Son of God. Grounds for calling the Davidic Messiah Son of God could be found by any Jew in 2 Sam 7:14. At any rate, it is doubtful that the Gospels think of "Son of God" on the lips of the high priest as offering any greater challenge to Jesus than "Messiah."

And what is Jesus' answer to this solemn charge? In Luke, it is obviously non-committal. At first he dismisses their question as inutile, then when pressed he replies, *You say that I am*. This is likewise the meaning of his answer according to Matthew: *You have said so*. As we know very well, "Messiah" was not a name that Jesus could answer to without qualifications. He was the Messiah—as he understood the significance of this figure in the saving purposes of God—and he definitely was not the Messiah as most of those about him, whether approving or disapproving, thought of the Messiah (see above on Lk 4:3–13 and parallel). Hence the sense of his reply is the equivalent of "As you wish . . . You say it, not I."

Mark, however, has him say unequivocally, *I am*. Actually, there are Marcan manuscripts that read "You have said that I am," which some scholars believe to be the original wording of Mark's Gospel (thus better explaining Matthew's text which is otherwise usually an adaptation of Mark's). Still,

we know that Mark has a special stake in the title "Messiah"
as applied to Jesus: the "messianic secret" (see above on Mk
1:22–28) for him is a vital page of the Gospel. The secret
has now been broken, and he would thereafter find it hard
to deny this title to his Lord, even though he would
understand it in a way quite different from that of the high
priest. "I am," therefore, is probably what Mark originally
wrote. In much the same manner, by an alternate arrangement of the dialogue between Jesus and his judges, Luke
has given special prominence to the title "Son of God" (see
above on Lk 1:34–38).

But having progressed thus far, we are still faced with the
fact that, whether positively or negatively or neutrally, Jesus
had committed himself to absolutely nothing that was actionable under Jewish law. If we are to look for an objective
basis for the charge of "blasphemy" that was immediately
hurled against him, we must seek it elsewhere in Jesus'
reply.

In all three Gospels Jesus goes on to speak of himself in
the language of Dan 7:13 and Ps 110:1. He is the Son
of Man, he is the mysterious Lord of whose enthronement
David had sung (see above on Mk 12:35–37a and parallels). In Mark-Matthew he speaks of his coming glorification, in Luke's version it is considered as already begun
(cf. Jn 12:31). Technically, this was still not the language
of blasphemy, but equivalent statements of Jesus had brought
down this imputation before (cf. Jn 8:59, 10:31–33). It is
important to observe that, not only in John's Gospel but in
the Synoptic tradition as well, and in the most solemn of
Jesus' declarations according to this tradition, he is represented as identifying himself by preference not as the Jewish
Messiah but as the glorified Son of Man (see above on
Jn 1:43–51). It was as such that he confronted the Sanhedrin, and as such that he was condemned.

By whatever evidence, probably on a confluence of motives and causes, Jesus was adjudged *deserving of death*.
It was a judgment made by men who in separate ways
saw him as a threat to their way of life, their profession,

their religion, their nation, their God himself. It was undoubtedly the judgment of men sincere as well as men
devious and guileful. It was a judgment made by Jews. It
was not, however, the judgment made by a people.

Mt 27:3–10   Following the story of Jesus' trial, the Gospels proceed to the next inevitable step in
the journey of Jesus to the cross, the ratification of his
sentence by the Roman governor. Only Matthew, however,
has inserted at this point a narrative which seems to have
been drawn from a Jerusalem tradition about the subsequent
fate of Judas Iscariot.

Probably a certain contrast is intended with the repentance of Simon Peter after his craven refusal to acknowledge
his Master in the high priest's courtyard. When the enormity
of what he had done was brought home to Peter, the
Gospels tell us that *he went out and wept bitterly* over the
collapse of the brave figure of loyal devotion in which he had
once fancied himself. Judas, too, seeing what had happened
to Jesus, *was* now *struck with remorse* over his betrayal.
Just why, we are not sure, since we know little of the
complexity of motives that had gone into Judas' action in
the first place, and neither this Gospel passage nor any
other informs us about them. At any rate, his bitter disillusionment is turned futilely against himself to a final act of
self-destruction. Just as a murderer will sometimes try to
destroy or to hide the weapon of death even from himself,
as though doing so would cancel out the deed, Judas' first
fixation is to rid himself of the incriminating *thirty pieces of
silver*, the sum which Matthew alone mentioned before (Mt
26:15).

It seems to be Matthew's thought that Judas tried to
return the money to the Sanhedrin itself, but it is *the chief
priests* who make the final disposition of it as temple property. According to this tradition they used it to buy a tract
of ground already known as *the potter's field*, doubtless
because its clay had served the needs of one or several
potters for some time, to turn it into *a burial place for*

strangers. These "strangers" would be Jews from outside Jerusalem who would chance to die in the Holy City or who had come there expressly for their burial, and who were dependent on public charity. For this reason, says Matthew, the ground came to be known as *the field of blood* —Jesus' blood, that is, as bought with the blood money paid to Judas.

In Acts 1:16–20 Luke records an alternate tradition, both as to the origin of the name of the field and as to the circumstances of Judas' death. The field, according to Acts, got its name from *Judas'* blood, because he died some sort of violent death there on the land he had bought. It is not evident from Acts that Judas committed suicide. It is pointless to ask which tradition is "right." The only point is that early Christian tradition associated the field with the money of Judas' treachery and that it reflected on the end of the betrayer in terms of his Old Testament prototypes (cf. Wis 4:19; 2 Sam 17:23; cf. also Ps 69:26 in connection with the story in Acts). These reflections came from a Jewish, hardly from a Gentile Christian community.

Matthew's discovery of a prophetic precedent for this event is particularly interesting, the fruit of the same kind of reflection on the Old Testament we have just noted. Matthew refers to *Jeremiah the prophet,* but verbally his quotation begins with a reminiscence of Zech 11:12 f., a prophetic allegory which provided a certain typology for the matter at hand. Jeremiah is present in his mind, however, through a further association of ideas (cf. Jer 32:7–9, 18:2–10, 19:1 ff.): dominating the passage is the thought of the potter's field, the price of Jesus' blood, a standing witness forever against these false *sons of Israel* in Topheth, in the dismal valley of Ben-hinnom (gehenna: see above on Mt 5:27–30). This interweaving of disparate strands of scriptural word and idea resembles nothing so much as the midrashic interpretation of the rabbis.

25. "WHAT IS TRUTH?"

Mk 15:1b After his trial before the Sanhedrin, Jesus
Mt 27:2 was taken *to Pilate the governor* and, as
Lk 23:1 John specifies, *to the praetorium,* a term
Jn 18:28–32 used later by Mark-Matthew also. The Sanhedrin presumably had met in its customary
meeting hall on the western side of the temple area, in a
sector and near a market place which the Jews called Gazith
(the corruption of a Greek word, *xystos,* which meant a
covered colonnade; similarly, Sanhedrin itself was a corruption of the Greek word *synedrion,* council). It is conceivable, however, that the trial of Jesus had been held in
the palace of Caiaphas the high priest, which was probably
somewhere in the southwestern part of New Testament Jerusalem, in the upper city where the homes of the wealthy
were. The geography of ancient Jerusalem is perforce often
very conjectural, dependent on casual historical references
and a good deal of guesswork, since the continuous and
dense habitation of the city has made the investigation of
much of its ground difficult if not impossible. The location
of the praetorium, for example, which could be quite relevant
to our understanding of the Gospel story, is by no means
certain.

The praetorium was the official residence of Roman authority, where edicts were dispensed and judgments given. The seat of the Roman governor of Judea was not Jerusalem but Caesarea; in Caesarea, then, was the chief praetorium of Judea (cf. Acts 23:35). The governor also maintained a residence in Jerusalem, however, which he visited especially in times of potential danger to law and order, such as the great pilgrimage feasts of Judaism. This residence would be the praetorium of the Gospels. As far as ancient records have anything to tell us about it, the governor's residence would have been in the Palace of Herod (the Great), on the western side of the city on an eminence now occupied by a citadel known popularly as the Tower of David, near the Jaffa Gate. Here was the second of the two garrisons maintained in Jerusalem, the other being at the Fortress Antonia adjoining the temple area.

A persistent Christian tradition, however, has long associated Jesus' passion with the Antonia region itself, and in the minds of many this tradition has been confirmed by the findings of archaeology, to establish that it was the Antonia that the Gospels call the praetorium. According to Jn 19:13, the praetorium of the Gospels was given the name *Lithostrōton* (stone pavement), and in Hebrew (that is, Aramaic) it was called *Gabbatha* (elevated place). Excavations many feet below the level of modern Jerusalem have certainly revealed the courtyard of the Antonia, marvelously preserved, and the courtyard was certainly paved with massive slabs of stone, on which it is still possible to see the marks left by chariot wheels, the scars made by Roman lances, and even the designs which the soldiers had sketched out for the games with which they whiled away the time. The possible relevance of this last detail we shall see later on. The Antonia was built on a rocky prominence, and therefore seems to correspond with John's description. However, the question remains open. The Palace of Herod was on a higher elevation than the Fortress Antonia, and while no excavations have brought to light its stone pavement, it undoubtedly had one; furthermore the fact that John speaks of it as *the* Stone Pavement might suggest that he had in mind a place better known to the people at large than the barracks of the Roman cohort.

Those who had brought Jesus to Pilate *did not enter the praetorium*, John says, lest they contract a legal impurity from contact with Gentiles and thus be unable to eat the Passover that evening (see above on Mk 14:12–17). Pilate does not hesitate to humor their scruples, as the Romans were usually careful to do. At the same time, the mutual contempt in which he and the Jews held one another is quite evident from the Gospel story. Neither does it appear, as we shall see, that Pilate is being introduced to the problem of Jesus for the first time. It is wrong to read the Gospels, as some have done, as though they conceived of Pilate as a man fundamentally disposed to justice whose hand was forced against Jesus. In a sense, his hand was forced, it is true, but if he had any thought of saving Jesus' life it was not from any devotion to justice. Like most of the provincial Roman governors, Pilate was selfish, rapacious, and corrupt. If he held office as long as he did, it was because of Tiberius Caesar's avowed and cynical principle that old governors governed best, having now the leisure to govern once they had squeezed their personal fortunes out of their subjects. In the drama of the passion Pilate plays no role that does not serve his own sordid interests and his taste for power. Jesus' enemies knew the temper of the man with whom they had to negotiate. His high-handed despotism that had got him into trouble before and would eventually bring about his downfall was this time kept under control, but it was the calculated control of one who owned allegiance to no principle outside himself.

The initial exchange between Pilate and the Jews as reported by John can be variously interpreted, depending on the sense of the avowal: *we are not permitted to put anyone to death*. Ordinarily this is taken to mean that in Roman Palestine the sentence of death decreed by a Jewish court such as the Sanhedrin would be recognized as having no validity unless ratified by Roman authority. Such procedure obtained elsewhere in the provinces of the Roman empire.

On the other hand, the Romans extended extraordinary
privileges to the Jews, and we have no clear-cut evidence
that they withheld the right of execution from the Sanhedrin;
in fact, there are some events that might suggest that they
did not (cf. Jn 8:7; Acts 7:58 f., 25:9–11). Even if they did,
one might suppose that the limit of Roman interest would
have been to certify the sentence and permit it to be carried
out in the Jewish manner, by stoning, not to insist on a
Roman trial and a Roman execution. Yet Jesus was executed
in the Roman manner, by crucifixion, and for a crime against
Roman law.

If this is, nevertheless, the meaning of the Jews' statement,
as it may very well be, then we are treated to the rather
unedifying spectacle of a sparring contest between two proud
parties over the innocent person of Jesus, who matters to
neither of them. Pilate asks, *What accusation do you bring
against this man?*, insinuating, of course, that his trial begins
here and now, that nothing that has been proved in any
Jewish court can have the slightest bearing on his jeopardy
to a death sentence. At this the Jews indignantly reply that
he has, indeed, been shown to be an evildoer worthy of
death. And thus Pilate is permitted to win the first round in
a mutually hateful encounter. An evildoer? Well, then, *take
him yourselves and judge him by your own law.* But this
they cannot do, and they are forced to the humiliating
admission that they cannot.

Others, however, understand John's story in another way.
It was not merely that Jesus' enemies wanted him dead; they
wanted him dead by Roman law and by a Roman execution.
Not only did they not want to face their own people as
responsible for his death, they hoped that he could also
serve as a scapegoat to satisfy the Romans that they were
being sufficiently vigilant over the rebellious people of Palestine, who now so obediently and loyally delivered over one
of its own refractory members who had got out of hand
(cf. Jn 11:49 f.). John himself seems to lean to this interpretation when he adds that *this was to fulfill the word
which Jesus had spoken to show what kind of death he was*

to die (cf. Jn 3:14, 8:28, 12:32 f.). In this construction, Pilate was simply demanding of the Jews a charge against Jesus that would stand up in a Roman court. Neither Pilate nor Roman law would take any cognizance of a merely Jewish crime (cf. Acts 18:14 f.). In either case, we might add, though in the latter especially, the possibility of prior collusion between Pilate and the Jewish leadership is always present.

Mk 15:2-5   The question which Pilate puts to Jesus
Mt 27:11-14   according to all four of the Gospels: *You*
Lk 23:2-5   *are the king of the Jews?*—probably with a
Jn 18:33-38   tone of contempt on both "you" and "the
Jews"—presupposes some kind of denunciation such as that which Luke alone records: *We caught this fellow perverting our nation, forbidding them to pay taxes to Caesar, and claiming to be Messiah, a king.* The charge is a mixture of truth, half-truth, and the utter falsehood that is so often the progeny of both. Jesus had made a pronouncement on tribute to Caesar (see above on Mk 12:13-17 and parallels); this much was doubtless common knowledge, whatever may have been the opinion about precisely what he had said. He had been hailed as king on more than one occasion. The credentials of most of those waiting on Pilate were probably quite acceptable for a denunciation of this kind. Belonging mainly to the Sadducean priestly families, their interests coincided with the Romans' in stamping out an incipient messianism whenever it should arise. This Pilate knew, quite in addition to whatever prior information he may have had about this particular case.

Jesus' answer to Pilate's question, according to all four Gospels, is again the non-committal *You say so;* John prefaces to it Jesus' explanation of the sense in which he may be considered a king. It is worthy of remark that at this juncture both Luke and John have Pilate explicitly affirm that he finds no cause for death in Jesus' teaching, and Mark-Matthew imply much the same by showing the need that his accusers apparently felt to multiply the charges against him. Pilate

was a Roman administering justice, and the maintenance of
the Roman system depended on a strict adherence to the
legal forms. He would later fall from favor, as a matter of
fact, through a miscalculation of this order, repressing as
rebels against Roman rule those who were able to convince
his Roman superiors they were no rebels at all. Jesus' reply
was accepted as satisfactory: whatever his "kingship" meant,
it was not deemed to constitute any threat to the empire.

The more extended dialogue which John ascribes to Jesus
and Pilate is very important to this evangelist. Here, finally,
the "world" to which Jesus has come to bring life and light,
and which of necessity has hitherto been an exclusively
Jewish world, now opens wide in the person of the Roman
governor who represents what to a first-century author would
have been the world par excellence, the *oikoumenē*, the inhabited earth, the empire (cf. Lk 2:1). Pilate is an earnest
of that vaster world of men in which and before which the
prophetic Word and Spirit were now incarnated in the
Johannine Church. But alas, Pilate is utterly indifferent to
the word. Jesus' invitation to him to consider the meaning of
this historical encounter and his part in it he dismisses with
the contempt of a Roman skeptic: *Am I a Jew?* Though he
can take in Jesus' words on the surface, to know that this
strange sort of king before him has nothing to do with his
world of intrigue and *Realpolitik*, his *What is truth?* shows
how completely he had missed the supreme opportunity of
his life. *Everyone who is of the truth hears my voice,* was
Jesus' final testimony. Pilate had heard nothing. He had not
even paid the truth the compliment of a rejection, so little
was his concern with it.

Lk 23:6–16   Luke alone tells the story of Jesus' being sent
by Pilate to Herod Antipas, a story that is all
the more credible because of our suspicion that more lies
behind it than even Luke knew. We have already seen that
the Herodians, Antipas' hangers-on and servants, were considered by the Gospels to have been involved in the plot
against Jesus' life, for whatever reasons of their own. Herod

certainly had cause to suspect Jesus' activity as adverse to his own interests (see above on Lk 13:31–33). It is not at all unlikely that if self-serving Jews and Romans could, to some degree at least, make common cause to rid themselves of one who disturbed them in various ways, Herod, who was a little of both Jew and Roman, might have found the same cause to his own advantage. Luke recalls that *Herod and Pilate became fast friends from that very day, whereas before they had been hostile to each other.* The friendship was, indeed, compounded over the body of Jesus, and it may well be that it was indicated rather than caused by Pilate's gesture, which really seems to have served little purpose beyond satisfying Herod's callous curiosity. The reason for their earlier enmity Luke does not explain, but it was quite likely some jurisdictional dispute or some action of Pilate's involving Galileans such as that described in Lk 13:1–9.

As Luke tells it, an apparently chance remark about Jesus' having begun his teaching in Galilee leads Pilate first to confirm that Jesus was a Galilean, *of Herod's jurisdiction,* and then to send him to the tetrarch who was in Jerusalem for the feast. Obviously this was nothing more than a courtesy on Pilate's part, as far as the legalities were concerned, since the governor retained full jurisdiction over any Jew in Judea. Evidently, too, however, he was looking for some help from Herod in determining what was to be the final disposition with regard to Jesus, against whom he now believed he had no capital case. Even though we pick up the Gospel hints that suggest a more complicated background to the death of Jesus than the dogged blood lust of a few Jewish plotters in high places, the same evidence prevents us from concluding that his fate had been irrevocably decided upon by others than these few. Roman soldiers might be easily hired for an illegal arrest, and Galilean officials might stand idly by when one of their subjects was bullied and harried, but there is no reason to think that the common interest extended on all sides to Jesus' literal destruction. That he should be discredited and repudiated, and his followers scattered, might be all that was needed. Murders, even judicial murders, have a way of remaining as evidence of untidy administration; Antipas seems to have had cause to regret the execution of John the Baptist (see above on Mk 6:14–29 and parallels). Thus, perhaps, Pilate's suggestion after Jesus was returned to him: *I will chastise him and then turn him loose.*

Whatever part Antipas was supposed to play in settling Pilate's mind, he seems to have contributed little or nothing. The tetrarch was almost certainly staying at the Palace of the Hasmonaeans, ancestral property of the Herod family, which Flavius Josephus locates for us as about equidistant from the Palace of Herod and the Antonia. Some, at least, of Jesus' accusers accompanied him to this place, but seemingly Herod paid little attention to them. His first interest in Jesus was as a captive magician who might enliven the boredom of the day by performing *some sign*. When, however, Jesus responded to his interrogation with the silence of the Lord's Servant that he had already shown before the Sanhedrin and before Pilate (cf. Is 53:7), Antipas quickly tired of the game and turned him over to the coarse amusement of *his soldiers* to be treated not as a dangerous criminal but as a lunatic and a fool. The *splendid apparel* in which Jesus was decked out to be sent back to Pilate was probably the clothing of royalty, by which his messianic pretensions were being mocked: these would have been as ludicrous to the Herodians as to the Romans. It is believed by some authors that it was at Herod's court that the sustained ridicule of Jesus as King of the Jews took place which Mark-Matthew and John, who have no story about Herod at all, later ascribe to the soldiers of Pilate. Luke himself prefers not to dwell on unpleasant scenes like this.

In verse 13 an anomaly is presented by Luke's text when Pilate is said to have *called together the chief priests and the rulers and the people* as those who had turned Jesus over to him for execution. Everywhere else in this Gospel, both prior to this verse (cf. 19:49, 20:6, 19, 26, 45, 21:38) and following it (cf. 23:27, 35, 48), the evangelist carefully distinguishes the people and its leaders as two opposed camps. It is the people who eagerly listen to Jesus, in fear of whom the leaders are hesitant to act against him, and who are shown never to have really consented to his death. Despite the lack of manuscript evidence, therefore, it has been plausibly suggested that Luke originally wrote here as he does elsewhere "the chief priests and the rulers *of* the people."

Mk 15:6–14   The four Gospels now tell of a development
Mt 27:15–23   which presupposes a custom at Jerusalem
Lk 23:17–23   of which they are our only historical in-
Jn 18:39–40   formants, but which we have no cause to
                doubt as having certain analogies elsewhere,
that *on the occasion of a festival* the governor *would release* to the people *one prisoner, the man they would ask for*. It has been conjectured that the custom began in Maccabean or Hasmonaean times and that the Romans had found it convenient to retain it; presumably a prisoner that might hope to benefit from such an amnesty was not one already under actual sentence of death—ordinarily only the emperor himself could grant a pardon of this kind—but one awaiting trial or sentence. It occurs to Pilate that there is a way out of his present quandary if he can invoke the custom in Jesus' favor. What puts it into his head, according to Mark-Matthew, is the gathering of *the crowd* for this annual purpose. It is to be noted that this crowd now appears for the first time, having up to this point had nothing to do with the discussion over Jesus; in John and Luke (if we accept the emendation of Luke's vs. 13) there is no crowd: they have in view simply the chief priests and elders of the people who have since the early morning resolved on Jesus' death.

It is at this moment that the name of *Barabbas* briefly enters the Gospel. Actually, Barabbas is not a name but a patronymic, like Bar-Jona, the patronym of Simon Peter. Its meaning was "son of his father"—lest the distinction be thought pointless, the idea was that this man bore the same given name as his father, somewhat unusual at a time when there were no surnames and the name of the father was depended on to distinguish one Simon or John or Joseph from another. Barabbas' name was undoubtedly Jesus: "Jesus Barabbas" appears in a number of manuscripts of Mt 27:16 f., and it is impossible to account for it there except as a matter of historical record; on the other hand, it is easy enough to understand why Christian scribes got it out of most of the other manuscripts. *Jesus Barabbas or Jesus the so-called Messiah,* then, was the choice Pilate offered to the crowd.

But why Barabbas as a choice? Probably because it was for Barabbas that the crowd had come to petition in the first place, and Pilate merely attempted to divert its attention to Jesus instead. Mark says that Barabbas had been *imprisoned as one of the rebels who had committed murder in the uprising*—alluding in passing to some well-known event in which, as usual, the Gospels otherwise evince no interest. Luke's description agrees substantially with this, while Matthew simply states that Barabbas was *a prisoner of note.* John's characterization of Barabbas as *a bandit* is meant to underline the sordid type of person whom "the Jews" preferred to Jesus; however, "bandit" was the term commonly used for the zealots or partisans among the Jews who opposed Roman rule by recourse to violence. Barabbas was without doubt a popular patriot, a leader in one of the many nationalist movements against the Romans, and suspected by the latter of complicity in activities that had led to bloodshed. As shown by his designation of Jesus to the crowd as *Messiah* and *King of the Jews,* in Pilate's mind Barabbas and Jesus were two of a kind, though he was now convinced that Jesus was harmless and *knew that the chief priests had turned him in out of jealousy.* From his standpoint it would make much better sense to release Jesus rather than the popular hero who was far more dangerous. But of course, his diversionary tactic was doomed to failure. Jesus' enemies had no difficulty in persuading the crowd to make a choice that was doubtless already to its liking. Those who were in sympathy with Barabbas were not likely to be enthusiastic over Jesus' kind of messianism.

Here and in subsequent passages the Gospels seem to go
out of their way to show Pilate more actively interested in
sparing Jesus' life than our knowledge of his character would
have prepared us to expect. Often this tendency is explained
as anti-Jewish bias, an attempt to minimize the part that
Rome had played in the crucifixion, understandable in a
Church that was engaged in controversy with Judaism and
which had to live in the Roman empire and by Roman law.
We have seen that there is, indeed, something of this tendency
in the Gospels. However, it is also true that we are hampered
by a lack of background information that, did we have it,
might make Pilate's intervention quite comprehensible. Of one
thing we may be fairly sure, that it was not prompted by
any abstract devotion to justice. One tantalizing allusion—if
it is that—to the more complicated history behind the Gospel
story may be seen in the story told by Matthew, apparently
making additional use of his series of Jerusalem traditions,
about the *message* sent to Pilate while *he was presiding on
the judgment seat* by *his wife,* a lady whom not too reliable
tradition identifies by the name of Claudia Procla. To many
this story is proof that the trial and passion of Jesus extended
over a much longer period of time than a single day and
involved others than the few whom the Gospels bring into it.
It does at least suggest the possibility that the name of Jesus
had been mentioned in Pilate's household before this fateful
day.

Mk 15:15   Having made its choice of Barabbas, there
Mt 27:24–26 was only one reply for the crowd to give to
Lk 23:24–25 the governor's further question, which he
                doubtless put to it in frustration and anger,
not unmixed with contempt: What then was to be done with
the one some called the Messiah? *Crucify him!* Preachers on
the passion of Christ have often dwelt on the fickleness of
the people of Jerusalem who on Sunday hailed Jesus as their
Messiah and on the following Friday demanded his death.
But in the first place, it is impossible to know how many of the
motley population of Jerusalem at Passover time, nine tenths

of which were pilgrims from every part of Jewry, had participated in the enthusiasm of Palm Sunday; probably most of it had been contributed by the Galileans who accompanied Jesus, few of whom, if the Gospels' chronology is to be taken at face value, were as yet even aware of his arrest. As for the present crowd which, altogether contrary to Pilate's expectations, the chief priests were able to turn into a mob demanding Jesus' blood, we have no reason to think that they either knew or cared much about Jesus. They had come to ransom a Jew held in a Roman prison, and they were not likely to be prejudiced in favor of someone whom the Romans evidently wanted to force on them and whom their own leaders were denouncing.

These remarks must be kept in mind when we evaluate the terrible cry which Matthew has recorded and which has been the cause of Jewish anguish ever since: *His blood on us and on our children!* Pilate's hand washing was a Jewish gesture, not Roman (cf. Deut 21:6 f.), and doubtless it needed no accompanying words to be understood. *All the people* present then assumed the responsibility which Pilate shirked. There is no doubt that Matthew heard in this cry a voice of prophecy echoed in the Synagogue of his day which was locked in struggle with the Church. It is for him a symbol of Jewish unbelief, a Jewish valedictory to Israel's hopes, the passing of the age of Israel which from now on becomes (as so often in John's Gospel) simply "the Jews" (cf. Mt 28:15), an alien religion. The solemnity of the passage as well as the structure of his Gospel as a whole forbid us to take Matthew's meaning in any other sense.

But to recognize the lesson that Matthew intended to draw from the passage for an embattled Church is not to dispense ourselves from the historical and theological task which his and the other Gospels set us in dealing with these events. "On us and on our children" was the legal formula by which liability was assumed that would also extend to one's heirs. In speaking thus the crowd intended, presumably, to acknowledge itself completely responsible for Jesus' death. But no one, of course, can make his children guilty of a crime he alone has committed. "All the people" who undertook this responsibility were Jews, it is true, but they were certainly not the whole Jewish people, nor even a very large part of the city of Jerusalem. They could speak only for themselves. Even the guilt which they must undeniably bear was unevenly divided among them. There is no basis in this or any other passage in the Gospels for a concept of the Jews, past or present, as a people laboring under an inherited curse: there is no such thing. Nor does the Jewish failure to accept Jesus as Messiah—which, in any case, he was in something of a non-Jewish sense—stem from these ill-considered words of a small mob or have any direct connection with the fortunes of the Jewish people throughout subsequent history. It must be candidly and humbly confessed that throughout most of their subsequent history the chief cause both of Jewish unbelief and of Jewish agony has been simply Christians.

In general, the Gospels do not say that Pilate sentenced Jesus to death, but rather that he *delivered him over* (Matthew and John both speak of the *bēma* or judgment seat, however, and Lk 23:24 used the word "sentenced"). The reason for this does not seem to be an intention on their part to minimize Pilate's part in the execution of Jesus but rather to stress the role of Jesus as the Servant of the Lord (cf. Is 53:12, "he was delivered over to death"); for the same reason, Judas is said to have "delivered Jesus over" (cf. Mk 14:18; Mt 26:46; Lk 22:21; Jn 12:4, etc.) and the Jews to have "delivered him over" to Pilate (cf. Mk 15:1; Mt 27:2; Jn 19:1; Acts 3:13, etc.). Jesus was certainly judicially sentenced by Pilate and suffered death at the hands of Roman soldiers and under Roman law.

Mk 15:16–20   At the end of the preceding section Mark-
Mt 27:27–31   Matthew tell us that, once Pilate had finally
Jn 19:1–3   had his mind made up for him, *he had
              Jesus scourged, then delivered him over to
be crucified.* The close sequence is undoubtedly correct. Crucifixion, originally an Oriental mode of execution which

the Romans had adopted as they did so much else and made peculiarly their own, was a disgusting and degrading torture reserved for non-Roman citizens convicted of exemplary crimes like treason. It was properly an occasion rather than a cause of death to the poor victim, who died— usually after several days—of exposure, exhaustion, hunger, and especially thirst. For this reason, some of the other brutalities that usually accompanied it, such as scourging and the breaking of bones that we will see later, were in their own way rough acts of mercy which would hasten death. Before crucifying a man the Romans would first give him a thorough lashing, then with whips drive him naked through the streets with the heavy wood of his cross across his shoulders until, half-dead already, he reached the place of execution.

The whipping which preceded crucifixion was a savage affair in which the victim frequently died. The whip, which could never be used on a Roman citizen, often had pieces of lead or bone attached to the multiple lashes, which tore the flesh horribly. There was no limit placed on the number of strokes: the soldier, or several soldiers consecutively who administered the punishment simply kept at it till their arms grew tired. The Roman practice was in contrast with the humane Jewish law which limited the number of lashes that a man could be given to forty (cf. Deut 25:1–3); scrupulous as ever on points of the Law, the Jews never went beyond thirty-nine (cf. 2 Cor 11:24).

All this taken into consideration, it is not probable that Pilate used the scourging as a means of placating those thirsty for Jesus' blood and, perhaps, of stirring up pity in their breasts, as John goes on to tell the story. The scourging, *flagellatio*, was not a cautionary but a terminative punishment. It would have taken place immediately before the crucifixion, as in Mark and Matthew. By the same token, however, neither in all likelihood would a man who had undergone a Roman scourging have been a fit subject for the cruel humor of Pilate's soldiers, as is now presupposed in the sequence of all three Gospels. The mockery itself is without doubt entirely historical, but there is much to commend the view that it had already taken place in the Palace of the Hasmonaeans, under the auspices of Herod Antipas (see above on Lk 23:6–16). Luke avoids saying anything directly about either of these indignities.

Whether administered by soldiers of Herod or those of the Roman garrison, the treatment accorded Jesus could hardly have differed very much. In both instances these were men recruited from the dregs of society, not Romans by birth but of every race and allegiance from the neighboring provinces, who by military duty could earn for themselves the coveted privileges of Roman citizenship. They shared a common hatred and contempt for the Jews: what was done to Jesus, we note, was as much an insult to the Jews as to himself personally. In this man who called himself —so they imagined—the King of the Jews, they saw a ludicrous object upon which they could vent their feelings for the whole race. The Gospels seem to describe a mock coronation. *They dressed him up in royal purple,* Mark says, which Matthew more realistically revises to *a scarlet cloak* of the type that soldiers wore: if sufficiently faded, it would resemble royal purple (John holds to *a purple robe*). The *crown of thorns* which they wove and crushed down on his head was probably in imitation of the laurel wreath affected by the Roman emperors. None of this grotesquerie, of course, was particularly subtle, nor is it therefore difficult for us to follow.

Those who locate the *Lithostrōton* at the Fortress Antonia, however, and who follow Mark-Matthew and John in identifying the soldiers who made mock of Jesus with the praetorian guard, may perhaps have some support for their views in the excavations that brought to light the paved courtyard of the Antonia. One of the games played by the Roman soldiers, the tracings for which may still be clearly discerned in the pavement (see above on Mk 15:1b and parallels), was the ancient Oriental jape of royalty called *Basilicus.* Having its origins in grim rites of myth and sympathetic magic, its sport consisted in the exaggerated ceremonial honors ac-

corded a "king" chosen by lot who at the end was obliged
to pay a forfeit—in ancient times his life itself, later a
banquet or a round of drinks which he stood for his fellow
players. Harmless vestiges of the ancient mythical ritual still
exist under many forms in the folkways of various European
peoples. The suggestion is that it was this customary game
of the praetorian soldiers that dictated their treatment of the
King of the Jews on this Good Friday.

Jn 19:4–16a John has, by exception, repeated these re-
pugnant details from the Synoptic tradition
because they prepare for the scene that follows which is
particularly suited to his portrayal of the Gospel story. We
can easily imagine it as taking place after Jesus had been
returned to Pilate by Herod Antipas, even though John in his
Gospel has nothing about the confrontation of Jesus and
Herod.

If it was Pilate's thought that the spectacle of the humili-
ated Jesus would satisfy the designs of the crowd, he could
not have made a greater mistake; for John, "the Jews" who
cry *Crucify him!* are *the chief priests and officials* who had
arrested him (vs. 6), since this evangelist has nothing in his
story about the crowd which had gathered to call for
Barabbas. *Here is the man!* on Pilate's lips is a piece of
Johannine irony. Pilate intends simply to point out a pitiable
object, but John wants us to remember that the Son of Man
is *the* Man.

Pilate's suggestion that the Jews *take him yourselves and
crucify him* can only be sarcasm, for whatever power the
Sanhedrin may have had to enforce capital punishment,
crucifixion was a non-Jewish form of execution symbolic to
them of their subjection to laws other than their own. The
taunt does elicit from them a statement on the sentence
passed on Jesus in the Jewish trial which John has not recorded: what had been done to Jesus thus far was all that
Jewish law could do, and it now remained for Rome to do its
part. *The Son of God* to Pilate would have had overtones far
different from the biblical sense of this expression. Skeptic

and cynic that he was, he doubtless shared in the super-
stitions of his class and age. Was this man somehow the
offspring of a god, like the divine Caesar? *Where are you
from?*, then, John sees as another piece of irony: Pilate is
unconsciously demonstrating once more that he is part of
that world which knows neither God nor his Son (cf. Jn
8:14, 9:29). Jesus maintains his customary silence during
this as his other interrogations, for in the circumstances an
answer would have been incomprehensible and have no
point. He breaks his silence, however, when Pilate asserts his
authority over life and death, to set the record straight,
much to the satisfaction of John the evangelist: it is Jesus
and not Pilate who is in real command of this situation. *The
one who turned me over to you* is doubtless a reference to
the Jewish leadership in general. It is the *more guilty* for
having abused a God-given power, misleading rather than
guiding the people entrusted to its care. As for Pilate, he has
already proved himself to be only dimly aware of the
magnitude of the drama taking place under his eyes, and in
a moment it will become evident how hollow was his claim
to have absolute discretion concerning what would happen to
Jesus. It is now the judge who is under judgment.

If you turn this man loose you are no friend of Caesar.
John's testimony to the ultimate persuasion used against
Pilate has the ring of absolute authenticity. This was an
argument which Pilate, who loved the glory of man rather
than the glory of God (cf. Jn 12:43), found quite un-
answerable. If he were to release Jesus against the will of
those who had handed him over, what would be reported of
him to Rome? That such reports were often made, and often
heard, we know as a matter of record. Of a sudden, therefore, Pilate's vaunted power has melted away. He goes
through the motions of the course laid out for him. He cannot
resist one final fling at the Jews. Pointing to the outwardly
dejected and degraded figure standing before him, he cries
with all the hatred of his soul: *Look at your king!* From
Pilate's point of vantage, this was merely a cry of frustrated
rage. However, it goads the Jews into a counterstatement

which John is able to report with his habitual irony. *We have no king but Caesar*, taken at face value, was the politic utterance of men prepared to deny their own heritage (cf. Jn 8:33) to gain their present objective through the power of Caesar. In John's day, a half dozen false messiahs later, with the temple in ruins and Jewish political power destroyed forever, the statement had its own more literal and more bitter truth.

Jn 19:16b–17a The actual story of the way of the cross
Mk 15:21 and the crucifixion is told with relative
Mt 27:32 brevity by all the Gospels. The passion
Lk 23:26–32 narrative, in the three versions that we
have in our Gospels, goes back to early Christian meditation and *kerygma*, considerably influenced by the relevance of Old Testament figures and types such as that of Ps 22, the theme of the suffering just man. So much is this the case, it is not always possible to decide to what degree the type has determined the course of the narrative rather than been kept in its place as illustrative. The Gospels were no longer concerned with these events as statistical facts well known to their readers. From the beginning, the story had the liturgical and instructive character that it has ever after enjoyed in the Church.

John emphasizes that Jesus was *carrying his own cross* because he continues to insist on Jesus' complete control of his destiny at all times. Actually, this picture accords with the usual practice. Crucifixion was a degrading spectacle from beginning to end. The condemned person, stripped naked and beaten along with whips, was forced to bear the heavy crossbar on his shoulders, sometimes already fastened to his hands and arms; the upright of the cross, or of several crosses, for that matter, was already permanently fixed at the place of execution. However, there is no reason whatever to question the story of *Simon of Cyrene* found in the Synoptic Gospels. Obviously the cross was too much for Jesus to bear in his weakened condition, hence the soldiers forced a chance passerby to take up its burden instead. A high-handed action, but the Romans were used to this. The intimation of the Gospels is that Simon carried the cross by himself and that he carried it all the way to Golgotha. He was evidently a Jew of the Diaspora in Jerusalem for the feast day, *coming into the city from the country* (Mark and Luke). That Mark knows him as *the father of Alexander and Rufus* might mean that his sons, at least, later became Christians. The Gospels, at all events, say nothing further about him.

The story of Simon of Cyrene and that of *the women* of Jerusalem told only by Luke are two of the traditional "stations" of the cross. The stations, composed of incidents taken both from the Gospels and from apocryphal legends and introduced as a devotion into the West apparently in the thirteenth century, are faithful to the genre of the narrative we have before us. The women of whom Luke speaks were probably those who made it their pious custom to accompany condemned criminals and render them charitable services. The cup of wine that was ministered to Jesus before his crucifixion was probably handed him by one of these women. It is typical of Luke's concern for the feminine element in the Gospel that he alone has recorded this story. We note, too, that besides the women, *a great multitude of the people were following him;* with only the apparent exception of verse 13 above, in Luke's Gospel "the people" are Jesus' well-wishers.

Jesus does not rebuke the women for weeping over his plight, for their weeping was undoubtedly sincere; but somewhat in the language of the Synoptic eschatological discourse (see above on Mk 13:3–8 and parallels), he tells them of the coming things over which they will have to weep even more bitterly as affecting them the more directly. His citation of Hos 10:8 (describing the destruction of Samaria) specifies his reference to the devastation of Jerusalem by the Romans in A.D. 70. *If they do this with green wood, what will they do with dry?* has been variously interpreted. The general sense is clear: if green wood, which is tough and resilient and hard to burn, can nevertheless be

so easily destroyed, by comparison what a blaze can be
kindled with old dry wood! But who are the "they"? In
context, Jesus is the green wood and Jerusalem the dry, and
"they" are probably the Romans. If they so treat one who has
offended them in no way, what will they not do with
rebellious Judea?

Only Luke mentions at this point the presence of the others
who were crucified with Jesus. Luke speaks, literally, of *two
other criminals,* a choice of words that caused no end of
embarrassment to early Christian scribes (and even to some
modern translators as well); however, legally Jesus was a
criminal, and he and his companions in suffering were on a
common plane. Mark-Matthew later identify them as *bandits,*
by the same word that John earlier used for Barabbas. It is
conceivable that they, too, were part of the uprising of which
Barabbas, presumably, had been leader (Mk 15:7). At all
events, the association—together with the title which Pilate
had affixed to Jesus' cross—without doubt gives us a strong
factual indication of the meaning that the crucifixion had for
Pilate and his Roman soldiers: the execution of a convicted
rebel against the authority of the state.

Mk 15:22–26 According to Mark, who alone of the
Mt 27:33–37 Synoptics makes a point of it, *it was the*
Lk 23:33–34 *third hour when they crucified him.* This is
Jn 19:17b–24 one of the celebrated conflicts of the Gospels, since John has already said (vs. 14)
that it was *on the day of Preparation for the Passover about
the sixth hour* that Jesus was condemned to death. John's
chronology is theological: it was after noon (the sixth hour)
that the Passover lamb was sacrificed on the day of Preparation (see above on Mk 14:12–17 and parallels). But
Mark's chronology is probably equally theologically motivated: Jesus is crucified at the third hour, but then (vs. 33)
there is darkness *from the sixth hour until the ninth hour*
(the "darkness at noon" of Amos 8:9) when all is con-
summated; Mark's sequence divides itself into the three-hour
periods of the Roman day (cf. the "terce," "sext," and

"none" canonical hours of the Roman breviary). If we had to make a decision between the two timetables, which we do not, we should doubtless opt in favor of John's, since it is hard to imagine all that we have seen thus far having taken place by nine o'clock in the morning. On the other hand, the visitor to Palestine to this very day is perennially surprised to find that when he turns out of bed at eight o'clock or so in the morning the day is already half over for many natives of the place.

The place of execution is called by all the Gospels *the Skull*, for which all but Luke give the Aramaic name *Golgotha* (more accurately, *golgoltha*). The name "Calvary" in common English use comes from the translation in the Latin Vulgate *calvariae locus*, "the place of the Skull." The place was so called probably not from any fancied resemblance to the configurations of a human skull, but because it was a height, a headland. It is likely that there is no better authenticated site among all of those mentioned in the New Testament than that of Jesus' death and burial, which, according to John (vs. 41), was one and the same. Here Constantine built the first Basilica of the Holy Sepulcher in the fourth century, depending, as he usually did, on far more ancient and reliable tradition. There is not much that modern-day archaeology has been able to contribute to strengthen or weaken the tradition, but what little it has had to say has been in its favor. Some maps of "Jerusalem in the time of Christ" may still be found on which an encircling line has been drawn about the traditional site of the Sepulcher to indicate that in the first century it was within the city walls, thus impossibly the place of Jesus' execution and burial both from the known laws and customs of the time and on the testimony of the Gospel (cf. Jn 19:17, 20). But this line was drawn by unscholarly prejudice from the beginning, and subsequent scholarly prejudice has not availed to justify it; what little archaeological evidence there is, which is admittedly scanty, indicates that the traditional Golgotha and Sepulcher were safely outside the walls of New Testament Jerusalem. We must stress that it is the site only of which we are now speaking: nothing that is at present to be seen in the Church of the Holy Sepulcher in Jerusalem, several times demolished and rebuilt in the course of the centuries, goes back to New Testament times.

The *title* which Pilate affixed to Jesus' cross, which in John's Gospel is the occasion of a last bitter interchange between the governor and the Jews, was in accordance with Roman practice. That it was fastened to the cross rather than hung about his neck as was sometimes done may indicate that the form of Jesus' cross was "Latin," that is, that the upright beam projected beyond the crossbar. The cross was probably not very high; wood was and is a scarce commodity in Palestine. There was no footrest on the cross as later artists have imagined. The feet of the crucified were either nailed separately to the wood or were tied there. Instead, there was ordinarily a projecting peg which the condemned person straddled; this took the weight from his hands and arms and supported the body. The hands were sometimes nailed to the crossbeam, either at the wrists or through the palms, and sometimes they were tied. Or both methods might be used. John takes it for granted that Jesus was nailed to the cross (cf. Jn 20:25–27), and this seems to be Luke's meaning as well (cf. Lk 24:39). The *wine mixed with myrrh* which was offered to Jesus according to Mark was supposed to have a narcotic effect to deaden the pain of the torture. Matthew, by substituting *gall*, has seen in this gesture the fulfillment of another Old Testament type (cf. Ps 69:22).

All the Gospels mention the distribution of Jesus' garments by the soldiers (cf. Ps 22:19); custom gave the executed criminal's clothing to the executioners. Only John notes that the number of soldiers was *four*. This evangelist also makes a point of the *tunic without seam* worn by Christ for which the soldiers cast lots rather than destroy it. It is probable that he is again thinking of Jesus' priestly role on the cross, since it was the high priest's garment that could not be torn (cf. Lev 21:10).

Christians have long followed the devotional practice of

collecting the last sayings of Jesus during his passion as recorded severally by the Gospels into "the seven last words." The first "word," Luke's verse 34a, is missing from some of both the oldest and the best manuscripts and may not be original to the Gospel; but it is one of those most in keeping with the spirit of the Jesus that is portrayed by the Gospels. *Father, forgive them, for they know not what they do* is not a condonation of evil but a plea for mercy. It does not deny the malice of those responsible for the crucifixion, but it extends pity to those who are most in need of it, to those whose prejudices and hatreds have blinded them to the enormity of the crimes they commit and which make them evil men while they deem themselves righteous.

Mk 15:27–32 John has no room in his Gospel for the
Mt 27:38–44 spectacle of the crucified Christ prey to the
Lk 23:35–43 insults and sneers of the bystanders, *wagging their heads* in the Oriental way of derision (cf. Pss 22:8, 109:25; Lam 2:15) and throwing in his face his own words or deeds or words and deeds ascribed to him (on Matthew's vs. 43 cf. also Ps 22:9). Luke has permitted us to see some of it, but for his own purposes and in his own way. In the first place, he distinguishes as usual between *the people* who *stood by watching* and *the rulers* who *scoffed at him*. Mark-Matthew supposes the cries of raillery to have been initiated by chance passersby, which is natural enough. Public executions, for a variety of psychological and other reasons, often enough bring out the very worst of which man is capable; then, too, it is usually the very worst of men who find their recreation in witnessing an execution. Natural, too, is Luke's information that the soldiers joined in the mocking of Jesus. These were crude, rough men who knew no way of dealing with criminals except cruelty. They merely aped the cries that they heard about them, hoping to draw a reply from the suffering man that would ease the boredom of their vigil. Luke brings in here the incident of the *sour wine*, apparently taking it as another instance of ridicule.

Luke makes another distinction. In Mark-Matthew's account, *those who had been crucified with him also were taunting him.* Common misery does not always ennoble men or make for brotherhood. According to Luke, however, only one of the criminals joined in the abuse. Writhing in pain on his cross, the poor devil was without doubt happy to find that at least someone in the world was in a worse state than he. At the same time, while his taunt was undoubtedly not to be taken seriously, he made it practical. Yes, let Jesus indeed save himself—and save his companions too. But the other one of the crucified, still according to Luke, was prepared, despite the abject appearance now borne by Jesus, to accept him at his own evaluation and recognize in him a Savior. His profession of faith draws from Jesus the second "word" from the cross: *Today you will be with me in paradise.* It would be beyond the evangelist's intention to read into this utterance a New Testament theology of the afterlife. "Paradise" meant various things in Jewish apocalyptic language, but always it had an association with a blessed immortality with God. The "good thief" had put his faith in Jesus and asked to have a share in his *kingdom*—we certainly need not presume that he had a better formed notion of what he was asking than Jesus' own intimate disciples had had (see above on Mk 10:35–45 and parallel). Jesus answers his request in the spirit in which it was made: he will, indeed, be remembered by Jesus, and even more, he will share his glory as he has shared his suffering, and that beginning immediately. This immediacy of the kingdom is Luke's contribution to "realized eschatology." For him as for John the important thing is that Jesus reigns from the cross, the dispenser of salvation.

Jn 19:25–27   The third "word" from the cross is John's, and very much a part of his theology. All the Gospels speak of friends as well as enemies of Jesus who witnessed his execution. Luke (vs. 49) has it that *his acquaintances stood at a distance* (cf. Pss 38:12, 88:9 f.)

WHAT IS TRUTH?"   259

along with *the women who had followed him from Galilee*.
Mark (vs. 40) and Matthew (vs. 56) include among these
women *Mary Magdalene, Mary the mother of James and
Joses* (Matthew: *Joseph*), one of the "sisters" of Jesus as
James and Joses were his "brothers" (see above on Mk 6:
1–6a and parallels), and one or two others. *Salome* (Mk)
may be *the mother of the sons of Zebedee* (Mt), and either
John's *Mary the wife of Clopas* or *the sister of his mother*
(if, indeed, John means to designate two women here) may
be the mother of James and Joses; but we cannot be sure
about these correspondences. At any rate, the Gospels presuppose various others present. John's most significant contribution to the list is Mary *the mother of Jesus*.

As in the only other passage of John's Gospel in which she
plays a role, Mary is addressed by Jesus as *woman* (see
above on Jn 2:1–11). Jesus' present action is not merely to
provide a home for his mother as he is on the point of departing the world in death. His designation of *the disciple
whom he loved* as her *son* is also a proclamation of Mary's
spiritual motherhood of the faithful, as the new Eve, the
mother of the living (Gen 3:20), a figure of the Church.
The beloved disciple, whatever his historical identity, bears
the character of every true Christian who is in the heart of
Christ as Christ is in the heart of God (cf. Jn 1:18, 13:23).
It is altogether fitting that this proclamation be made at the
moment of Jesus' expiration (cf. John's vss. 30, 34 below),
the beginning of the saving work of the Church through the
power of the Spirit.

Mk 15:33–35   Quite different from this is Jesus' fourth
Mt 27:45–47   "word" as given by Mark-Matthew. This is
Lk 23:44–45a   another of those utterly authentic sayings
               ascribed to Jesus which, far from being the
creation of early Christian theology, have posed problems for
theology ever since. Luke no more than John can bring
himself to transmit it, but restricts himself to the description
of the *darkness over the whole earth from the sixth hour*

until *the ninth hour* when Jesus spoke his word: the traditional *tre ore* of the passion, from noon till mid afternoon.
As far as this and the subsequent phenomena described by
the Gospels are concerned, while we need not conclude that
they are purely symbolic, neither would it be faithful to
the Gospel accounts to interpret them as the record of
statistical facts. They use the language of apocalyptic, which
habitually described the great deeds of the Lord in terms of
cosmic disturbances and perturbations, imitating in this the
usage of the Old Testament prophets (cf. Is 2:2, 40:4 f.;
Ezek 47:1–12; Mi 1:3 f., 4:1, etc.). On the "darkness at
noon," cf. Amos 8:9; Jer 15:8 f.

Both Mark and Matthew quote Jesus' cry in two slightly
varying forms of a Hebraized Aramaic; it is not possible to
decide whether Jesus spoke in Hebrew that was Aramaized
in the Gospel tradition, or vice versa. The words are the
beginning of that Ps 22 which has so influenced the writing
of the passion narrative. It has often been pointed out that
this psalm is, in the ultimate analysis, a prayer of confidence
in God and trust in his mercy, and that, whether or not
Jesus recited the entire psalm, as is conceivable, his quotation
of it was evocative of its final word of faith and trust. This is
indeed true. But it is also that these are words that express a
sense of dereliction. It is the dereliction of a man of faith,
but dereliction nonetheless. We must not attempt to explain the words away, but rather accept what they have to
tell us about Jesus. They tell us that the Christ of Christian
faith who suffered and died for us did so as a man in the
fullest possible way, for all that this faith also assures us that
he was something beyond man. It is the former rather than
the latter affirmation of faith that this "word" impresses upon
us. Just as at Gethsemane, Jesus' "loud cries and tears"
(Heb 5:7) on the cross were wrung from a heart conscious of
a terrible aloneness, an aloneness which even included that
bewilderment before the inscrutable ways of God and his
personal involvement in them that the man of faith knows
as being abandoned by God.

Mk 15:36–37　The fifth, sixth, and seventh traditional
Mt 27:48–50　"words" now follow in quick succession.
Lk 23:46　　　Mark and Matthew have their casual by-
Jn 19:28–30　standers catch Jesus' agonized prayer as a
　　　　　　 call for help to *Elijah,* who was so often
featured in messianic thought (see above on Jn 1:19–24).
Perhaps the confusion may indicate that Jesus spoke the *Eli*
of Matthew (Hebrew or Aramaic) rather than the *Elohi* of
Mark (Hebrew, approaching the Aramaic *Elahi*). It has
been often debated whether the mistake was in good faith or
another form of ridicule, but the Gospels indicate that it was
honest. These, after all, were uninvolved people, the "no
opinion" percentage of the popular polls on good and evil,
war and peace, God and Devil. Jesus' sufferings had provided them diversion against an idle afternoon and they had
been the first to laugh at the pathetic spectacle on the cross,
a demonstrated failure. But they had nothing against him,
really. Perhaps, after all, he could bring off his summons
of Elijah. It was certainly a possibility worth waiting for.
Therefore they protested vigorously when some tried to put
an end to Jesus' suffering by offering him drink—*Wait! let's
see whether Elijah comes to save him.*

This relationship of events is somewhat obscured for us
by Mark, who may have misunderstood the purpose of the
sour wine; in verse 36 Luke also seems to have taken it as
part of the persecution of Jesus (there is, for that matter,
an allusion to Ps 69:22 in the incident). But it is clear
from Matthew and, especially John, where the wine is
offered in response to Jesus' *I thirst,* that the gesture was
kindly meant. It was popularly believed, on whatever authority of experience, that drink hastened the death of a
crucified person. In John's Gospel Jesus takes the drink
knowing that all was now finished: he himself decides when
it is time for him to die. Probably (explicitly so in Luke) it
was one of the soldiers who proffered the wine as an act of
rough kindness. The wine in question (*oxos*) was the cheap,
vinegary thirst-quencher such as soldiers commonly carried
with them on duty. According to Mark-Matthew the wine

was raised to Jesus' lips by means of a soaked *sponge* thrust on *a reed*. For "reed" John has substituted *hyssop*. This is initially incomprehensible, since hyssop is a limp, leafy plant unsuited to be the conveyer of anything. However, John is still thinking of Jesus as the sacrificed Passover lamb (see on Mk 14:12–17 and parallels and cf. Jn 19:14); it was with hyssop that the blood of the Passover lamb was sprinkled on the doorposts of the faithful (cf. Ex 12:22).

Immediately after drinking the wine, according to John, Jesus says, *It is finished*. Again he himself pronounces that the moment of his death has come; his sacrifice is ended with his carrying out of the divine decree. The Synoptics mark the time of passing with Jesus' utterance of *a loud cry* of sudden death, to which, nevertheless, Luke adds the words of Ps 31:6. The *expired* (Mark and Luke) or *he gave up the spirit* (Matthew) of the Synoptics probably means nothing more or less than "he died"; but when John writes solemnly that *he handed over the spirit*, we are probably meant to recall that through Jesus' glorious death the Spirit has been delivered to the Church (cf. Jn 7:39, 20:23).

Mk 15:38–39   The Synoptics conclude their apocalyp-
Mt 27:51–54   tic dramatization of the death of a
Lk 23:45b, 47–48 Savior: if men do not know how to
                 mourn this thing that they have done,
then the elements do. *The veil of the temple was split in two:* but which veil? One veil, at the entrance of the temple, separated the interior of the temple from the profane gaze of Gentiles. Are we to understand, then, that the death of Jesus has torn this veil asunder as it also broke down the "wall of separation" (Eph 2:14), uniting Jew and Gentile in one principle of salvation? There was also the veil that separated the Holy Place of the temple, where the priests offered incense, from the Holy of Holies, the most sacred spot in all Israel, where God was thought especially to dwell, and which was entered by only the high priest once a year. Do we take the Gospels to mean that now the Old Testament priestly distinctions are at an end, their functions

subsumed and fulfilled in the sacrifice of Jesus (cf. Heb 6:19, 10:20)? At all events, the death of Christ has changed the significance of the temple, and what now matters is no longer the temple, but Christ the Lord (cf. Jn 2:19).

Matthew's vision is the boldest of all. *The earth quaked, boulders split, tombs opened, and many bodies of saints who had fallen asleep were raised. Coming forth from their tombs after his resurrection, they entered the holy city and appeared to many.* This again is imagery (cf. Heb 12:26), utilizing Old Testament figures (cf. Is 26:19, 52:1; Ezek 37:12; Dan 12:2, etc.) in the perfect genre of New Testament apocalyptic (cf. Apo 11:11–13, 20:4–6, 21:2–4, etc.). In non-apocalyptic, non-descriptive language, Paul has put it otherwise: "Christ has been raised from the dead, the firstfruits of those who have fallen asleep" (1 Cor 15:20).

It is Mark, our oldest of the Gospel historians, who has told us what ultimately prompted the "confession" of *the centurion* in charge of the soldiers who saw to the execution of Jesus. It was, he says, *seeing how he died.* At the same time, Mark and Matthew after him have not resisted the temptation to put on the centurion's lips the affirmation of Christian faith—*Truly, he was Son of God*—in place of what comes much more naturally from Luke's account: *Surely, this man was innocent!* The centurion was undoubtedly a pagan, no better and no worse than the rest of his kind, whose level was not high. But he had seen what he had seen. Right is right, after all. Jesus had died no raving, screaming death of a maniac, but with the dignity fitting the claims he had made for himself. Equivalently, he had been proved right and his enemies wrong: the testimony of the Spirit had begun (cf. Jn 16:8–11).

26. GOD AND LORD OF ALL

Jn 19:31–37 This concluding chapter begins with the Gospel accounts of the immediate aftermath of the crucifixion. While the Romans had no scruples about letting an executed criminal gasp out his life for days, if necessary, the Jews did. The Law forbade a dead body to remain on the gibbet overnight (cf. Deut 21:22 f.: the Jewish law, of course, did not envision the impalement of a living person). Now the Sabbath would soon be upon Jerusalem, at sunset, after which the work of burying the dead could not take place. Besides, this coming Sabbath was *a solemn day*, the Passover, in fact. It was not to be tolerated that the solemnity of the feast should be marred by the sight of the three crosses with their sorrowful burdens on the hill of Golgotha just outside the walls of the festive city. Hence the Jews petitioned Pilate to hasten the death of the executed men that they might be safely laid away before the close of day. Pilate acceded to their request; he was no doubt as anxious as they were to avoid any potential trouble rising from the Passover celebration.

The customary manner of carrying out this apparently merciful measure was the brutal one of beating the helpless victim with iron rods. John calls it *breaking their legs*, because in fact that is what usually occurred; the legs were the part of the body the soldiers could most conveniently reach as the person hung on the cross. This beating was inflicted on the two others who had been crucified with Jesus, for they were still alive. But Jesus was already dead, and hence his bones were not broken. John sees in this fact another fulfillment of the typology of the Passover lamb, the bones of which were not to be broken (cf. Ex 12:46; Num 9:12).

Though the soldiers omitted the breaking of Jesus' bones, recognizing him to be dead, nevertheless one of them *pierced his side with a lance,* just to be sure. From the wound *immediately poured out blood and water*—the water, in medical opinion, would be actually either pericardial fluid or the clear serum of a pleural hemorrhage. For John this is another "sign" witnessing to the meaning of Christ's death. In 1 Jn 5:8 "water and blood" sums up the redemptive life and death of Jesus. It was a common patristic interpretation that the flow of blood and water symbolizes the life-giving ministry of the Church which derives its efficacy from the death of Christ, and it is most likely that John had something like this in mind. In fact, his previous use of the symbols of water (cf. Jn 3:5, 4:10, 14, 7:38 f.) and blood (cf. Jn 6:53–57) encourages us in the belief that he was thinking of the sacraments of Baptism and the Eucharist, both of which he has featured in his Gospel. The piercing of the side of Jesus itself he connects with Zech 12:10 (a word concerning one who, in John's thought, was probably identical with the Servant of the Lord).

Thus even in death the Word of God rules and saves, as these mute witnesses testify; and to their testimony the evangelist adds his own, which is part of it.

Mk 15:40–47 The Synoptic Gospels have introduced the
Mt 27:55–61 disciples and Galilean followers of Jesus,
Lk 23:49–56 and especially the women (see above on
Jn 19:38–42 Jn 19:25–27), as witnesses both of his
crucifixion and his burial. All our narrative sources are in agreement as to the identity of the man who

buried Jesus, though they describe him somewhat variously.
Joseph of Arimathea, a wealthy man who had come from an
obscure little town in Judea, was, it is agreed, a leading
member of the Sanhedrin. Neither Mark nor Luke ever says
in so many words that he was a disciple of Jesus, though
Luke approaches such a statement in verse 51; both Matthew
and John explicitly identify him as one of Jesus' followers.
From this variation some scholars have concluded that Mark
had the right of it at the beginning: that Joseph was simply a
Jew faithful to the law of Deut 21:22 f., who saw to the
burial of Jesus as a disinterested work of piety (so, too,
the pious Jews—not Christians—of Acts 8:2 who buried the
protomartyr Stephen); the later Gospels which make Joseph
a disciple contain the embellishments of an expanding tradition. While this is conceivable, it would be difficult to explain even on Mark's account why Joseph went to all the
trouble he did for someone in whom he did not take a personal interest; furthermore, Mark's observation that *he too
was looking forward to the kingdom of God,* we may be sure,
was not idly written.

As a disciple, however, he was not a particularly heroic
one. Luke's saying that *he was a good and just man* is not a
blanket endorsement of his life. We are left to imagine the
figure he cut as a member of the Sanhedrin that judged Jesus
worthy of death—though, for that matter, his involvement in
that action may have taken no more positive form than the
flight of the Twelve who had left Jesus alone and defenseless. John appropriately associates with him the timid
Nicodemus (cf. Jn 3:1 ff., 7:50 f.), also a member of the
Sanhedrin and also a secret disciple of Jesus. It was doubtless of these men among others that the evangelist was thinking in Jn 12:42. At least, they do now come forward and
declare themselves by their actions.

As relatives or friends of the deceased had a right, Joseph
petitioned the governor for the body of Jesus that he might
save it from the common burial ground or charnel heap into
which the bodies of executed criminals were commonly cast.
The request may have been made at the same time that

the Jews asked for the executions to be speeded up in view
of the impending feast. Pilate, at first understandably surprised that Jesus was so soon dead, readily acceded to the
proposal of an important man that cost him nothing.

The tomb, John says, was *in a garden near the place
where he was crucified,* and, according to Matthew, it was
Joseph's own tomb, probably one which he had had prepared for himself and his family: that it was *a new tomb in
which no one had yet been laid* is perhaps John's and Luke's
way of agreeing with Matthew. The proximity of the tomb
to the place of execution is natural enough, since both had to
be outside the city walls according to law. There are still
visible in Palestine many tombs contemporary with and like
the one the Gospels describe. It may have been at first a
natural cave which was then further hollowed out till a
sizable room was made, then fitted out with several individual
resting places for the deceased. These were simply slabs of
stone, sometimes with headrests, and sometimes with foot-
rests as well. It was in such a tomb that the body of Lazarus
had been laid according to the story of Jn 11:1–44, and
the Gospels now described Jesus as swathed in linen cloths
as Lazarus' body had been. The opening of the tomb was, as
usual, covered by a round flat stone—old millstones sometimes served the purpose—which could be rolled aside in a
groove fixed for it.

The major discrepancy between the Johannine and the
Synoptic accounts of the burial of Jesus concerns the circumstances of the embalming of his body. All the Gospels
stress the haste of the burial, but while in the Synoptics
this serves to explain the deferring of the customary preparation of the body for the tomb—a deferment which, in fact,
was never actualized because of the intervention of the
resurrection—John, nevertheless, insists that everything of *the
burial custom of the Jews* was, indeed, done by means of
the superabundant *mixture of myrrh and aloes, about a
hundred pounds,* provided by Nicodemus. The reason for
the difference, which is chiefly due to John's theology, we
have already seen above (on Jn 12:1–8 and parallels). As

John saw it, the burial for which Mary's precious ointment had been kept was not this "Jewish" interment of his dead body but his submersion in the life of the Church.

Mt 27:62–66 Matthew has another story (completed in Mt 28:11–15 below) from his collection of Jerusalem traditions which he uses to complete the narrative of Jesus' passion and death preparatory to the common Gospel testimony to the resurrection. The purpose of the story, as is obvious, is to counter an objection that the tomb of Jesus was found to be empty only because his disciples had come and spirited away his body. Even though the narrative is a free composition by the Christian community—the conversation between *the chief priests and Pharisees and Pilate,* for example, must have been reconstructed on imagination, since it is hardly to be thought that any one of the principals would have furnished a transcript for the Gospel tradition; furthermore, taken on the surface, the priests and Pharisees have a more vivid recollection of Jesus' promise of resurrection *after three days* and a greater expectation of its fulfillment than did his own intimate disciples!—still, in its own way it is a witness to the historicity of the empty tomb. That such a story had to be told shows that the point under debate between Christian and Jew was not the fact of the empty tomb, but rather how it came to be empty. The tradition of the empty tomb certainly belongs to the Jewish era of the Church: in Jewish thought, but not in the Greek thinking of the Gentile world, survival and reappearance after death necessitated a bodily resurrection.

Matthew's way of referring to Saturday as *the day after the Preparation* is curious—almost as though he was conscious that this was, indeed, the Passover as it appears in John's Gospel, but was inhibited from calling it this in view of his portrayal of the Last Supper as a Passover meal; otherwise we would expect him to have simply *the Sabbath,* as he later does in company with the other Gospels. Mk 15:42 also refers to the day of crucifixion as *the Preparation,*

but there it is made to mean *the eve of the Sabbath*.
The intervention of the Sabbath-Passover partly explains why
a Roman *guard* (cf. Mt 28:14) was requested for the tomb
when otherwise the temple police or other Jewish guards
might have been employed: throughout for "guard" Matthew
uses the Latin word *custodia*. Also, of course, the tomb
was private property, and therefore some kind of official
approval was needed. Pilate's *you have a guard* is to be
taken to mean "here and now you are given a guard."

Mk 16:1–8   As is also the case with other Gospel events,
Mt 28:1–8   both those of great importance such as the
Lk 24:1–12   institution of the Eucharist and those of rela-
Jn 20:1–13   tively secondary concern such as the story of
             Peter's denials of the Lord, the resurrection
narratives of the four Gospels are materially discordant and
it is absolutely pointless to think of harmonizing their many
variant details. Also, that kind of consistency was never
within the purview of the Gospel writers, who wrote down
the traditions as they had come to them without bothering
their heads about such discrepancies or attempting to give
us any help toward resolving them (some of their copyists,
to be sure, did make the attempt). A fifth record of the
tradition (1 Cor 15:3–8), the oldest of the lot as a written
document, set down at a time when there were still living
witnesses to the events recalled in it, merely compounds the
confusion by contributing discordances of its own. We simply
have to face the fact that such matters as to whom the
risen Lord first appeared, and in the presence of whom,
and under what precise circumstances, were not historical
issues for the New Testament traditions of the resurrection.

Comparing the traditions one with the other, however, we
find that there is a consensus not only on the underlying
essentials, but even on certain points of detail. First of all,
there is never any attempt—as there is in later apocryphal
literature—to describe the resurrection itself. The resurrection
is allowed to remain the mystery that it is, its "mechanics"
unsubmitted to speculation. The empty tomb is a sign of the

resurrection, but only after it has been determined by the revealed word: "He has been raised." The essence of the resurrection is not that a dead body left the tomb, but that a living person who had been dead, Jesus of Nazareth, lives once more, now transformed and glorified with God. He has passed from this earthly sphere and entered into the heavenly realm, for all that he continues to live in his Church through his Spirit. But both in the Semitic conception of things and, more than we often realize, according to our own "Western" conceptions as well, the body of man *is* his human personality. Thus the meaning of the empty tomb for the evangelists.

It does not seem to be true that the tradition of the empty tomb represents a later stage in resurrection theology, an attempt to provide objective evidence for the spiritual experience that the first Christians had of their living Lord after his death and burial. A resurrection without an empty tomb would have been as incomprehensible to St. Paul as to these other Christians: if the discussion in 1 Cor 15 is read attentively, this becomes very clear. Though the words "empty tomb" do not occur in the tradition which Paul recalls in verses 3–8, the idea is certainly there. That Jesus was known to have been raised up *on the third day* and not immediately indicates an awareness of the part played in the history of the resurrection by Jesus' burial and the tomb. The empty tomb does not figure in the Gospels as an argument to settle doubts and silence incredulity; rather, as Matthew has already shown, it was the occasion of controversy as well as a sign for belief.

Another point on which the Gospels are agreed is that the resurrection was wholly unexpected by Jesus' disciples. Though the Gospels have recorded Jesus' prophecies of his resurrection, they have also shown that the prophecies were not understood: these Gospel accounts are redactions of Jesus' words in the light of post-resurrection faith. Any idea of the resurrection of Jesus as a wish-fulfillment of the early Christian Church, therefore, must call for evidence that is contrary to that of the Gospels, evidence which they had far less reason to invent than simply to remember with mixed emotions.

The time of the discovery of the empty tomb is roughly the same in all the Gospels: *very early in the morning on the first day of the week* (Mark *ad litteram;* the substance in Matthew, Luke, John). Only two of the Gospels offer an explanation of the coming to the tomb of *the women who had come with him from Galilee* (so Luke's "they," cf. Lk 23:55; Mark, Matthew, and John mention *Mary Magdalene* explicitly and certain other women—even John, cf. the "we" of vs. 2). According to Mark and Luke (cf. also Lk 23:55 f.), they came to anoint Jesus' body. John, we know, has reason to omit such a detail, and Matthew, for some reason of his own, omits it as well: perhaps he saw a difficulty in an anointing and embalming so long after burial. Even though Joseph of Arimathea has been, explicitly or implicitly, identified by the Gospels as one of Jesus' followers, he was evidently unknown to the women and there had been no communication between them (cf. Mk 15:47; Lk 23:55). The Gospels say nothing further about him or Nicodemus.

When the women reach the tomb they find *the stone* (mentioned now for the first time by John) already *rolled away* from the door. The purpose of this intervention was not to suggest the manner in which the Lord left the tomb, but to show that he had indeed left it; this is also the purpose of the much more graphic story by which Matthew describes the way in which the stone was rolled away and the Roman guards about the tomb were routed. This story as well as those which Mark and Luke go on to tell are variant forms of "angelic annunciation" (so also John's vss. 11–13), not dissimilar from others we have seen earlier in the Gospels, especially in the Gospel of the Infancy (see above on Lk 1:8–12). The descriptive details are fairly conventional for such stories (cf. Dan 10:5–9; 2 Macc 3:26, 33; Acts 1:10 f., 10:30–32; Apo 3:5, 7:9, 19:14, etc.), which have in view to communicate the word by which the empty tomb is constituted a sign to believers: *He is not here; he has been raised up!*

The most serious discrepancy in the Gospel accounts of this annunciation is as regards the indication they give of the locale of the post-resurrection appearances of Jesus. Mark and Matthew understood that the Lord would make himself known to his disciples once again *in Galilee,* where, as far as they were concerned, the Gospel had begun. Luke and John, however, take it for granted that he appeared to the disciples in Jerusalem (although John's ch. 21 without explanation shifts the scene to Galilee). Having once adopted these viewpoints, the Gospels stick to them fairly consistently. Since it does not seem possible that they can be harmonized, most commentators have felt that one or the other must be chosen as historical, and of these probably the majority has opted for the Galilean tradition. After the crucifixion, it is felt, the scattered disciples fled to their Galilean homeland —a three days' journey from Jerusalem—and it was here that the risen Lord gathered them again into his Church. The post-resurrection focus of interest was later switched to Jerusalem, according to this hypothesis, because the Church in Galilee did not long flourish and the center of Palestinian Christianity speedily became Jerusalem in any case. It can be added that both Gospels which feature Jerusalem do so for theological reasons: for Luke Jerusalem is both the beginning and the end, and for John it is the center of Jesus' public life. There is much to support this argument; however, it can neither be proved nor disproved on the Gospel evidence, and contrary positions are also tenable. We are reduced simply to taking the Gospel narratives singly as we have them.

Mark disagrees with the rest of the Gospels at this point. According to him, the women *fled from the tomb* and *said nothing to anyone because they were very much afraid.* It is possible, however, that Mark is merely emphasizing the awe that had gripped these first witnesses to the empty tomb, and that he is not precluding their later report to *his disciples and Peter* as they had been instructed. At any

rate, the other Gospels say that they did run to take the
news to the disciples. Luke records that their word was not
believed (his vs. 12 is probably not original, but is an addition to his text modeled on Jn 20:3–10).

John's narrative becomes not only incoherent with the
other Gospels but also somewhat with his own sequence: it
is not entirely clear how verses 11–18 concerning Mary
Magdalene are to be fitted into the chronology he has
established for himself. According to his version of the story,
the news of the empty tomb was first brought by Mary
Magdalene (and other women?) *to Simon Peter and the
other disciple whom Jesus loved,* who hastened to verify
the report with their own eyes. This story itself, as it
happens, there seems to be no reason to regard as anything
other than what was originally the recollection of an eyewitness; Lk 24:24 appears to refer to it. *He* (the beloved
disciple) *saw* the linen cloths in the empty tomb *and* (he
also, along with Peter?) *believed* might suggest that the
mute evidence of the empty shrouds (preserving the outline
of the figure that had lain in them?) offered some kind
of visual evidence of a resurrection even though *they did
not yet understand the Scripture.* The "understanding" of
the Old Testament as having relevance to the resurrection
of Christ (cf. Acts 2:24–36, etc.) is part of the rereading
of the Scripture in the light of Christian fulfillment (cf.
Lk 24:27, 32, 45); in precisely the same way, contemporary
Judaism had reread the Old Testament in its own favor.

Mt 28:9–10　　With verse 8 above the original Gospel
Jn 20:14–18　　of Mark, to the extent that we now pos-
[Mk 16:9–11]　　sess it, has come to an end. We say "to
the extent that we now possess it," for
hardly anyone is prepared to believe that the Gospel originally ended so abruptly, even though it does end so abruptly
in our oldest and best Greek manuscripts. For whatever
reasons, it is agreed, the original ending of Mark's Gospel
has disappeared, leaving behind no provable trace in the
manuscripts. On the law of averages, it was not very

lengthy, probably not even as lengthy as the verses 9–20 which are found in most of the manuscripts, which the Church has traditionally regarded as inspired and canonical, but which were assuredly not written by Mark. These verses the Church itself has contributed to serve as a conclusion to the Gospel: they are a composite of what is elsewhere found in Matthew, Luke, and John. By the critics they are sometimes called "the longer ending" in distinction to an ending of only a few lines substituted for or combined with it in some few manuscripts.

At least part of the lost ending of Mark's Gospel may have been preserved for us in the verses copied from it by Matthew, according to which Jesus himself appeared to the women hastening from the tomb to reinforce the angelic instruction that they carry the good news to his disciples. The passage fits better in Mark than it does in Matthew, as a matter of fact. In Mark it might have served to break the silence of fear that had descended upon them at the tomb, whereas in Matthew it somewhat interferes with the climax of the Galilean appearance of the Lord in the Gospel's final verses.

That the women who saw the risen Jesus are said to have *embraced his feet* is probably one indication that this passage is the Synoptic parallel to John's story of the appearance to Mary Magdalene. Mary at first does not recognize Jesus, taking him to be the one who owned the garden in which the tomb was situated (Jn 19:41). Partly this misunderstanding follows the pattern of the Johannine dialogues; however, Lk 24:16, 37 ff. also indicate that there was something about the appearance of the risen Lord that did not make him immediately recognizable. But perhaps we should not expect logical coherence in a story of this kind which is describing a human situation that need not be logical. Mary is distraught from grief and bewilderment. The thought that Jesus' body has been moved and that she must *take him away*—we do not ask how she expected to manage this—has become a fixation for her. In any case, it suffices for Jesus to call her by name for her to know

him at last (cf. Jn 10:3 f.). She gives the glad cry of
recognition, *Rabboni* (so Mk 10:51; an alternate form of
the "rabbi" otherwise frequent in the Gospels), and falls
to her knees at his feet. *Do not cling to me* is Jesus' way
of telling her of the changed relationship in which they
now stand, somewhat like his words to his mother in Jn 2:4,
when the same kind of change was anticipated. No longer
is he merely a rabbi with his disciples at his feet. His
glorification is not yet complete. He must now *ascend to my
Father and your Father, to my God and your God:* the
disjunction is calculated, to remind us that God is our
Father only because he is first the Father of Jesus Christ,
through whom we have eternal life. As in Mt 28:10, Jesus
now calls the disciples *my brothers* (cf. also Jn 2:12 and
Mt 12:49 f.).

The verses in the supplement to Mark, it seems to be
evident, are a summary statement based on John's story,
with the help of Lk 8:2 and 24:11.

Mt 28:11–15   Matthew now continues with another story
              that was not in Mark's Gospel, the conclu-
sion of the Jerusalemite tradition about the empty tomb
which he began in Mt 27:62–66 above. As we have already
observed, a story of this kind can only be a free composition by which the Christian conviction as to what had
taken place was translated into narrative form. The earliest
Christian apologists of patristic times testify that the explanation of the empty tomb which Matthew ascribes to the
suborning of the Roman guards was, indeed, current among
the Jewish adversaries of Christianity.

Lk 24:13–35   Luke also has a proper story of his own
[Mk 16:12–13]   concerning the post-resurrection appear-
              ances of Jesus which has been hastily
summarized—not, however, without some conflict—in the supplement to Mark. It is a rather strange story which he has
not entirely integrated into his Gospel, but at the same
time it contains a number of details which for that very

reason are all the more interesting for their being quite uncalculated. Some have thought that it is the vestige of the tradition known also to Luke, though not used by him, that the word of the resurrected Savior was first brought to Jerusalem from outside. The reference in verse 34 to a prior appearance to Peter looks like an afterthought in line with 1 Cor 15:5, since there is nothing else in the Gospel about this. Whether or not this is so, Luke has repeated the story because of other values that it had for him. We shall try to see those values briefly.

That very day is presumably Sunday, the day following the Passover, when pilgrims to the Holy City could make their return to their homes far and near (so vss. 21b–24, if these were part of the original story). *Two of them* has no immediate antecedent; *Cleopas* (not the Clopas of Jn 19:25) and his companion were certainly disciples of Jesus, but their relation to the Twelve and the others of his intimate band of followers is not clear. Their conception of Jesus' mission was without doubt that of most of his disciples, including the Twelve, despite the hints that he may have given them of the larger dimensions of his character: *a prophet mighty in deed and word before God and all the people . . . we were hoping that he was the one who would redeem Israel.* Obviously they had no idea of a suffering Messiah, of Jesus as fulfilling the ideal of the Servant of the Lord. It is this same limited christology that Luke ascribes to the apostles at the very moment of the ascension (cf. Acts 1:6). The application to himself of the relevant themes of Old Testament prophecy Jesus now proceeds to reveal to them as he enters their company with the easy democracy of the East and engages them in conversation.

After *the breaking of the bread* the disciples recognize Jesus in the mysterious stranger and they also realize how *he opened to us the Scriptures.* It is unquestionably here that Luke sees the chief significance of this story, which he has used like one of the Johannine narratives to find in it a "sign." The meal that the disciples had with Jesus at Emmaus was, of course, not the Eucharist—"the breaking of bread" was a common idiom for taking a meal just as it later became a Christian term for the Eucharistic celebration. But even as Christ showed himself to his disciples in the breaking of the bread, Luke wants his readers to recognize how something of the same kind happens in their Eucharistic assemblies. Furthermore, it is on such occasions that the meaning of the Scripture is made clear.

From the historical point of view, certain details of the story cause problems. Most of them revolve about the location of *the village whose name was Emmaus, about sixty stadia from Jerusalem*. There is only one site in Palestine which can reasonably be identified as Emmaus, as it has been from the earliest Christian times; it is still known by that name, in the Arabic form *Amwas*. But Amwas is considerably farther away from Jerusalem than sixty stadia (say seven miles): the distance is more like twenty miles to the west. It is true, there are some manuscripts of Luke which read *one hundred and sixty stadia*, but this reading is generally thought to be an adjustment of the text to fit the geography of Amwas. On the other hand, it is possible that Luke did originally write "one hundred and sixty stadia" and that the figure was later altered to "sixty" for the same reason that would cause a modern commentator to question its accuracy, the improbability, namely, that having already traveled twenty miles and come to Emmaus toward evening (vs. 29), Cleopas and his companion could after supper return the twenty miles to Jerusalem and that same night find the apostolic band still gathered together. Improbabilities, it must be admitted, are not necessarily impossibilities. It is almost certain that Luke never adverted to the difficulty at all. Other proposed sites of "Emmaus" in Palestine have little to recommend them except that they are in closer proximity to Jerusalem and were close by the pilgrim routes of later times; the latter criterion has always been a powerful one in establishing alternate traditions for "the holy places."

Lk 24:36–43   It is as a sequel and continuation to the
Jn 20:19–23   preceding story that Luke now tells of the
[Mk 16:14]   Lord's appearance in Jerusalem to *the Eleven
and those who were with them* (vs. 33).
It is not certain whether the parallel story in John's Gospel
was intended to reflect precisely the same tradition; at any
rate, there are several similarities between the two accounts
other than the one of their general situation. As usual, copyists have tried to make the similarities even closer: Luke's
verse 40 is suspect as an addition to the text modeled on
Jn 20:20, and the greeting of Jesus in verse 36 has probably
been borrowed from that of John's verse 19. The summary
verse in Mark's supplement seems to refer to the Lucan
story; however, the rebuke for disbelief in the resurrection
has been considerably heightened in contrast to Luke's account, according to which *they still disbelieved for joy.*

Luke is intent on showing the reality of the resurrection,
the idea of which was doubtless still somewhat grotesque
to various of his Gentile readers, and consequently he lays
emphasis on the signs which Jesus gave to the unbelieving.
Lest they should think that they had experienced an hal-
lucination, he had them note the wounds in his *hands*
and his *feet* and *touch* the solidity of his body (this
seems to be the meaning of vs. 39, even though only in
Jn 20:25 is there explicit mention of nail wounds in his
hands). Even then, as they could scarcely credit their senses,
he ate in their presence, taking the food that they themselves
had prepared that they might be sure there was no illusion.
The story has as its obvious purpose to "objectivize" the
resurrection in meaningful human terms (cf. 1 Jn 1:1);
Luke offers no theories on the constitution of what Paul
called the "spiritual body" of the raised (cf. 1 Cor 15:42–50).

John also brings in the physical evidence of the resurrection, though he makes a point of Jesus' appearance despite
the fact that *the doors were shut* (so also in vs. 26 below).
His main stress, however, is on the resurrection as fulfillment
of Jesus' promises. *Peace be with you* is the conventional
Jewish greeting, but it has added significance in view of Jn

14:27 and 16:33. Similarly, his consecration of which he
spoke in Jn 17:18 now finds its culmination in the mission
of his apostles: *As the Father has sent me, so I send you.
He breathed on them* expresses sacramentally what is determined by the words: *Receive Holy Spirit* (cf. Gen 2:7;
Jn 3:8). This action shows that, in John's view, the ascension
to the Father of which Jesus spoke to Mary Magdalene
in verse 17 above has now taken place, the glorification
which is necessary for the giving of the Spirit (cf. Jn 7:39,
15:26, 16:7; 1 Cor 15:45). John has nothing in his Gospel
of the symbolic chronology of Luke by which the resurrection
is separated from the ascension by forty days, and the coming of the Spirit by another ten days (cf. Lk 24:49–53;
Acts 1:3–11, 2:1 ff.). Christian liturgical celebration of these
mysteries has followed the Lucan chronology for the same
reason that the evangelist first employed it, to focus attention
on one or the other separable aspect of a single spiritual
reality. John, too, has separated the aspects, but without the
chronology.

The specific activity to be exercised by the Church
through the power of the Holy Spirit is here defined in
terms of the forgiveness of sin (cf. Mt 9:8, 16:19, 18:18).
This the Church does alike in its preaching of the Gospel
of salvation and in its ministry of the sacraments of forgiveness, baptism, and repentance.

Jn 20:24–29   John has a complement to the story he has
just told, with which he originally concluded
his Gospel: the episode ends with the most explicit act of
faith in Christ to be found in all of the New Testament. It
takes place on the Sunday following, a device by which
the evangelist is probably suggesting the rapidity with which
the first day of the week became the time of Christian
assembly in perpetuation of the Easter mystery. *Thomas
called the Twin* has been introduced before (cf. Jn 11:16,
14:5) as a member of *the Twelve* (John still uses the
traditional designation). In John's mind Thomas' objection

was probably not one of skepticism with regard to the reality of the Lord's presence, but was concerned with its manner; as was Lk 24:37, John is disposed to make a point of the resurrectional appearance of Jesus as more than "spiritual."

Thomas' conditions for belief were rigorous, and Jesus' words are almost ironic as he invites the inspection which the disciple had demanded. But apparently the sight of the risen Savior was enough for Thomas. *My Lord and my God* is a culmination of the faith of apostolic Christianity expressed in a formula explicit both in the language of the Old Testament and in that of the Hellenistic world of the Gospels. This is the meaning of Jesus' acknowledgment: *Because you have seen me, you have believed. Blessed are they who have not seen, yet have believed.* The resurrection appearances, and the entire Gospel narrative itself, are the testimony of the first Christians to what they had seen. But though to believe was to see, to see was not necessarily to believe: John's "book of signs" is evidence of this. In the ultimate analysis, belief is the acceptance of a word, not on external proof but on the power of the word itself to convince. Those who followed Jesus in his earthly ministry did so because they believed in his word. Those who now follow him do so out of belief in the same word, which is the word of the Gospel.

Jn 20:30–31   And thus John gives us at the end the purpose of his Gospel: *that you may believe that Jesus is the Christ, the Son of God, and that believing you may have life in his name.* Once more we understand what he has meant by speaking of Jesus' *signs,* some of which he has written down, most of which he has not. What Jesus did and said—adequate motives for belief for all who are called by God and disposed to be his children (cf. Jn 8:47)—is available in the living witness that the Church gives in its ministry of the sacraments, its proclamation of the word of life, and its total life of the Spirit.

Jn 21:1–14   The final chapter of John's Gospel is a supplement, though not in the same way as verses 9–20 are a supplement to the last chapter and the Gospel of Mark. These passages are within the same tradition as that used by the evangelist of the Fourth Gospel, and so much in its spirit and style that many have believed that the original author himself has supplemented his own Gospel. It seems more plausible, however, for reasons that will later become more apparent, to see in this chapter a parallel redaction of Johannine material that was added to the Gospel after the death of the great John on whose testimony it ultimately depends. Probably, for that matter, it was part of the Gospel from the first in its published form. But there has been no real attempt to integrate the chapter fully into the scheme of Jn 1–11.

We see this immediately when without any warning except that it was *after these things* we suddenly find ourselves with the disciples *by the Sea of Tiberias* (so called only here in the Gospels) in Galilee. Present, among others, are Peter, Thomas the doubter, Nathanael, and *the sons of Zebedee* (a Synoptic term not elsewhere used by John). No explanation is given for the transition from Jerualem to Galilee. That the disciples did, indeed, go back to Galilee after the apparent disaster of Golgotha, and that they would inevitably have reverted to their earlier ways of living, these things are easily credited. It seems equally evident, however, that the view of events reflected in this chapter is quite independent of that of the Jerusalem appearances of Luke and John's chapter 20. What is being described here is a first appearance of Jesus to his disciples, despite the "again" that has been inserted in verse 1 and the "third time" in verse 14 which set up a perfunctory connection between chapters 20 and 21.

The encounter of Jesus and his disciples in this story bears certain resemblances to that of Lk 5:1–11, there a narrative of the initial call of the disciples to follow Jesus. As we saw (above on that text), there is some difficulty in harmonizing Luke's account with that of the other Synoptists (in any case, a Galilean call of the first disciples stands in contrast to the Johannine chronicle of the ministry which is antecedently more probable: see above on Jn 1:35–42), and some commentators even believe that the Lucan story is a displaced narrative of a resurrection appearance which the evangelist could no longer use because of its Galilean situation. Whatever the case may be, John's story is completely natural in its details. After the disciples had fished all *night and had caught nothing* they heard a stranger hailing them familiarly from the shore. There is no more normal greeting in the world than that with which the fisherman is habitually accosted: "Any luck?" And it was likewise normal for someone on shore to suggest likely places to cast the net, for sometimes he could see fish in the water to which those in the boat just above would be blind; besides, it is a rare fisherman who is unwilling to follow anyone's suggestion to try anywhere else, just once more.

But now *the disciple whom Jesus loved* recognizes in the stranger the risen Lord: the superabundant draught of fish is evidently seen as a "sign." He communicates his perception to Peter, and Peter the impulsive cannot wait for the boat to reach land: he throws himself into the water and rushes to meet Christ. The other disciples, no less eagerly but perhaps more practically, bring the boat in with the fish. They had been standing offshore *about two hundred cubits* —about a hundred yards—when they first saw the Lord. Their haul consisted of *a hundred and fifty-three large fish*. In view of the Johannine proclivity for symbolism, most commentators both ancient and modern have felt that this number means something of itself, but they have never been able to explain satisfactorily just what it does mean. In general, the scene is doubtless intended as a foreshadowing of the success of the apostles as "fishers of men." The Gospel also notes that *the net was not torn:* perhaps another symbolic detail (cf. Jn 19:23 f.), but also a practical consideration to fishermen who spent almost as much time repairing their delicate nets as they did casting them for fish.

The meal on the shore does not seem to have the same meaning as that of Lk 24:42 f. Here Jesus is not said to eat, but he *took the bread and gave it to them, and so with the fish.* This recalls the language of Jn 6:11, the miracle of the loaves which had taken place beside this same lake, and which was already established as a sign of the Eucharist. Thus the closer Lucan parallel is Lk 24:30–35.

Jn 21:15–19   Apart from telling of the appearance of the risen Lord to his disciples in Galilee—a version of the events which is probably more primitive than that adopted in the main part of the Gospel—the Johannine supplement also takes the occasion to conclude certain other unfinished business of the Gospel. First of all, it deals with Peter, whose name has once more been prominently introduced into the narrative.

The primacy of Peter in the apostolic Church is a common teaching of the Gospels (see above on Mk 8:27–30 and parallels), as it is, indeed, of the entire New Testament. If the testimony of Matthew's Gospel is the most detailed and explicit, it is nevertheless by no means unique or isolated. We have already proposed that the major Petrine passage of the Matthaean tradition is an artificial unity, combining the actual conferral of the primacy along wth the change of Peter's name (which John has in Jn 1:42) and Peter's own great confession of the Lord (the Johannine equivalent of which is in Jn 6:68 f.). Specifically, that Christ should have explicitly designated Peter as head of the apostolic community that succeeded him accords better with this Johannine perspective of a post-resurrection experience of the risen Lord of the Church than with Matthew's context of Jesus' public ministry.

Three times—as Peter had denied him thrice—Jesus asks Peter if he loves him. The first time it is, *Do you love me more than these?*, perhaps a delicate reminder that Peter had never been slow to assert himself and to compare himself favorably with the other disciples (cf. Mt 14:29).

With a sudden lack of impulsiveness, Peter is content to say only that he loves his Savior; for the others he dare not speak. Asked a second time for a declaration of his love, he replies humbly but confidently that the Lord knows he loves him. When he is asked the third time, possibly the full significance of these questions is brought home to him, and remembering his past weakness he cries out, troubled, that the Master who knows all things must know now that he does indeed love him, and that his betrayal has been bitterly repented. Each time Christ has repeated his commission to Peter: *Feed my lambs, tend my sheep.* To Peter Jesus transmits his own office as shepherd of the flock (cf. Jn 10:11 ff.; Acts 20:28; 1 Pt 5:2–4). As are all the offices in the Church, it is founded on love and service (see above on Mk 10:35–45 and parallel).

Jesus has an additional word for Peter. The true shepherd also lays down his life for his sheep (cf. Jn 10:11). There is no doubt, as verse 19 makes quite explicit, that the extent of Peter's following Jesus will be even to the end, to the death. Materially, Jesus says nothing more than that a man who is young and has all his faculties unimpaired girds himself and walks as he pleases, unaided, whereas an old man must stretch out his arms to be led, and needs others to care for him and help him. But this is Johannine irony. *You will stretch out your hands and another will tie you* would be recognized by John's readers as referring to Peter's crucifixion. There is good reason to accept the tradition—to which this Gospel passage is probably our oldest written attestation—that Peter was put to death in Rome under the emperor Nero either in A.D. 63 or 67.

Jn 21:20–23   The other bit of unfinished business concerned *the disciple whom Jesus loved,* who quite obviously in this passage emerges as the one on whom the Johannine tradition depends. What of him? This, indeed, is the question asked by Peter, who *turned and noticed him following them.*

It was an honest question, not born of envy but of friendly interest in a person who had often shared his confidences (cf. Jn 13:23 f., 18:15 f., 20:2 ff.). But it was not Jesus' practice to satisfy this kind of curiosity. *Suppose I would like him to remain until I come, what is that to you?* is as ambiguous as the prophecy of Peter's death. It neither affirms nor denies the possibility. What these verses are concerned with, however, is to lay to rest a popular belief that the Lord had, indeed, made a very firm commitment with regard to the beloved disciple.

The most logical interpretation of the background of this supplement is that this disciple—the John who is traditionally named the author of the Fourth Gospel—had recently died, the last, perhaps, of the known apostolic witnesses to the Jesus of Galilee and of the resurrection appearances, and that this event had upset a widely held conviction that such a thing could not occur before the *parousia* of the Lord. One of the stages in the Church's development of a theology of the "delay" of the *parousia* (see above on Mk 13:3–8 and parallels) without doubt involved the ever dwindling number of "first generation" Christians who had actually seen the Lord and lived with him. Surely, he would return before he had called all of them to himself? (That he had called any of them at all was problem enough to some, cf. 1 Thes 4:13–18.) Here we are being told, therefore, that Jesus had never really promised that the *parousia* would coincide with the end of the Johannine age.

Jn 21:24–25   Once again and finally, then, John's Gospel comes to a close. Those who are responsible for putting it in order testify to their dependence on an eyewitness authority—*he who wrote these things*—and to their acceptance of *his witness* as *true*. It is, as all the Gospels are, a fragmentary account: their intention is not so much to apologize for the brevity of the Gospel as to excuse their failure to plumb the full depths of all that Jesus had done and said.

Mt 28:16–20
[Mk 16:15–18]

Matthew also ends his Gospel in Galilee, at *that mountain to which Jesus had summoned them* (see above on Mk 3:13–19 and parallels; Mt 5:1 f. and parallel). This evangelist shows no concern whatever for certifying the reality of the resurrection (except for the note that *some had doubted* before this event). He is intent, rather, on setting forth its consequences for the existing Church. These are: (1) That the apostles now go forth with the *authority* and in the person of Christ (cf. Mt 9:6, 11:27 [=Lk 10:22]; Lk 5:24; Jn 20:21–23). (2) That the Gospel may now be brought to *all the nations* of the earth (cf. Mt 24:14 [=Mk 13:10]; 26:13 [=Mk 14:9]; see above on Mk 7:24–30 and parallel, etc.), following its definitive rejection by Israel (cf. Mt 27:25). (3) That, on the one hand, this is a ministry of sacrament: *baptizing them in the name of the Father, and of the Son, and of the Holy Spirit.* This formula undoubtedly speaks for the Church of Matthew's time. While it had been sufficient to baptize "in the name of the Lord Jesus" in the earliest days of the Church (cf. Acts 10:48, 19:5, etc.), very soon it became necessary to employ a trinitarian formula to distinguish Christian baptism from the many alien rites of the Hellenistic world. (4) It is also a ministry of *teaching* as well as of proclaiming. As a semi-permanent institution awaiting *the end of the world,* the Church must present to man an ethical and moral doctrine that is in conformity with the way of life. This Matthew has given, as one example, in the Sermon on the Mount.

The Marcan supplement adds to these essential characteristics certain signs that attended the apostolic Church (cf. Mk 6:13; Lk 10:19; Acts 2:3 f., 10:46, 19:6, 28:3 f.; 1 Cor 12:1–11, etc.) and which, on occasion, have attended the Church in every age, according to need. Miracles are not excluded from the life of the Church, but neither are they the life of the Church. This life Matthew has best described.

Lk 24:44–53   Luke's conclusion is a summary, and the
[Mk 16:19–20]   ending of Mark's supplement is a sum-
                     mary of it. No indication is given of a
change of scene or of a passing of time since the immediately preceding episode of Jesus' appearance to the disciples in Jerusalem, still on that first day of his resurrection.
The conversation which the Gospel ascribes to Jesus and
the disciples on this occasion, however, corresponds to the
forty days' instruction of which we read in Acts 1:3. Luke
is preparing for the story of the apostolic Church, the Gospel
of the Spirit, which begins where the Gospel leaves off, *in
the temple* (cf. Acts 2:46) where the Gospel also began
(cf. Lk 1:9). Through the Christ-event of the Gospel the
temple, where we first saw Zechariah offering the sacrifices of
the old dispensation, has now become a place of Christian
worship; and through the Gospel of the Spirit the temple
of Jewish Christianity will eventually be replaced by the
world itself as the "place" of the Church's life and action.

Only Luke has felt it necessary to describe a departure
of the risen Lord, a visible ascension (Acts 1:9; Lk 24:51b
may be an addition to the Gospel text). Apparently it occurred neither to Matthew nor John, nor presumably to
Mark, nor to their readers, to ask about the subsequent
whereabouts of the resurrected Christ. But even Luke is
only an apparent exception. The question, "Why do you
stand looking into heaven?" (Acts 1:11), focuses our attention where it belongs, where Matthew and John would have
it, where all the Gospels have placed it all along.

Despite their purpose of insisting on the reality of the
resurrection as the bedrock of the Church's unshakable
faith, by means that at this remove may seem at times somewhat naïve, the Gospels have never left us in doubt as to
what is the real heart of this great mystery, to which no
amount of description can be applied other than as an
approximation. The risen Christ is to be seen in the members
of his Church: this is not only the Church's glory, but also
its most imperative call to holiness and to showing forth the
God whom it incarnates. He is in the world, which often

sees him not. He is in Galilee, preaching the word of life, the good news of the coming kingdom, healing, and bringing hope. He is in prison, in the hospitals, in hunger and in thirst, wherever there is human need, of whatever kind. He is the eternal Son of Man whom we see in every man, for whom Sabbaths were made, whom it is blasphemy to treat with contempt or injustice or lack of concern. When we would see the resurrected Christ the Gospels turn our eyes back to the ministry of Jesus of Nazareth. He is one and the same. That, after all, is what the resurrection stories intend to say. Christ lives, our Savior, our Teacher, our Judge.

INDEX OF GOSPEL PASSAGES

In each instance the first page number is given on which the relevant passage is under discussion. The Roman numeral preceding each page reference refers to the volume of this edition in which the page reference is to be found.

GENERAL INDEX